Imagination and
Invention

A Univocal Book

Drew Burk, Consulting Editor

Univocal Publishing was founded by Jason Wagner and Drew Burk
as an independent publishing house specializing in artisanal editions
and translations of texts spanning the areas of cultural theory, media
archeology, continental philosophy, aesthetics, anthropology, and more.
In May 2017, Univocal ceased operations as an independent publishing
house and became a series with its publishing partner the University of
Minnesota Press.

Univocal authors include:

Miguel Abensour
Judith Balso
Jean Baudrillard
Philippe Beck
Simon Critchley
Fernand Deligny
Jacques Derrida
Vinciane Despret
Georges Didi-Huberman
Jean Epstein
Vilém Flusser
Barbara Glowczewski
Évelyne Grossman
Félix Guattari
Olivier Haralambon
David Lapoujade
François Laruelle
David Link
Sylvère Lotringer

Jean Malaurie
Michael Marder
Serge Margel
Quentin Meillassoux
Friedrich Nietzsche
Peter Pál Pelbart
Jacques Rancière
Lionel Ruffel
Felwine Sarr
Michel Serres
Gilbert Simondon
Étienne Souriau
Isabelle Stengers
Sylvain Tesson
Eugene Thacker
Antoine Volodine
Elisabeth von Samsonow
Siegfried Zielinski

Imagination and Invention

Gilbert Simondon

Translated by Joe Hughes and
Christophe Wall-Romana

A Univocal Book

UNIVERSITY OF MINNESOTA PRESS
MINNEAPOLIS • LONDON

The publisher and the translators wish to acknowledge the work of Nathalie Simondon in compiling and editing the contents of this volume.

Originally published in French as *Imagination et invention*. Copyright Presses Universitaires de France.

Published by the University of Minnesota Press
111 Third Avenue South, Suite 290
Minneapolis, MN 55401-2520
http://www.upress.umn.edu

ISBN 978-1-5179-1445-5 (pb)

A Cataloging-in-Publication record for this book is available from the Library of Congress.

Printed in the United States of America on acid-free paper

The University of Minnesota is an equal-opportunity educator and employer.

31 30 29 28 27 26 25 24 23 22   10 9 8 7 6 5 4 3 2 1

Contents

Preface

A Theory of the Image in Light of the Notion of Invention, a Theory of Invention in Light of the Notion of the Image
Jean-Yves Chateau

1. The Place of the 1965–1966 Course in the Teaching and Work of Gilbert Simondon

Imagination and Invention is a course that was given at the Sorbonne in 1965–1966, in the Institute of Psychology at the rue Serpente.[1] It was part of the Certificate in General Psychology, which was then the foundation for a license in psychology and one of four certificates required to teach philosophy. I was able to benefit from this system just before it was ended at the close of the following year, in 1966–1967. In philosophy, it was replaced by a three-year program from which all teaching of psychology was removed. This course, then, is a final testament to what could be done in the General Psychology classroom toward the end of this period, when general psychology constituted an important element in the formation of philosophers; more precisely, it is a testament to what Gilbert Simondon could do, for one must not underestimate the force of his personality and his originality.

Simondon's 1965–1966 course is a study of both imagination *and* invention. From a certain point of view this could be seen as limiting in principle the breadth of the analysis, the level of development and the level of detail devoted to each theme—even if what is presented here is, as we will see, a theory that organically reunites the two areas of reflection, a theory in which neither are, in principle, diminished by the attention given to the other. Moreover, there are additional resources dealing with the imagination and with invention which were available at the time to students and which might be considered as complements to this course—alongside the additional material that is now available to us thanks to the publication of Simondon's later courses.

(a) Concerning imagination: In 1964–1965, the year prior to the course on imagination and invention, Simondon had taught a course on perception at the Sorbonne. In that course he discussed the relation between perception and imagination in a way that anticipates the perspective and the theses of the 1965–1966 course and what is most new and radical in them.[2] The second part of *Imagination and Invention,* on the "intra-perceptual image in the perception of forms" and "subjective contours," explicitly refers us back to the course on perception.

On the other hand, in the "suggested readings" and Part III of *Imagination and Invention,* Simondon refers to a course on the imagination that had been taught in 1962–1963 by another Professor of Psychology, Juliette Favez-Boutonier, and which had been published by the Centre de documentation universitaire in 1965. Favez-Boutonier's course presented the major classical theories of the imagination in philosophy and the work of psychologists whose work was influenced by philosophy (mostly after Taine: Ribot, Bergson, Sartre, Husserl, Freud, Jung, Eliade, Lacan, Ortigues, Bachelard, Piaget). Because of this recent course, then, Simondon can assume his students are familiar with these different doctrines, and he often refers to them without going over their elements or their details. In the first sentence of the Preamble he characterizes his course as the presentation of a "theory." In contrast to the course presented three years earlier, Simondon develops a highly original project. The course is both fueled by a large number of international references to works in scientific psychology, and rather than merely introducing to students a number of philosophical positions, Simondon examines, discusses, analyzes, and situates them. This course is more technical and scientific by virtue of the information it introduces, then, and it is more theoretical and philosophical by virtue of the conception of the whole that it proposes.

It is ultimately the philosophical import of the different philosophical and scientific doctrines studied here that Simondon constantly seeks out, the manner in which they allow for the construction not of a theory in the sense of a doctrine that would exclude others, but of a general overview which would draw on the details of other doctrines to the extent that they are useful or related to the essential; often when they are presented, it is to show the range of problems related to an inquiry into the imagination. Simondon does not put much faith in the ability of the dialectic or a refutational discourse to advance toward truth or to even exhibit it. Not all theses are equal, of course, and his "theory" disqualifies a certain number of them, but it always looks for what is positive in other positions, and, whenever possible, for a point of view that would allow for conflicting theses to appear as positions which contain an element of truth—a partial truth—that can be rendered whole when one is capable of uncovering a neutral point in relation to which they are divided. The theory Simondon is attempting to sketch or decipher is one that would allow for things to be grasped in a sufficiently global manner so that diverse realities and diverse levels of analysis can be distinguished without necessarily separating them, enabling them to be set in relation. This is Simondon's "genetic" method.

The following course then, is precisely characterized by the scope of the conception it proposes. It is grounded in scientific psychology, as it is usually understood, psychoanalysis, genetic psychology, and animal psychology—but also biology, zoology, ethology, literature, aesthetics, and sociology—and all to the same extent that it is grounded in philosophy. Nor does the introduction of contemporary scientific work prevent Simondon from returning to and justifying positions of earlier psychologists like Taine or Ribot from within his perspective—an approach that is quite distant from the tendency of certain thinkers, however less learned, to disregard that work or declare it "surpassed" (a frequent attitude of Sartre's). The scope of his project is also visible in the way it presents, as Simondon often does, an account that is homogeneous with respect to living animals and humans, infants and adults, individual psychology and group behavior (and, indeed, facts of culture and of civilization), even as he underlines the differences between them; it is applicable across the different biological and psychological levels in the analysis of the living and across the different psychic functions which are usually isolated, like motricity, sensoriality, perception, imagination and the intellectual functions (which are sometimes called "superior"). Importantly, it is not a question here of taking "imagination" and "invention" as two terms

that are near synonyms, nor of taking the imagination as a faculty intervening into the domain of invention from the outside; nor is it, more generally,
a matter of studying the relation between the two through simple analysis of
their concepts; it is a question, rather, of establishing their effective relations
as determined in the cycle of a genesis.

   (b) Concerning Invention, notably in technics: Beyond the courses Simondon was to teach after 1965–1966, and which are now available to read in
L'invention dans les techniques, cited above, Simondon's students could read
On the Mode of Existence of Technical Objects, which had already been published in 1958, and which Simondon refers to, briefly, in *Imagination and
Invention.* That work, which was his secondary thesis, presents a theory of
the invention of technical objects and specifies the relations between invention and imagination. The first chapter of the first part of *On The Mode of
Existence of Technical Objects* studies, as its title suggests, the "process of
concretization" characteristic of the genesis of the technical object: it is that
which exists at the end of "a specific genesis proceeding from the abstract
to the concrete."[3] The second chapter, studying the "evolution of technical
reality" whose mode of existence has just been characterized, shows the
relation between processes of concretization (the objective technological
point of view) and of invention (the point of view of the inventor, related,
in this sense, to psychology): two points of view which are, in some sense,
united, and even equivalent. As Simondon writes, "invention is the mental,
psychological aspect of this proper mode of existence."[4] The second and third
sections of this second chapter present the relations between imagination and
invention in a highly synthetic manner, from a perspective which corresponds
to the one developed in the 1965–1966 course: a genetic unity founded on
a transductive dynamism of the image.

   At the time that this course was taught, useful complements could be
found in other texts that were as illuminating and equally concerned with
imagination, invention and their relations. But one can see above all, and
for reasons of principle, that in linking together these two notions, imagination and invention, the course is not adding an extra burden or extending its
object, as it would not have been possible for Simondon to separate these two
notions even if the title of his course had referred only to one or the other.
It presents a theory which, without confusing the two notions, decisively

unites imagination and invention as successive moments in the development of a single organism.

2. The Genetic Unity of Imagination and Invention

The aim of this course is not to analyze the relations between these notions, but to study each in light of the other, for that is the only way to discover the nature of each. Both are considered as phases of the same cyclic, genetic process: that of the image. Simondon's task becomes therefore a question of constructing a genuine theory of the imagination, one which is able to account for invention (for both the *possibility* and the *fact* of invention), just as much as it is a question of constructing a theory of invention which can shed light on the nature of the imagination and the mental image. It is not a theory of the imagination and of the image from which one might draw, secondarily, consequences for creation or indeed for invention; nor is it a theory of creation and of invention which would envelop or suppose an uncritical concept of the imagination and of the image.

The risk of partiality is indeed real: "imagination" is a term which presents a certain ambiguity—and Simondon notes that its ambiguity presents both advantages and disadvantages. In constructing a theory of imagination, one might focus on the imagined and construct an account of an imaging or imagining activity which it presupposes and which corresponds to it; or one might focus on the activity of imaging or imagining and "draw some conclusions" about the nature and the status of the imagined object. The theory Simondon develops does not participate in this ambiguity. It is a theory of the imagination and of the mental image from beginning to end, even in the fourth part of the present work which bears the title "Invention";[5] and, conversely, it is a theory of the movement and the activity guiding creation and invention, even in the first three parts which bear explicitly on *the image* according to the different points of view corresponding to the three stages of its development. Simondon notes in the conclusion that it is obviously not a matter of confusing an invented thing with an image, because an invention is what draws the image out of the interior of the living being so that it can be realized in a milieu (a difference of ontological kinds: they do not have the same "mode of existence"), and yet this "tendency to transcend the individual subject which actualizes itself through invention is, in fact, virtually contained in the three previous stages of the image cycle."[6] To put it briefly, before developing the point below: independently and outside of the moment of invention, the image, in all its forms, tends to transcend itself and to go out of itself, as in the case of invention; while invention, properly speaking, prolongs this essential movement of the image—always possible even within the most static image—thus revealing the latent potential within every image and which is the general regime of the development of the image.

In the different domains where it is studied, and above all in technics, invention is neither a consequence nor an application under specific conditions of the activity of an imagination one might study in general and without attending to these differences; its analysis reveals and allows us to understand the nature of the imagination and of the image in their effective, living, genetic, concrete reality. The imagination and the mental image are studied here by considering the fact that they are not always related to an object that has already been perceived, which one remembers and which one "reproduces" in a manner that is more or less deformed or recomposed, nor to an object that one imagines in a creative way (that is, as "productive," and not "reproductive"), but sometimes to an object that one is about to make real materially, in exteriority, and which sometimes (unlike an object or a work of art) is susceptible to *functioning* technically. How are we to think the mental image so that this would be possible? The reproductive imagination and the productive imagination are not opposed to one another—but nor should they be conflated with one another. The same could also be said regarding the productive or creative imagination in general and the imagination which invents effective technical realities. It is a question, rather, of thinking the image in such a way that one might grasp its possibility in these different cases, but without conflating its different regimes.

This is how the problematic of the 1965–1966 course may be characterized in the most general way but also, as we will see, in the most decisive way: Simondon's course studies the nature of the imagination in relation to the nature of invention. It takes into account, in the structure of the problem it poses, the need for a theory of the imagination and of the image to account for the functioning of the creative imagination, as producer of works. In this respect, certain parts of Simondon's theory seem to follow or reflect the concerns of classical French psychology, beginning in the second half of the nineteenth century.[7] In posing the problem of the imagination they attempted to connect the nature of the imagination to creation, and indeed, to invention. And while Simondon always attempts to uncover what is still of interest among authors stretching all the way back to antiquity, his work possesses a striking originality. On the one hand, more than any other thinker, and with an exceptionally detailed and erudite eye, he accords an eminent place to technical invention, thus taking into account the demanding requirement for a theory of imagination, namely, to be valid for technical invention as well. On the other hand, the relations between imagination and invention are not only well balanced, their link is intimate, radical, decisive, no longer under the jurisdiction of identity or difference, but of an organic, genetic, transductive unity.

3. The Mental Image and the Imagination: Some Problems

Simondon's desire to study imagination and invention as an organic totality, one that is genetic and cyclic, does not prevent him from addressing certain problems raised by the image and imagination in a detailed manner— even if he does so within a framework and capacious conception all his own. Among the most notable issues is one that confronted psychologists and philosophers in the last half of the nineteenth century and which they confronted in turn. It is an issue that is difficult to determine with precision: the problem of the relation of imagination and invention to perception.[8]

Let us begin by noting that for Simondon, it is not a matter of approaching this question in the form of a discussion of possible definitions leading to the elaboration of one which would allow us to provide an account of what experience seems to teach us. Here, we begin straightaway with what the broadest experience claims to teach us, observing things in different ways and not always coherently; one claims through this method to learn above all from experience itself, before any systematic construction or pregiven definition that would obviate the errancy of research. Only through a finely tuned practice of listening to one's experience, in all the ramifications it offers, can the nature of the image be determined in a way that neglects neither the variations which belong properly to it nor the possibility of its evolution. A definition of the image which would prohibit the hypothesis of a genetic

evolutivity essential to it would fall unwittingly under a metaphysical prejudice and a definition of the essence of the image that would exclude possible
variations or forcefully reduce a heterogeneous form to a unity. One must
recall that for Simondon questions concerning the definition of concepts
are not the most important element of his research, and in any case, they
cannot be taken as given or settled from the start. For reasons of principle,
he does not begin his inquiries by seeking to establish a definition, which
one could use later as an instrument without revisiting its validity. He begins,
in the Preamble and the Introduction, by underlining the problems that are
posed, and which risk remaining hidden by the very definitions and basic
meanings attached to words like "image," symbol," "perception," "desire,"[9] or
"imagination."[10]

Some definitions may be skillful and coherent constructions but still
bar access to the real in its effective complexity, rather than encouraging
it, because they do not follow, despite appearances and an often highly elab-
orate argumentation, the articulations of the real (as one might say in a
Platonic register) nor its genetic dynamism (indeed, it is only in this way
that its articulations truly reveal themselves). The risk is that the most strict
and rigorous definitions, by their very nature, turn away from following
what is most characteristic of and most essential to reality: its evolutivity,
its genetic character (here, it should be noted that in spite of any critique
he might level at Bergson, Simondon maintains a principled position that
is profoundly Bergsonian). This of course does not dispense of the task of
elaborating definitions; rather, it increases the difficulty. To define something, one must take into account the possibility that what has been accu-
rately defined at a given moment contains, in itself, its own potentials which
will make it exceed or escape that definition. The risk lies either in reducing everything (everything, for instance, that we call "image" in everyday
language) to a single definition, to a single model, a single essence, to which
one then tries to reduce by force all diversity; or, conversely, in needlessly
multiplying entities (for example, judging mental images to be absolutely
heterogeneous to materialized images, perceptual images, etc.). In short,
"Ockham's Razor" must be handled with care and in a way that is recurrent,
or rather, transductive. In order to avoid the difficulty of this principle as much
as possible, Simondon's approach is characterized, here and elsewhere, by

the recognition of the maximum number of differences in reality as it is offered to us by experience. His approach gives reality its due not (only) by gathering it up into the unity of the concept and the definition, but in a transductive unity, one that operates from place to place and which closely follows the genesis, evolution, and even the disparation of its object. There is some advantage in calling very different realities "images." If we did not, we might conceal a real family resemblance between them, as well as an actual genetic continuity, though its notion would be difficult or stultifying to fix within a common genus (it would make it an impoverished generality). One must, rather, follow the differences between images, all the while rendering visible their connection, not as genus to species or as essence to a species of the same genus, but as phases in a quasi-organic process of development.

Simondon had already broached the question of the relations between imagination and perception in his *Course on Perception* which was taught the previous year and which has a great deal in common with *Imagination and Invention*.[11] One cannot separate *perception* and *imagination*; one must think them together without confusing them. Such a thesis will be just as important for the course below.

Most notably, Simondon's thesis directly contradicts the central idea defended by Sartre who was still a very prominent and highly influential thinker during the era, particularly for his theory of the imagination. One of the foundations of Sartre's doctrine was that "image and perception, far from being two elementary psychic factors of similar quality that simply enter into different combinations, represent the two great irreducible attitudes of consciousness."[12] For Sartre, "existing *in image*" is absolutely opposed to "existing *in fact*."[13] Or, as he says again clearly: "The formation of an imaging consciousness is accompanied . . . by an annihilation of perceptual consciousness, and reciprocally."[14] From the very first lines of *The Imaginary*, Sartre defines the imagination as the "great 'irrealizing' function of consciousness" of which the imaginary is the "noematic correlate."[15] It is through reference and opposition to the "function of the real" in Pierre Janet that this originary characterization of the imagination and of the image acquires the sense of an opposition and a radical incompatibility with perception.

However, for Simondon, one cannot truly separate imagination and perception, even if one can distinguish their concepts: "The capacity to perceive is hardly distant from the force of imagining, unless the sense one gives to this word is from a fictive construction."[16] Perception and imagination are not identical, as the words chosen to characterize each indicate: "capacity" and "force." But as soon as one does not exclusively consider the imagination's power of fiction, we will see that they are also not very different, that they are tightly linked, the one to the other, *in act*. Perceiving is not that different from imagining to the extent that it is impossible to perceive without imagining, and that the imagination entertains multiple relations with perception, which one must not begin by trying to reduce. An accurate conception of both perception and imagination is required to grasp this great proximity, an intimate bond, if not an identity.

Sartre is able to distinguish the image from perception to the extent that the latter is analyzed as a consciousness of passivity, a consciousness of something which is imposed, a consciousness of a certain objectivity which is given. The object of the imagination is not really a real object: "the image is a consciousness" which means that it is *only* a consciousness, not an objective reality.[17] The image is "a certain way in which the object appears to consciousness, or, if one prefers, a certain way in which consciousness presents to itself an object."[18] But, precisely, this "way" is characterized by the fact that the object given here is not given in its flesh and bone; it is given as absent: one cannot really observe it, it can only be the object of a "quasi-observation."[19] While "the object of perception constantly overflows consciousness, the object of an image is never anything more than the consciousness one has of it; it is defined by that consciousness . . . ."[20] The image is not a perception: one only finds what one puts there, which is what constitutes its "essential poverty," a poverty in *objective reality*. One could thus say that "the imaging consciousness posits its object as a nothingness": it intends it *[le vise]* as irreal, it irrealizes it.[21] For Sartre, this is not simply an observed property of the image: it is its necessary and essential definition. There is, for Sartre, a necessity to find within the image's "inner nature, an element of radical distinction" with respect to perception, almost as if there were a vital danger of confusing them (hallucination, illness).[22] Sartre's entire theory rests on this foundation. The "spontaneity" of the image is only "a kind of indefinable counterpart to the fact that the object gives itself as a nothingness."[23]

Thus, for Sartre, the imagination is an annihilating, "irrealizing" function. It is opposed to the function of the real, of which perception is the major form. He strives to show that philosophers and psychologists made the mistake of thinking the imagination on the basis of perception, and, in contrast to them (a difference of degree), Sartre appears to have taken the opposite view in a radical and systematic way. But perhaps he had enclosed himself too exclusively within this problematic. This led him, in *The Imagination*, to clearly position himself against Bergson (who had, however, clearly affirmed in chapter III of *Matter and Memory* that there is only a difference of degree between memory and perception) to the extent that Bergson had made the image a reality existing in the external world, in the first chapter of *Matter and Memory* (all reality is image, to the extent that it is susceptible to being perceived, even if it is not currently being perceived).[24] That the image might exist within an objective exteriority, independently of the activity of a consciousness, other than as a consciousness, an "imaging consciousness": this appears, to Sartre, impossible, indeed, absurd, and he speaks of it as of a blunder, a philosophical and psychological archaism.

It is precisely on this fundamental point that Simondon, while clearly recognizing the significant merits of Sartre's position, refuses to follow him. He calmly recalls that Sartre's thesis corresponds to a current use of "image," but one that is not entirely justified:

> The word "image" is generally understood as designating a mental content of which we can be conscious; this is the main difficulty, because in some cases such a conscious appearance of the image is indeed possible for the human subject—partially in a situation of anticipation, and especially in that of a memory-symbol; but there is no evidence that even in the best cases this consciousness exhausts the entire reality of this local activity. To the contrary, we might surmise that the conscious aspects of the local activity are cases of an almost exceptional surfacing [*affleurement*] connected to a continuous framework.[25]

Simondon agrees with Sartre in essentially linking the imaging function and the symbolic function—in contrast to certain psychoanalysts, Sartre says, and specifically, Simondon adds, to Lacan (to whom he devotes several pages below).[26] And Simondon will state that he thinks Sartre's "interpretation is extremely interesting" to the extent that "it emphasizes a relation of existence and of action between the object and subject, one woven in images and symbols rather than, as in most other doctrines including Husserl's, relations of signification which to a greater or lesser degree associate images and symbols with signs."[27] But it is Sartre's formulation of his conception of the "imaging consciousness" as a constitutive problem that is debatable for Simondon. It is then the very tool which Sartre used in his radical refutation of Bergson that is contested and turned against Sartre himself. If the word "imagination," which refers to a "faculty psychology," is useful at all, it is to the extent that it "presupposes that mental images result from a certain power, that they express an activity that shapes them, and that they imply perhaps the existence of a function that utilizes them."[28] It is from this point of view, too, that Sartre's analyses are interesting. But Sartre's conception of the "imaging consciousness" (to which he reduces the image) leads him— in according an absolute "spontaneity" to the image (which is to say: to the imaging consciousness)—to the refusal, in the very same gesture, of all objective reality of images. This conception of the "imaging consciousness" gives the subjective character of images their full share—but that is too much because, at the same time, it grounds the impossibility of recognizing in images a mode of existence that is sufficiently consistent and autonomous.

As is his practice, Simondon does not oppose specific theses: he tries to show, rather, that every thesis has an element of truth, even if it is insufficient. One must find the point of view from which it can be completed, or, rather, from which *reality* appears as *complete*. Now, unless we wish to deny the reality of images as it is commonly experienced, we must acknowledge that images have an exteriority and a kind of objectivity. Simondon thus levels a critique against Sartre's theory that is comparable, on this point, to what one can object to in "faculty psychology": it places too much importance, at the level of principle, on subjectivity. This is, he says, the fault of the word "imagination." It can be misleading to the extent that it exclusively attaches images to the subject that produced them and tends "to exclude the hypothesis of a primordial exteriority of images in relation to the subject."[29] Here, then, we find that the Bergsonian thesis of the exteriority of the image is restored: in itself, there is nothing absurd about it, and it corresponds to the most common experience; it suffices to complete it with an account of that which is subjective in the image if one wishes to provide an integral account of its nature, as we will see.[30] Simondon does not proceed by way of a meticulous refutation of Sartre, comparable to the kind Sartre directs against his adversaries. Rather he locates Sartre's argument within a far more ancient perspective, and he goes well beyond Bergson's attempts: to deny all objectivity in the image and to repudiate all of the force belonging to the world of images would be to go against common sense, a sense grounded in an experience as old as humanity itself. Certainly, "it is a common attitude among contemporary thinkers for whom an image refers back to an 'imaging consciousness,' to invoke Sartre's terms," to reject the exteriority of images.[31] But against this recent intellectual fashion Simondon invokes the antiquity of human experience since Homer: the "independence and objectivity of the image struck the thinkers of antiquity."[32] It was not only in the seventeenth century that "the description of images in terms of subjectivity imposed itself."[33] Simondon asks of Sartre, who proposes in the first lines of his method to abandon prejudices, to "describe" images, and to "leave theories to the side" (remarks that recall, precisely, those of Bergson at the beginning of the first chapter of *Matter and Memory*), to not begin by altering and simplifying experience: "Why should we exclude as illusory those characteristics whereby an image resists our free will, in which it refuses to let the subject's will direct it, and presents itself according to its own forces, living in our consciousness like an intruder disturbing the order of a household?"[34] One can readily see Simondon's usual manner of proceeding: it is not a matter of polemicizing or of refuting Sartre's position in detail, but of making his *differend* bear on the *principle* which constitutes the compendium of *experience*; it is the ancient weight of this experience that he invokes and which exempts him from having to further discuss or dialecticize.

We should note that, despite the force of the argument itself, founded on testimony of the earliest human experience, had Simondon wanted to find support in a contemporary thinker celebrated for their work in this domain, he could have evoked, for example, Gaston Bachelard's conception of imagination, which he doesn't himself present here, but which he cites in his bibliography—where Simondon recommends reading all of Bachelard's works, and particularly *The Psychoanalysis of Fire*.[35] In a certain sense,

Bachelard might resemble Sartre, in having grasped, as he says in *Air and Dreams,* that "perceiving and imaging are as antithetical as presence and absence. To imagine is to absent oneself." Yet Bachelard parts ways with Sartre by adding: "to launch out toward a new life."[36] Certainly, we often "have no guiding principle for our absence and do no persevere once we have set out," but the genuinely poetic imagination is an *invitation to journey* toward another world, certainly, but to a real world, even if it has been buried since,[37] and it establishes an effective relation with what it finds there: "And how many times has that [buried] world suddenly answered me . . . . O my things! What conversations we have had!"[38] This imagined world is not without existence or without force for the dreamer, for "the realism of unreality is evident *[s'impose].*"[39] Bachelard affirms, in response to Sartre, that one cannot separate the "function of the irreal" from the "function of the real": "Difficulties with the function of the unreal *[l'irréel]* have repercussions for the reality function."[40] Sometimes the "dream is stronger than experience";[41] but it always precedes every objective experience which must be won on and against it. Rather than seeking to think imagination on the basis of perception (envisaged as a repetition of perception or in its difference from perception, whether a difference of kind or degree), one must show the "primitive character, the psychically fundamental character of the creative imagination": such is the task Bachelard sets himself at the beginning of *Earth and the Reveries of Will.*[42] For when the real is present in all of its force, as in perception, one is led to forget all that is unconscious and which is unburdened in conscious life, and it becomes necessary to "redouble attention if we want to discover the prospective activity of image, if we want to place the image before even perception, as an adventure of perception."[43] Images are not repetitions or representations of what has been perceived; there are also images that precede and inform perception: creative images.

The imaginary world thus described is quite far from Sartre's "annihilation" and his conception of the imagination as an "irrealizing function." We are dealing with two different intellectual atmospheres and two different sensibilities. Here images depend on the force of the imagination, but they also have their own force, they are what dreams are *made* of, they constitute a world that one can contemplate and explore, in which one can live and with which one must reckon—it would be "neurotic" to try to escape from it, according to Bachelard's diagnosis: in his description, consciousness is not "imaging" as in Sartre, it is "imagining," we might say, consciousness can be genuinely creative, and the creative (not the reproductive) imagination is that which precedes all perception and can inform it: it is prospective of the real. "The human psyche is primitively formulated in images."[44] Bachelard prioritizes the force of the creative imagination but without, for that reason, neglecting the force of images, of the imaginary as a world. Whereas Sartre's psychology of the imagination, entirely centered on not just an opposition to perception but an incompatibility with it, seems unable to truly grasp the possibility of a creative imagination (other than in its works, or rather, its results, after they have been given to perception or, better, received)—and still less of an effectively functioning inventive imagination, as in technics: the objective real is, for it, the object of perception, of receptivity of passivity; it never seems to be thought as a possible product of a realization, a becoming-real on the basis of imagination.[45] Considering imagination as an "irrealizing function" (in opposition to the "function of the real" the perception would essentially be) seems to prevent one from being able to grasp it as a function of realization.

4. The Theory: The Primacy of the Image.
The Cycle of the Image and of Invention

If one wishes to describe the reality and the experience of images, then, in setting prejudices and theories aside from the start, one is indeed led, according to Simondon, to recognize the "relative independence of images:" "they can only be governed indirectly"; "they maintain a certain opacity"; "displaying, to a degree, will, appetite and motion, images almost seem to be secondary organisms within the thinking being: parasites or a surplus, they are like secondary monads, sometimes inhabiting the subject, other times leaving it." One can be haunted by certain images, possessed by them, and not always easily delivered from them. In sum: one must refuse the choice between the thesis of a radical subjectivity of the image and the affirmation of its purely objective character; it is necessary to say that the image is at once *objective and subjective,* at once *concrete and abstract*; or, indeed, that sometimes it appears to be an *intermediary reality* between the objective and the subjective, between the concrete and the abstract, between the self and the world.[46] Images can be purely mental, but also materialized in "image-objects" (institutions, products, wealth). Thus "images impregnate civilizations and energize them with their power *[force]*." The image is not only a "result" (as if it depended entirely on a pure "spontaneous imaging consciousness"), it is also a "germ": images have "a complex mode of existence and proliferation." They cannot be reduced to a single status, for example, that of being the revival and the reproduction of that which has already existed; one must distinguish images which are turned toward the past (memory), those that are turned toward the future (anticipation, waiting, invention), and those that are turned toward the present (perception), without being thereby led to forget that they are, in general, formed and developed in close relations between themselves.

In this situation, in order to avoid reducing all of the different kinds of image to a single essence, in order to give the polymorphous diversity of images and the unending evolution of images and of the imagination their due, and to avoid neglecting or confounding their difference, the method consists in examining the extent to which one can form a genetic conception, following from beginning to end the manner in which each moment or phase renders the next possible by constituting original conditions for its genesis (this is what Simondon calls the "transductive approach"). For the word "image" can be understood in different senses: the mental image, the material image, schema, etc.; and, Simondon notes, rather than the term "image," it is sometimes necessary to say "symbol," "perception," even "desire," and so on. And yet, it is not a matter of reducing these different forms to an identity, but of showing that, in a sense, "the aspects of the mental image, which have been the object of conversations and of published studies, do not correspond to different types of reality, but to different stages of a single activity undergoing a developmental process."[47] Nor is it a question of "reducing the whole of mental activity to the image in the process of genesis, but of showing that, during anticipation, then in the course of the perceptual-motor relation, and ultimately within memory and later in invention, there exists a local activity making of the subject a veritable generator of signals meant to anticipate, then receive, and finally preserve and 'recycle,' through action, the incoming signals from the milieu."[48]

The image is therefore conceived as a "quasi-organism... dwelling in the subject and developing in it with relative independence from unified and conscious activity."[49] Mental images would be "like structural and functional subsets of this organized activity that is psychic activity."[50] Thus the observed characteristics of image, which sometimes appear contradictory, can find their compatibility and their coherence in this frame, which seems to dissolve traditional oppositions by changing the sense and value of traditional formulas: one can now say that the image depends on the subject and, at the same time, that it has its own dynamism, that the image sometimes seems to be confounded with consciousness in its relation to an exterior object and that it sometimes seems to be in the subject and one can observe it as though it were an exterior object. In its quasi-organic development, (1) the image is first of all, at the beginning of life, a sheaf of *motor tendencies,* a long-term *anticipation* of the experience of the object. This is a genetically programmed behavior, which guides the young living being in its milieu, before any experience and any recognition of an object, in a pure motor spontaneity, of which the image consists. (2) Then the image becomes a mode of receiving signals and information coming from the milieu and a source of schemata for responding to these stimulations, the different images progressively organizing into subsets under the effect of *experience* (this is the phase of perception). (3) Finally, images are organized and *systematized* in a "veritable mental world," (notably under the influence of an affective-emotional resonance), through which "the subject possesses an analogue of the exterior milieu." (4) *Invention* can the appear as a *change of organization* of the system of images, allowing the subject to approach the milieu with new anticipations: it marks the end of a cycle and the beginning of a new one. "What characterizes an image is that it is a local endogenous activity, and this activity exists just as much in the presence of the object (in perception) as it does before experience, as anticipation, or afterwards, as memory-symbol."[51] The fear of seeing the notion of the image associated with that of anticipation, memory, or perception, clings to anti-associationist reflexes, but it is "faculty psychology" above all that presents a difficulty "because faculties were defined on the basis of dominant tasks: anticipating, perceiving, and remembering; to those three moments in time correspond perception, memory, imagination."[52] However, one must not confound imagining and

perceiving, and if "among memories not all are images," the image plays—
or can play—a role, each time different, in each of these functions.

Because Sartre conceives of the image as consciousness and as an essence
that is determined above all by its relation to and contrast with perception,
his conception can only appear insufficient to Simondon.[53] Now, not only
can one say with Bachelard that the imagination is more primitive than perception (the reproductive imagination is not the model or the essence of the
imagination, only a particular case), but, still more radically, it is necessary
to recognize that sensoriality is not primary, that it is preceded by motricity.[54] Perception and, generally, behaviors of *reaction* to the milieu are not
primary; it is the *spontaneous* motor behaviors that are primitive, which one
misrecognizes when perception is made to be an exclusive, *sui generis* essence
of any influence of the imagination and, more originary, of all motor spontaneity: images do not first come from antecedent perceptions, and the worry
of confounding them with perception is not decisive in defining them; they
come from spontaneous movements—and as for their relation to perception: they precede it and inform it.

It is necessary then, if one does not want to defend at all costs and against
the facts a conception which denies the primacy of life and movement with
respect to consciousness and perception in living beings, including humans,
to accept the idea that the first images are not conscious, not in the sense
at least in which perception is conscious, since they precede perception (the
reception of signals coming from the milieu), they are motor, linked to the
most simple behaviors through which the living take possession of the milieu
and proceed to the first identification of the (living or non-living) objects
they encounter. But this does not mean that primitive motor behaviors are
accompanied by images (considered as conscious representations which, for
example, could motivate and orient these movements, give them an end, as
will be the case later, when perception, memory, and experience are present); the primitive motor images have no other content than the movements
themselves (autokinetic, non-finalized image), such that they are organized
in a way that conforms to the specific programs of the individual and as a
function of the chance encounters which occur within the frame of the milieu
in which it finds itself.

The organism is a set of behavior schemas as clearly definable and with as sharp a taxonomic value as the shape of exoskeletal spurs, the number of claws, etc. Such action schemas thus exist in living beings as anticipations of possible behaviors, as partial programs of behavior, and, employed virtually, they can provide a content to anticipations in the guise of preparations for situations in which the object is encountered or the anticipation of responses; the organism can, more or less fully, rehearse its comportments before applying them to a real object; getting up, attacking, fleeing, or confronting: these are sequences whose program a living being possesses in itself the way it possesses its own body.[55]

The objects, whether living or non-living, which are identified in the milieu are not initially perceived, given as data in the mode of that which might be received, and then progressively recognized (according to an empiricist explication). They are distinguished, constituted, instituted, identified, either in a very short amount of time (in the case, for example, of "imprinting," of "*Prägung*," of the maternal function)[56] or progressively and in a differential manner, through the autokinetic *motor activity of exploration,* of which the subject is capable in light of their organic equipment and the vagaries of discovery in their milieu. It is through this local activity coming from the subject that it constitutes the objects that its behavioral programs render possible for it (good or bad objects, predators or prey, resting places, the maternal figure or a substitute, and so on), and it does so by recruiting them in the course of encounters occasioned by its autokineses. This process cannot correspond to a perception (the reception of a signal coming from an object in the milieu), as long as this recruitment and this constitution are not sufficiently advanced: it first appears as an anticipatory behavior, an activity of the *imagination.* "An anticipation cannot be merely an initiative; it is an organized initiative, with a structure, a consistency with respect to itself, a form."[57] Motor activity deserves the name "image" under conditions in which it is not purely trial and error but finds itself organized and structured with a minimum of constancy and where it leads to the identification of an object (it is only then that the possibility for perception will be attained). The image in this case precedes perception and consciousness (in any case, the consciousness that characterizes perception as presence to that which irrecusably imposes presence); it is not determined by the object (perceived or quasi-perceived), since it is situated before perception and consciousness (and escapes the traditional muddled problems concerning the relations between imagination and perception). It is the image, we could say, that makes the object come to pass for the subject, which it constitutes as an object susceptible to being perceived, identified, recognized, studied. It is produced by a local activity of the nervous system which can, during the encounter with the milieu, "constantly generate sketches of nascent movements which are not responses to stimuli, and which thus constitute the postulate of all new behaviors;"[58] it is an "anticipation of the object," a "sketch of perception," "categories of perception," perhaps. One has to say that it does not *receive* its object as a donation, but that it *recruits* the object (it encounters it, retains it, elicits it in fact) in the course of motor behavior and the activity of generating signals in the direction of the milieu which accompanies it, without which there would be no grouping of signals which could exist in the milieu and thus no signal coming from the milieu would be received as such. The image in this case is "the first form of the *a priori* image whose content is essentially motor."[59] Motor images refer to a "body schema," radiating from it and inherent to it.[60] "To summarize, the primordial source of the *a priori* appears to be, in the form of anticipations of movement, the organism. Such anticipations take the form of a projection of motor images into the milieu coming from this unique and primary source that is the organism with its motor schemas radiating out of the body schema."[61]

A profound reform of traditional psychology and of a certain phenomenology is implied here. Perception is not primary, neither is consciousness; it is rather life, movement, and, when movement is organized, the image. The donation of the object in perception has a condition of possibility in the local activity of the subject, of endogenous origin, which is nothing other than a certain kind of life, of vitality, a barely organized and constant movement: the first form of the image. It is through this that the encounter with the object properly speaking, which is called perception, is possible: it is what *recruits* it. If one has understood that the image, in a primitive, pre-perceptual motor situation, cannot be confused with reception or consciousness, in principle, because it precedes them, and gives rise to its object through anticipation and, properly, recruitment, then perhaps one will not be surprised to see now that the image inevitably and essentially has a place in perception ("intra-perceptual images"), something that might appear impossible and absurd for a Sartrean phenomenology. It is not a question of confusing perception and imagination, nor of readopting an "associationist" point of view, but of taking account of the fact that perception, whether it be the most simple motor-perceptual behavior or the most highly elaborated perception, is not a static relation to the object, but endlessly susceptible to evolving, as a function of the activity of the subject in all of its dimensions. In these conditions, how could the anticipatory activity of the imagination, which is observed even before the existence of perception, be eliminated during perception, which every activity of the subject can cause to evolve? "Images appear, then, in the form of perceptual anticipations of potentialities, as more general than individual objects,"[62] including in the most simple perception (motor-perceptual behaviors), to the point that they can be compared with concepts. But, above all, the intra-perceptual image plays a role in the "constancy effect" which insures the feeling that the object does not change its form when varying its position and thus what is in "view" as a circle that one pivots around the axis of one of its diameter continues to be seen as a circle and not as an ellipse.[63] But it is not only a matter of stating that the perception of an object presupposes those faces of the object that remain unperceived (which one could relate to memory or to a general knowledge of the structure of space). Certain perceptions can, "in a single glance," fill out a complex situation in which the number and the entanglement of factors is too great to be perceived (what one sometimes calls "intuition"); this happens in the case of the carer who "sees that their child is coming down with something" or of the shepherd who sees, without counting, that he is missing several sheep. These are cases of "differential perception."[64] There is a rich and complex image which serves as the ground for the figure of what is perceived and which makes the difference in relation to what was expected immediately apparent. But, above all, the consideration of the "subjective contour" or of the "associated image"[65] makes it apparent that one cannot, without artifice, separate perception and image in experience. One cannot account for what is effectively perceived without bringing into play the power *[puissance]* and the activity of the imagination and of the image. This is a point on which Simondon had already insisted in the earliest pages of the *Cours sur la perception* of the preceding year, to which he returns here: when, in perception, the figure-ground relation appears, the effect of a contour appears, even when this contour is not at all materialized in objective reality. The grouping of perceptual unities, their classification and organization in a figure and its contour resembles an "intra-perceptual induction," but one that is instantaneous, "not requiring a later work on images subsequent to perception," but operating "at the interior of the perceptual field itself, during perceptual activity." It would then be correct to say that the subject contour is a veritable *intra-perceptual image*; this image is not an element, nor is it given by elements taken one by one, rather, perceptual activity elicits it as expressing a configuration conforming to the distribution and the valence of the elements (one can see clearly that this analysis is not at all associationist, but gestaltist, and that not even a phenomenologist would be able to reproach it with anything essential). "The intra-perceptual image is elicited in perceptual activity" with facility and spontaneity, it is isomorphic with the representation of the subject, with the dimension of the subject of perception, and it belongs to an intermediate order of magnitude that lies between the world, which envelops everything and escapes manipulation, and the elements, which are manipulable; it is that in which the structure of the object appears, structure responding directly to the subject of perception. This page from the *Cours sur la perception,* which rewards attentive rereading, makes the difficulty of separating the activity of perceiving and of imagining apparent, if one analyses them closely, beyond the conceptual distinctions with which one begins.

We could then say that in perception the image is still what ensures perception is not a pure passivity, but a differential activity, which recruits that which reaches out to it from the given, or at least that which might leave the given at any moment. It participates in the vitality of perception. It is not the germ of nothingness within perception; it does not necessarily destroy its relation to the real. The possibilities of remembering, of symbolizing, of anticipating, constitute the major forms of this tendency of the image to transcend itself. Now, within symbolization, this tendency takes the form of an *analogon* of the milieu, which allows it to be *simulated* in a realistic and efficacious way—a condition of technical invention. The fact and the power [*puissance*] of symbolization and of technical invention are an irrefutable proof that the imagination can be a function of the real, of realization. One sees the decisive importance of taking invention and its strict connection with the imagination into account in developing a theory of the image. If that theory is to take account of the possibility of a genuinely creative imagination, one that produces works and is capable of inventing effectively functioning technical objects, then one cannot attribute to the image, in its universal essence, the necessity of having a derealizing relation to its object, in whatever sense one understands it.

The first behaviors are motor, spontaneous behaviors, and images are first of all motor, leading to the recruitment of objects from the milieu fulfilling its programmed expectations. Then, in the second phase of the cycle of the genesis of images, they play a decisive role as "intra-perceptual" images. Finally, they are organized among themselves as a system of symbols, to which one is effectively related as to an analogue of the world. It is this which makes the arrival of invention possible. In each phase of the image cycle, there is the possibility of a recruitment from reality, the image thus being a potential process of amplification of the present givens at each moment. During the phase of symbolization, there is a passage to a universalization of this possibility: symbolization allows the reconstruction of the real in an objective and calculated way, and it can be communicated as such to everybody else. There is, in invention, a change in the order of magnitude: in the effective invention of a technical object, it is effectively a new being, hitherto unseen, that can be recruited, even if that must first of all be rendered possible (the ontological dimension of invention). One grasps the form of the unity of the image, imagination, and invention that this theory proposes.

"According to this theory of the image cycle, reproductive imagination and invention are neither separate realities nor opposed terms, but successive phases of a single process of genesis, comparable in its unfolding to the other genetic processes the living world shows us (both phylogenesis and ontogenesis)."[66] However, in invention there occurs, within images and between them, "a change of structure which is also a change in the order of magnitude": "Invention is distinguished from the images preceding it by the fact that . . . it does not stay within the living being as a component of its mental equipment but steps over the spatio-temporal limits of the living to connect with the milieu which it organizes."[67] However, we must note that

> the tendency to transcend the individual subject which is actualized through invention is, in fact, contained virtually in the three previous stages of the image cycle; the amplifying projection of the motor tendency, prior to the experience of the object, is an implicit hypothesis of deployment within the world; the perceptual classes, serving as a subjective system for the reception of incident information, posits a universal application; finally, the symbolic bond of memory-images, while it expresses the attachment of the subject to the situations that constituted its history in a centripetal direction, it also and above all prepares for the use of reversibility, which converts this bond into a pathway towards things. In none of the three stages of its genesis is the mental image limited by the individual subject who carries it.[68]

The image, in each of its stages, even before that of invention, tends to transcend and to leave itself, and invention, properly speaking, prolongs this movement in objectively revealing the general regime of the development of image: "Genuine invention transcends its own end; the initial intention of solving a problem is only a trigger"; invention recruits more than it anticipated: *in the successful invention, some measure of being itself is recruited,* and the change in the order of magnitude has ontological ("ontogenetic") implications. "If invention were merely the organization of a given situation, without the creation of an object, this incorporation of supernumerary functions within the universe of producible things would not occur since organization would be confined to the resolution of a problem; but as soon as a separate object arises, the constraints of that object entail a long detour, a larger unit of measure, that performs an incorporation of reality in the same way the evolution of life proceeds according to Lamarck: by incorporating within organisms properties that were left to the random effects of the milieu, properties which become, in more complex organisms, the source of regular functions."[69]

The *Cours sur la perception* made perception appear "to be a privileged modality of the living and thus active relation of the human being to its world," as Renaud Barbaras forcefully put it in the first page of his preface. The course on *Imagination and Invention* shows that one could say the same of the imagination, and even more radically for the reasons that we have briefly recalled here, since, to a degree, the vital function of perception and its relation to the first motor structures from which it comes, passes through the image. This theory makes the image and the imagination appear as a fundamental vital function, as the path by which mind *[psychisme]* arises in the living (and not only the human). It is the radicality and the coherence of its biological signification which is expressed in the fact that the image itself appears as a kind of organism in development. The theory of the imagination and of invention presented here allows us to grasp, in a particularly clear and synoptic way, the thematic and problematic unity of Simondon's thought.

Imagination and
Invention

Preamble

This course proposes a theory: the aspects of the mental image, which have been the object of discussion and of published studies, do not correspond to different types of reality, but to different stages of a single activity undergoing a developmental process.

A mental image is a relatively independent subset within the living being qua subject *[être vivant sujet]*; at its birth, an image is a sheaf of motor tendencies, a long-term anticipation of the experience of an object; during the interaction between the organism and its milieu, it becomes a receptor system for incoming signals, and it allows the perceptual-motor activity to exercise itself in a progressive mode.[1] Finally, when the subject is again separated from the object, the image—enhanced by cognitive contributions and integrating the affective-emotional resonance of the experience—becomes a symbol. From the internally organized universe of symbols, which tends towards saturation, there may then spring an invention, which consists in putting into motion a more powerful, dimensional system capable of integrating more complete images according to a mode of synergetic compatibility. After invention—the fourth phase in the becoming of images—the cycle starts again with a new anticipation of the encounter with the object—which may well be its production.

According to this theory of the image cycle, reproductive imagination and invention are neither separated realities nor opposed terms. They are successive phases of a single process of genesis, comparable in its unfolding to the other genetic processes that the living world shows us (both phylo-genesis and ontogenesis).

The central difficulties encountered by this theory of the image cycle comes from two sources.

(1) The same word, "image," seems to be applied to different and un-related realities. We should then specify them accordingly as "symbol" or "perception" or "desire" . . .[2] In fact, it is not a matter of reducing the whole of mental activity to the image in the process of genesis, but of showing that, during anticipation, then in the course of the perceptual-motor relation, and ultimately within memory and later in invention, there exists a local activity making the subject a veritable generator of signals that are meant to antici-pate, then receive, and finally preserve and "recycle," through action, the in-coming signals from the milieu. Faculty psychology creates the conceptual barrier, because faculties were defined on the basis of dominant tasks: antic-ipating, perceiving, and remembering; to those three moments in time cor-respond perception, memory, and imagination. What characterizes an image is that it is a local endogenous activity, and this activity exists just as much in the presence of the object (in perception) as it does before experience, as anticipation, or afterwards, as memory-symbol. Among memories not all are images.

(2) The word "image" is generally understood as designating a mental content of which we can be conscious; this is the main difficulty, because in some cases such a conscious appearance of the image is indeed possible for the human subject—partially in a situation of anticipation, and espe-cially in that of a memory-symbol; but there is no evidence that even in the best cases consciousness exhausts the entire reality of this local activity. To the contrary, we might surmise that the conscious aspects of the local activ-ity are cases of an almost exceptional surfacing [*affleurement*] connected to a continuous framework; they are connected to an infrastructure that carries them along after having prepared them, like the visible part of a mushroom which is supported by the more durable, essential, and universal mycelium, for there are mushrooms that do not produce this visible part above ground; and yet they proliferate, and their action on the milieu is no less powerful.

Finally, there is an important terminological issue that must be cleared up to avoid confusion: the relationship between sign and symbol. A sign, in relation to the reality it designates, is a supplementary term which is added to that reality; a blackboard exists and is complete in itself in the absence of the word designating it; we can leave by the wayside the question of *The Cratylus* concerning the rectitude of nominations that may be either arbitrary, conventional, or based on some intrinsic resemblance or analogy between the structure of the sign and that of the named thing, which would make of the sign the cipher [*chiffre*], the formula of the thing. A symbol, by contrast, maintains an analytical relation with what it symbolizes; symbols come in pairs, which means that a symbol is a fragment of a primordial whole divided along an accidental line; put together, the two complementary symbols reconstitute their primitive unity; each symbol moves towards the other, drawing its meaning from the reunion with its complement. Originally, symbols were the two fragments of a divided object, as in the rites of hospitality where a stone was broken; each family preserved and transmitted the fragment it received on to its descendants; the gapless reunification with the other fragment authenticated the relation. The relationship between a key and a lock is of this kind. A key without a lock or a lock without key are not complete realities; they only become meaningful through their reunion. The relationship of the human couple is thus interpreted by Plato, in the myth of the *Symposium,* as reconstituting the primitive unity of the "Androgynous." This original meaning of the word "symbol," its strong meaning, reappears when the word signifies a criterion for a gathering, allowing the authentication of those who belong to a group; the Apostles' Creed [*Symbole des Apôtres*] or the Nicene Creed [*Symbole de Nicée*] are professions of faith producing the mental coincidence of multiple people while keeping heresy at bay.

In the study of the genesis of images, we will call those memory-images resulting from an intense exchange between a subject and a situation "symbols"; having fully participated in an action, or a situation, a subject gives something of himself to this reality; in exchange he preserves an image that is intense enough to be a fragment of the situational reality and, to some extent, allows for its reactivation; such is the memory of a fight, a great danger, or a house where one once lived; a symbol is nostalgic, tending towards the milieu where its counterpart is located; it implies a tendency towards the reconstitution of a primitive unity. The symbol-image may have recourse to the materiality of objects: a "souvenir," be it a metal fragment from the battlefield, a remnant or a relic (a part for the whole), is a mode of access to the whole; it is a way of eliciting it; from this point of view we can understand the value of symbolic objects that concretize the memory-image, the way a flag does for a veteran. They derive their meaning from the mental memory-image, which is really the symbol. In a material way, symbols, the fragments of objects in which the part stands for the whole and communicates with it, are the basis of magical spells; a mere lock of hair or the shred of a garment taken from a person are a fragment of their reality and can act on this person remotely through the intermediary of a symbolic relation. Even without added materialization, mental images may be used as hexes. The symbol is never *flatus vocis*; it presupposes an implicit realism.

This section stands as a symbol for the course.

Introduction

A. The Image as Intermediary Reality between Object and Subject, Concrete and Abstract, Past and Future

1. Object and Subject

The word "imagination" refers back to "faculty psychology"; it is, however, a felicitous word, since it presupposes that mental images result from a certain power, that they express an activity that shapes them, and that they imply, perhaps, the existence of a function that utilizes them. On the other hand, the term "imagination" can lead to misunderstandings, for it connects images to the subject who produced them, and it tends to exclude the hypothesis of a primordial exteriority of images in relation to the subject. This is a common attitude among contemporary thinkers for whom an image refers back to an "imaging consciousness," to invoke Sartre's terms. But why should we exclude as illusory those characteristics whereby an image resists our free will, in which it refuses to let the subject's will direct it, and presents itself according to its own forces, living in our consciousness like an intruder disturbing the order of a household?

This independence and objectivity of the image struck the thinkers of antiquity: in Book VI of *The Odyssey*, Homer describes the vision [*songe*] in which Athena appears to the young princess Nausicaa, prompting her to go wash clothes on the very beach where the shipwrecked Ulysses will soon land, as though it took place at Nausicaa's bedside. The vision [*songe*], with the dream [*rêve*] figures that animate it, is not merely what we would call a subjective event; it makes manifest a certain power, an intention, or a reality that isn't anchored in the subject, but which, on the contrary, comes to him and seeks him out. The image that overcomes the subject is an apparition; it can be stronger than him and change his destiny through a warning or a prohibition. Nor is it simply something of the pedestrian and quotidian real; it has a charge of foreboding; it reveals, makes manifest, declares something beyond the order of quotidian realities; it is of the "numinous," halfway between the objective and the subjective. The belief in ghosts and apparitions may be an attenuated remnant of the relation to the "numinous"; yet it adequately renders and concretizes the aspect of the image's relative exteriority. Any strong image is in some sense endowed with ghostly power, since it can superimpose itself on the world of objective representation and of the present situation, as we say of a ghost that it can walk through walls.

Rites of invocation like the Greek *nekyia,* the representation of the dead through images, or the temporary replacement of the absent through their *colossus* (a statue that was honored like the person it stood for) all reinforced the image density of the numinous world with perceptions. But it is worth noting that the more rationalist ancient philosophers tried to explain this aspect of the exteriority of the image through physical causes rather than denying it. In Book IV of *De rerum natura,* Lucretius explained the different images formed spontaneously in the atmosphere (vapors, clouds looking like giants or tall mountains) through physical causes alone. The simulacra, emitted by objects that have since ceased to exist, can preserve and combine themselves at random over their wayward course; like spiderwebs or gold leaves, they fuse together to produce Centaurs, Cerberuses, or Scyllae: the Centaur results from the fusing of horse simulacra and human simulacra. In the dead of night, these weak and old simulacra can move the soul that receives no intense stimulation; the eye of the mind is like the eyes of the body. The simulacra that produce dreams exist in reality, even though the beings from which they come have vanished; the error of dreams consists only in attributing a present life to the object they represent; if we think we see dream figures move, it is not because they are alive now (IV, 767–76), but because we receive a great number of successive simulacra representing progressively varying postures that reconstitute the impression of motion. Such an explanation, entirely objective and objectivist, respects the potency of the exteriority and relative independence of images with respect to the subject. It is only starting in the seventeenth century that the description of images in terms of subjectivity imposed itself.

In fact, images are not as limpid as concepts; they do not follow the mind's activity with the same flexibility; they can only be governed indirectly; they maintain a certain opacity, like a foreign population in the midst of an orderly state. Displaying, to a degree, will, appetite and motion, images almost seem to be secondary organisms within the thinking being: parasites or a surplus, they are like secondary monads, sometimes inhabiting the subject, other times leaving it. They may prove to be, against a person's unity, a seed of splitting [dédoublement], but they might also bring their reserve of implicit power and implicit knowledge to moments when problems must be solved. Through images, mental life contains something social, for there exists stable or mutating groupings of images in the process of becoming. We might surmise that this character of images, at once subjective and objective, translates, in fact, the image's status as a quasi-organism, dwelling in the subject and developing in it with relative independence from unified and conscious activity.

2. Concrete and Abstract

The image is not a reality devoid of force, efficacy, or consequences; in meditation or contemplation, images entering consciousness might not be forceful or be endowed only with a weak "ideo-motor power." Yet, in action, in constraining situations and intense situations—replete with danger, need, desire, or fear—images can intervene forcefully. Montaigne and Pascal noted how the pomp of the powerful brought prestige to those who surround themselves with commotion and armed guards. The intensity of sensorial stimulations and spontaneous reactions brings a motor power to the image of justice, of the deployment of force, and so on, even when these concrete aspects are merely evoked rather than perceived. Malebranche was wary of the power of a strong imagination, for he knew how much images can inflect the path of our lives. Spinoza found one of the principles of human bondage in the inadequate knowledge that images provide (see in particular his analysis of jealousy). The path towards freedom begins with knowledge according to the order of causes.

In situations of urgency and worry, or, more generally, of intense emotion, images take on their full vital relief and lead to decisions; these images are not perceptions, they do not correspond to the pure concrete, since in order to make a choice one has to be at a certain remove from the real, to not find oneself already engaged; the semi-concrete dimension of images comprises anticipatory aspects (projects, envisioning the future), cognitive contents (the representation of reality, and details heard or seen), and finally, affective and emotional contents; the image is a sample of life, but it remains partly abstract because of the patchy and partial aspect of this sample. In the choice of a profession, the life sample provided by the image of each envisioned profession has elements of anticipation (the lure of travel, the pursuit of power) that are the triggers for potential activities, cognitive data (examples of people in these professions, models), and finally, an affective resonance (the impression of security, of purity). In this sense, the image, as an intermediary between the concrete and the abstract, synthetizes, in a few features, motor, cognitive, and affective charges; this is why it allows for a choice, because each image has a weight, a certain force—and we can weigh and compare images, not concepts or perceptions. Thanks to this synthesis that images operate, means can become homogeneous with ends, where conceptual thought separated them. One can choose an activity by thinking about the image of a train or high-speed transport allowing one to reach the city where the activity will take place.

Abstract thought is mainly a braking mechanism, a means of refusal: it calculates and shows complications, distant consequences; perceptions provoke an entrainment by the situation; only the image is truly regulative, for it is sufficiently abstract to disengage the subject from intense [*prégnantes*] situations, yet concrete enough to provide a sample likely to reflect them. The best situation for making a choice is one allowing the formation and use of a truly mixed image, equally abstract and concrete, one which implies a middle distance in relation to the object. Children generate such semi-concrete representations for people who live in a middle distance (educators, peers), and by becoming models these representations play a determinant role in organizing behavior. Realities that are too purely day-to-day and concrete cannot become so strongly normative: no prophet is accepted in his own country.

Clichés, or stereotyped images—what one calls in English "stereotypes" —intervene in the relations between nations and ethnic communities (according to a UNESCO report). In peacetime, such semi-concrete representations express perceptual tendencies *[allures]* in a static manner, rather like a caricature: a Frenchman in Germany is "a man decorated with a legion of honor insignia who doesn't know geography"; for the French an Englishman is a traveler with a patterned suit and big teeth; and the Frenchman, for the English, is a snail and frog eater. Such images, as a matter of fact, express different degrees of social distance: the imaginary degree of non-hygiene corresponds to remoteness, and proximate populations (the English as seen by Americans) are considered clean; they also express general attitudes or fears: in certain regions of the United States the French are perceived as "Don Juans." In times of war, the affective-emotional charge of such images comes to the fore; the image of the enemy is applied to any individual attracting attention through a physiognomic feature or a detail of clothing, and becomes the spy or secret agent. Fauconnet has shown in *Responsibility* how, especially in primitive societies, responsibilities are attributed; he also cites medieval texts stating as supplemental presumptions of guilt "the bad mien" of a defendant, his taciturn appearance, or "the ugly name he bears." In some cases a phenomenon of cumulative causality occurs which ultimately brings into existence, as an actual attitude and an objective social state, a stereotyped image whose origin is purely mental and subjective: this was documented by Gunnar Myrdal in his important investigation of the status of African Americans in the United States; the prejudices of white employers and landlords regarding the qualities and deficiencies of African Americans predetermine the possibility or impossibility of certain behaviors (professions, for example); conversely, and here in an objective way, professional choices predetermine a certain mode of education for children, a certain level of literacy, and the definition of ideals; after a few recurring cycles going from the image to the real and from the real to the image through perception, the original image becomes real and finds, in social conditions, sufficient justifications to become stabilized. This phenomenon of cumulative causality has played an important role in the stereotyping of minorities such as Jews in western Christian states, women in patriarchal societies, and currently teenagers in our own societies: the fear and animosity of adults trap them in a narrow role, materialized in the "image of youth" that adults generate. The image of the slave in antiquity was also a phenomenon of cumulative causality that stabilized for centuries, until the forceful realization of Seneca.

If we may consider the whole of economic exchanges as an action, the role played by images in decision appears clearly: a commodity or an object is clothed in images (of social status, of foreign provenance) that are superadded to their actual characteristics. Commerce willfully creates conditions that give an imaginary life to those commodities whose characteristics are insufficient to determine a choice; when a commodity is sold in a package, the package is the bearer of images (laundry soap, for instance); if the commodity (gas, for instance) is sold to a distributor, it can be colored (Azure's blue petrol, for example) or given images by the distributors themselves: the Exxon tiger, for example, with a striped ribbon around the exhaust, and tiger tails to be attached to cars. Each of these images is developed in motor and affective elements; azure is the color of the sky, and the tiger, symbolically placed into the engine, for all of its peace and calm is capable of leaping at will.

Collective phenomena like fashion imply the existence of the semi-abstract character of the image. By adopting a given fashion, a person chooses a set of attitudes, limits, and possibilities—a certain lifestyle; the look of Chanel implies different values than that of Courrèges, in women's fashion; through the cut of their clothes, individuals are perceived as traditional or modern. In their particular features, each person carries the concrete aspects rendering him or her recognizable; but through the use they make of fashion, as a set of attitudes exhibited and made perceptible, a person affirms his or her belonging to a group and his or her adherence to a partially conceptualizable and abstract set of norms. Clothing functions as a selector: it adapts to certain gestures, forbids others, preserves from rain or cold, or, to the contrary, makes one vulnerable; this prosthetic role reduces the number of possibilities, but also develops and heightens the possibilities targeted, like a theatrical mask that immobilizes the expression of physiognomy at the same time that it gives the voice a greater range. Clothing, masks, and personas place the organism at a middle distance from things and stabilize the relation to the physical and social world by mediating it.

In this sense, anything that functions as an intermediary between subject and object can attain the value of an image and play the role of a prosthesis in both the adaptive and restrictive sense. Today, the particularities of speech, of accents, the professional jargon draw less attention than they did in the seventeenth century (in Molière's comedies); the uniform has also tended to disappear. Yet the imaginal value of the intermediary between subject and object is transferred to marks of social status, to cars, or other details like hairdos. Indeed, the image as an intermediary reality between abstract and concrete, between self and world, is not merely mental: it materializes to become an institution, a product, wealth, that is relayed both by commercial networks and the "mass media" diffusing information. Its intermediary character, made of both consciousness and object, bestows on it an intensified capacity to propagate; images imprint [imprègnent] themselves in civilizations and energize them with their power [force]; in a way, images express social and economic facts (for instance, the use of plastic fiber in clothing), but as soon as they are materialized and objectified, they also constitute a charge and introduce a tension that partially determines social becoming. For this reason, phenomena such as the evolution of fashion are far from superficial; we cannot consider them as a pure result, an expression, an epiphenomenon, a transitory aspect of the superstructure; the image is a resultant, but it is also a seed: it can become the trigger for concepts and doctrines. The circular causality that goes from the mind to objective reality through social processes of cumulative causality also goes from objective reality to the mind. Any image is susceptible to incorporation into a process of materializing or idealizing recurrence; deposited in fashion, art, monuments, technical objects, the image becomes a source of complex perceptions triggering movements, cognitive representations, affections, and emotions. Almost all man-made objects are in some way image-objects; they bear latent meanings, not merely cognitive but conative and affective-emotional; image-objects are quasi-organisms or at least seeds capable of being reborn and developing in the subject. Even outside of the subject, they multiply through group exchanges and activities, propagating and reproducing themselves in a neotenic state until they find the opportunity to become reabsorbed and redeployed until they reach an imaginal phase in which they are reincorporated into a new invention.

The study of imagination must research the meaning of image-objects since imagination is not just an activity of image production or evocation, but equally the mode of receiving images concretized as objects, the discovery of their sense, of the perspective of a new existence for them. Image-objects—artworks, clothing, machines—become obsolete, larval memories, ghosts from the past that slowly vanish with the vestiges of lost civilizations. Aesthetic analysis and technical analysis go in the direction of invention, for they operate a rediscovery of the meaning of these image-objects by perceiving them as organisms, and rekindling the invented and produced reality of their imaginal plenitude. Any complete and true discovery of meaning is at the same time a re-installation and a recuperation, an effective re-incorporation into the world; consciousness is not enough since organisms do not only have a knowable structure, they have tendencies and develop. It is a philosophical, psychological and social task to *save the phenomena* by re-installing them in becoming, relocating them in inventions, by deepening the images they harbor.

The concreteness of invented reality is not, indeed, arbitrary and subjective like a flight of individual fantasy; it tends towards universality because it is plurifunctional; the image-object, whether aesthetic, technical, or prosthetic, is a weave of the now linked to the network of contemporary realities; the least stable in appearance—fashion for instance—is a real invention insofar as a piece of clothing integrates economic availabilities and operational or perceptual norms into a unity; white winter boots and a white raincoat correspond to the availability of dyed synthetic plastic, insuring chromatic stability and high visibility in low lighting environments; there is a family relation between such clothing and the clothing of road workers, an analogy between white reflective bands, or the signals and runway signs used for aeronautics or rockets; this clothing is "opticalized" more or less ostensibly, meaning it declares itself as a prosthetic for outdoors, for all terrains and climates, rather than as street or indoor clothing.

It is this charge of invention that can be redeployed when the image-object is rediscovered and analyzed, possibly by means of transposition: what was used in garb or clothing for the perception of social rank may be rethought for street or indoor clothing according to norms of perception connected to the functionalism of road traffic, factory, or construction work.

The object-image is a true intermediary between the concrete and the abstract when it condenses several functions into one (for a single function it remains abstract) and uses solutions linking it to the network of contemporary realities; its reality is here paradigmatic, allowing for the understanding of other related realities with which it is articulated and solidary.

The existence of different categories of image-objects, a third reality between objective and subjective realms, calls for a particular mode of analysis we might properly call phenomenological since this type of reality has the aim of manifesting itself and imposing its image character.

3. Past and Future

The numerous metaphors for images, drawn from the domain of the living and from the world of the non-living (crystallization), signal a complex mode of existence and proliferation, one that makes images—whether purely mental or materialized in image-objects—intermediaries between past and future, for both the individual subject as well as for the group.

In individual life the image may stretch towards memory, manifesting itself primarily as a reference to the past, under the aspect of a revival of complex sensations. This aspect was studied by Taine in *On Intelligence*: an image is a spontaneously reborn sensation, usually less energetic and precise that the sensation itself; each of the senses has its own images. The image and the corresponding sensation have equal and similar effects. If the image differs from the sensation, it is not in its content or its mode of appearing, that is, in itself, but through the effects of image reductives [*réducteurs*],[1] which promptly rectify the illusion accompanying the image, which would otherwise develop into a hallucination. An image always involves a hallucination of greater or lesser duration, but in most cases, the hallucination is destroyed by antagonistic sensations, by memories, or by general judgments, all of which form, in their cohesion, a corpus of auxiliary reductives, while the antagonistic sensation is the special reductive. The polypus of images that is the mind is thus comparable to the polypus of cells that is the body: cells interact with each other; as do images; they lead, in the reasonable wakeful state, to a mutual equilibrium. The image is the substitute of sensation, a more manageable instrument of mental activity than sensation itself.

Conversely, the image is the basis of anticipation, allowing the prefiguration of near or distant futures, and symbolic attempts at solving anticipated
problems. The activity of anticipation differs from the use of the image as
memory in its meaning and mode of deployment: in anticipation, the reductives are less effective, and there can an amplifying proliferation of images,
comparable to what happens in La Fontaine's fable where Perrette already
sees the "calves, cows, hogs, chicks" until the milk jar shatters, acting as a
violent reductive.[2] The imagination of artists and writers can pre-form a new
state of society, a new face of life, as we find in *romans d'anticipation*. To a
greater extent, invention is so strongly stretched towards the future that it
brings to existence, outside of the subject, a new mode of reality.

Nonetheless it is quite rare for imagination to be either purely reproductive or purely creative. The evocation of the past is a new life, schematized
differently than the old life, polished and formalized by active memory as
in engravings of historical scenes or the Épinal prints celebrating the legend
of the Napoleonic epic. Such an evocation presents ideals, vehicles for values, and projects itself into the future as an example to be followed by future
generations: the memory-image seeks to reincarnate and perpetuate itself,
it carries a subjacent anticipation and, to a certain extent, does violence to
the present in guiding it to open itself toward a future of revival [*reviviscence*].
Anticipation, in turn, reprises old dreams and contains the echo of old aspirations already materialized in old object-images, such as anticipations of
human flight and travel "towards celestial signs," to which the legend of Icarus
and the Promethean adventure correspond. For humans, the wing is as much
a memory as it is an invention, remembrance as much as anticipation.

For collective life, too, the image incorporates part of the past and can
make it available for prospective work precisely to the extent that mental
images materialize themselves not only through processes of cumulative causality, but through paths of invention, creating aesthetic, prosthetic, and technical image-objects. Forward planning in collective life (in corporations,
even nations) corresponds to the function of projects and rational anticipations in the short, mid, and long term: there are specialists in forward
planning according to the time span under consideration. . . . This effort of
collective rationalization of the gaze projected onto the future is one of the
characteristics of the world today: during the last century, appeals to the

future were associated with a strong affective and emotional charge, colored by social ideas, inflated by hope; the dimension of the future remained mythical and contained a veiled recourse to transcendence, a haven for longing towards eternity. Only the past had become a topic of science, for scientific historians. The necessities of long-term forecasts [*prévision*] for action have introduced rationalization into the dimension of the future and have driven out mythical thinking, at least in the domains of economics and demography; time begins to be organized like space; the future is annexed to knowledge and no longer the privileged field of the optative, of desire, or of volition. Nonetheless, the image recovers its density and force which carries it towards the anticipation of the collective future, beside and beyond the prospective rationalizations, which are not true inventions, but extrapolations.

Science fiction is one of the ways the image recovers its futural power, that is to say, its prophetic function; science fiction is the image of the real world grasped as a tendency and pushed further, truly anticipated, grasped prospectively in its cognitive and emotional aspects rather than merely supposed. What is lacking for forward planning to become an actual anticipation is this qualitative power, this *physis* that bestows on the future its true dimension of a development in process. To foresee [*prévoir*] is not just a matter of seeing, but of inventing and living: true forecasting [*prévision*] is to a certain extent a *praxis,* a tendency to development of an action already begun. The image, as a reservoir of oriented emotion linked to a specific knowledge, ensures this continuity of the act faithful to its own progression; it adds to forward planning a "proactive" force.

An old and forgotten form of the image is that of religions, particularly in the prophetic act as well as in sacrificial practices. Religions, however, are modes of being according to which past and future communicate and lend each other their force through the constituted image. What was destroyed will come back, what had died will be reborn, and what was corrupted will bloom again in an immense cycle. In *Maccabees,* as one of the first followers is ready to die, drained of his blood, having ripped and thrown his intestines to the crowd, he shouts out that God will bring him back to life and he will be reborn. We can also recall the Biblical saying, "unless the kernel of wheat falls into the earth and dies . . ." The painful consummation of the past prepares a rebirth. Death prepares a birth; the complete image of death declares and prophesizes the call of a birth. The blood of martyrs is a seed. Prophecy as a verbal image accompanies and expresses this subterranean cycle that runs from past to future the way fall cycles to spring.

This order of *third reality* is neither fully perceptible nor entirely conceptualizable: the study of the image in this area must be complemented by the evocation of the myths of becoming, like the high road and low road among ancient Greek philosophers, the rhythm of conflagration and deflagration, the return of the Great Year, and even the notion of Nemesis.

Part of the reality of groups is made of images, materialized as drawings, statues, monuments, garments, tools, and machines, as well as turns of phrase, formulas like proverbs that are true verbal images (akin to slogans). Such images ensure the cultural continuity of groups and are constant intermediaries between their past and future: they are both vehicles of experiences and knowledge as well as specific modes of waiting.

B. The Hypothesis of the Genetic Dynamism of the Image: Phases and Levels

Studies of ontogenesis have shown that growth processes do not cover the organs and functional systems of a living being in a uniform way: there are lags in each partial growth relative to the others, and there are different speeds, especially among complex organisms, so much so that it is difficult to establish the exact moment at which an organism reaches its complete adult stage; moreover, growth and development display stages and cycles, separated by periods of transition in which a dedifferentiation is followed by a reorganization. Such processes are very clear in the metamorphoses of some living species, yet they also take place in the organic development and the ontogenesis of human behavior.

Could we not then posit that mental images are like structural and functional subsets of this organized activity that is psychic activity? These subsets would thus possess a genetic dynamism analogous to that of an organ or a system of organs on a trajectory of growth, and we could essentially distinguish three stages: first, that of pure and spontaneous growth, prior to the experience of the object to which a functional activity is pre-adapted; this would be, in the image, the equivalent to the embryonic stages of organic growth; each image, as an embryo of motor and perceptual activity, develops itself for itself here as a non-controlled anticipation, through reference to the experience of the milieu, and to a free state, which is to say without strict correlation to other subsets of psychic activity. It displays pre-adaptations but not adaptations. The image then becomes a mode of receiving [*accueil*] information coming from the milieu and a source of response schemas to these stimuli; in perceptual-motor experience, images become effectively and directly functional; they organize and stabilize themselves in internally correlated groups according to the dimensions of the relationship between the organism and the milieu. Finally, after this stage of interaction with the milieu corresponding to a learning process [*un apprentissage*], an affective-emotional repercussion completes the organization of images according to a systematic mode of linkages, evocations, and communications; a veritable mental world is constituted, with regions, domains, qualitative key points through which the subject commands *an analog of the external milieu*, one that has its own constraints, its own topology, its complex modalities of access. In other words, images would undergo successive mutations that would modify their mutual relations by making them pass from the status of primitive mutual independence to a phase of interdependence at the moment the object is encountered, to a final state of systematic and necessitating linkage in which primitively kinetic energies have become tensions within a system. Invention could then be considered as a *shift in the organization* of the system of adult images, returning mental activity to a new state of free images, through a change of level, thus allowing a genesis to start again: invention would be the rebirth of the cycle of images, one that permits an approach to the milieu with new anticipations from which adaptations will emerge that were not possible for primitive anticipations, and then a new internal and symbolic systematization. In other words, invention operates a change of level; it marks the end of a cycle and the beginning of another, each comprising three phases: anticipation, experience, and systematization.

Each phase of the genesis of the image can be placed in relation to a dominant activity or "function":

Before the experience of an object borne by the milieu, the image, as anticipation, is rich in endogenous motor elements; it is connected to the hereditary coordinations of movement revealed by ethological studies; its

intensity may thus vary according to levels of motivation, up to a hallucinatory mode of appearance and action (as in the case of *Leerlaufreaktion*, or
vacuum activities, in ethology). In this sense we can speak of *a priori images*,
and the predominance of primary motor elements in this activity is to be
associated with the fact that in species development, and perhaps individual
development too, motricity precedes sensoriality as a long-term anticipation
of behaviors.

In the direct relation with the milieu, the image provides the local activity
that is a mode of reception of incident information. This short-term anticipation, constantly adapted and readapted to the situation, adjusted to the
structure of objects in the form of a pre-perceptual or inter-perceptual schema,
is marked by the predominance of cognitive contents. By analogy, and an
extension of the vocabulary, we might speak of *a praesenti images*, which
may, in some cases, be manifested in a separate state, in the form of errors or
illusions, but which, normally, pass unperceived since they are at the service
of perceptual activity.

After perception, the affective-emotional effect, or resonance, takes priority; the image is then the remarkable point that is preserved when the situation no longer exists; we might speak of a memory in this *a posteriori image*,
and indeed the category of memory-images, with their capacity to revive
situations from evocations of the image, is not new in psychology. But we
should note that not all memories are images. A memory is a true *a posteriori*
image when it appears as an imprinting *[prégnance]* and with an intensity
that endows it with an organizing power; this particular memory is a remarkable point that holds a meaning for a topology of the system of past experience in the process of organizing itself; it is a source of attitude reactivation,
it has a qualitative power, and presents itself as a sample of a situation rather
than as memory of an experience. Through this image that preserves an
objective density and contains a reference to the alterity of experienced reality, the subject preserves and retains in himself an *analogon* of external reality, one that may materialize itself as a caricature, a devotional image, or
a work of art. The emotional density and the sheaf of qualitative nuance
incorporated in this particular memory constitutes a charge, a state of the
system that conserves and condenses at once both the spontaneous, endogenous movement of long-term anticipation of the *a priori* image, and the

heterogeneous plurality of the perceived, brought by experience. This synthesis in equal proportions of endogenous motor energy and information coming from the milieu is a concrete symbol of the relation between subject and milieu; this particular mix represents a point of insertion of mental activity in the milieu; it condenses a situation, preserves it with its network of forces and tendencies, and allows that situation to be recreated. In this sense, the world of memory-images produces a true mental universe, or rather, constitutes the terminals [bornes] and the wiring [voies] of a mental universe that is polarized [polarisé] and under tension [tendu].

This universe, in which movements linked to exogenous structures have become forces and energies in a state of suspension, in the mode of potentiality, is an analogical organization of symbols; when the subject is saturated, unable to receive new experiences, he must modify his structure to find larger, more "powerful" dimensions of organization able to surmount the felt incompatibilities. When invention, as a change of level, is unable to take place and develop a new cycle, the failure of the structural change of the symbolic universe manifests itself in pathological modalities.

Such a general hypothesis of the genesis of images might lead to a dialectical interpretation (the a posteriori image has the characteristics of a synthesis), but the dialectical aspect of the relations between organism and milieu is only a partial aspect of the process of genesis; the thetic phase, anterior to experience, translates the spontaneity of the organism and the preexistence of an anticipating activity deployed prior to experience; experience is already an antithetical phase corresponding to the tightest relationship between organism and milieu. In other words, one might think that a deeper study of the relations between organism and milieu might help us understand the origin of the dialectical schema, and consequently lead to situating it, to relativizing it, rather than preserving it as the unconditional principle of the intelligibility of becoming. If the idea of dialectical evolution can be conserved, it is above all as an affirmation of a progressive succession of modes of organization of images across different phases, such modes of organization being so many "logics" capable of providing anchor points for reflective and systematizing thought.

If invention can effect a change of level, we need to define the main levels at which the dynamic genesis of images might be located.

The primary level might be called biological or vital: it implies the participation of the entire organism as a means of actualization and it engages that organism in situations through categories like the relation to predator, to prey, or to partner; anticipation is in this sense the preexistence of hereditary coordinations of instinctual action, like aggression or flight, that imply the participation of the organism as a whole. Perceptual experience is directed by innate forms or "patterns,"[3] grasping the corresponding sense of situations according to the primary modes of danger, feeding, partnering, and domination or submission in social species. Resonance consists mainly of intensive apprenticeships, limited, however, to typical situations such as those from the phenomenon of imprinting *[Prägung]* studied by ethologists.

The secondary level, which may be called psychological, though the term is far from satisfactory, involves a more specialized participation of the nervous system in the local activity producing images; instead of directly engaging the whole organism in each situational relation with the milieu, it develops a mental analog of this primary relation. Anticipation, rather than awaking instinctual activity, manifests itself in the form of motivation and conscious anticipation, of desire, of felt needs, of action plans, and through a succession of images that prepare the encounter with the object. In experience, the local activity producing images no longer functions as a mode of reception of primary categories of existence, but of the recognition and analysis of the object, of the perception of its present state, of the appreciation of variations and differences, and of the high differential processing of incident signals; the image functions here as an instrument of adaptation to the object; it presupposes that there is an object and not just a situation. After experience, the properly psychical image is the affective-emotional symbol of the object, comprising the association of a representative trait with a modality of reaction in the subject. For instance, after a conversation, the images of a few words remain, a typical expression with a specific intonation by the interlocutor joined to a specific affective-emotional valence. This memorial complex serves as a reference for the organization of the representation of the milieu with its valences in the subject.

Finally, there may also be a third level of the activity of images that must be called formal or, in a certain sense, reflexive, because they operate systematizations effectuated from the point of view of the subject dominating its relation to the milieu. As anticipation, the *a priori* image appears under the form of a motor intuition, a projection schema issued from an active center of spontaneity and radiating towards the plurality of situations or objects. Such intuitions are found in the principle of philosophical doctrines like Platonism, Plotinus' doctrine, or that of Bergson's *élan vital*; through reflexive intuition the subject identifies with the singular and unconditional source of projection, of procession or evolution; the subject returns, at the level of ideas, to the absolute origin of present existence and experience, and operates a pure anticipation. This same level of formal activity manifests itself in the modality of present experience through an abstract schematization of classification, impelled by an analogical transfer from level to level, as one sees at work, for instance, in the application of the hylomorphic schema; in this case, the monism of *a priori* intuition is opposed by the permanent duality of two heterogeneous principles taken together; the reciprocal situation of matter and form is comparable to the exogenous input of incident information, coming from the milieu, informed by the local activity that confers a unity upon it. Finally, if the implicit logic of *a priori* images provides the primitive model of intuitive reflexivity, while that of intra-perceptual images is the trigger of an inductive or deductive systematization, the world of *a posteriori* images seems indeed to be the principle of amplifying reflexivity, capable of ideally reconstructing the genesis of events and their history from a limited number of reference points endowed with a specific valence; it is this type of organization of images as an *analogon* of the universe that takes place in philosophical systems of a dialectical kind; they presuppose, as a source of intelligibility and development, a complex experience whose origin comes from historical situations.

The sketch of a link between reflexive modes and the activity of images, taken as a non-exhaustive example of the formal level of such activity, aims not only at foregrounding the relativity of intuition, of discourse, or of dialectical thought, but also at showing that none of these three systematizations fully coincides with the activity of invention, which is too unstable to serve as a paradigm. At a less elevated level of formalization, the *a priori* activity of images is deployed in the various kinds of initiation-based thought, while their *a posteriori* use fuels the structuring of figurations and myths with broad collective meaning; in this sense, the study of the image could be directed towards the analysis of cultural contents.

C. The Fields of Application of the Notion of Genetic Cycle of the Image; the Image Exterior to the Individual

In Nature we observe that cyclical activities tend to synchronize, that is, to become attuned to recurring phenomena apt to interfere with them. Can we observe such synchronizations in the genetic becoming of mental images?

1. Synchronization with the Circadian Rhythm

The alternation of days and nights modulate human activity in varying degrees (depending on lifestyle, the degree of urbanization . . .). To a certain extent, each day takes on the appearance of a complete cycle that carries along a continuous variation in predominance of this or that category of images. The images of evening, coming after the day's intense activity, are those of memory; the involuntary evocation of the past may acquire enough relief to evince apparitions out of the images of lost ones; situations experienced a long time ago or recently recur and take on a new life; the day, and more broadly, life, is recapitulated when action ceases or relaxes. Its chapters are to images and faces, the past becomes systematized, ordering itself in sets according to an emotive-affective topology qualified by regret or satisfaction. By contrast, the first lights of dawn chase away this crowd of images from the past; after sleep and before activity begins, the anticipations of movement, images that are but projects and triggers of realization are predominant; it is the time when the individual feels the most pressingly what motivates his actions and that he is the origin of his behavior, experiencing a sense of freedom in the inchoate phase of his relationship to objects; the day's perspectives project like rays diverging from a single center, focus, and source: future action is envisioned in an *a priori* mode, and the encounter of real objects arises and orders itself within the amplifying expansion of the project. The unity of motor intuition structures the anticipation of the activity. The direct relation to the milieu, when one is working, corresponds instead to images that are the most directly inserted into perception; finally, night is the time of a cycle change wherein changes of structure sometimes occur which represent major or minor inventions that lead to seeing situations under a new light; one "sleeps on it," as the saying goes, because night reveals solutions that did not appear to belong to the waking world.

2. Life as Cycle of the Genesis of Images

If life is compared to a day in which youth would be morning, it is because the character of unlimited freedom of motor power, the principle of anticipation, is common to both. The development of the individual discloses a plurality of powers that constitute so many postulates of the encounter with the object, so many anticipations of life's situations imagined according to the contours of desire—at the same time that it shows those powers as successively diverging from a common origin. In the *élan* of a young being, unlimited will projects the envelope of all possible realities over an entire lifetime. Later, as reality is experienced as limit and obstacle, the sheaf of potentially projected actions becomes diffuse, reflected or refracted; the object emerges within an organization whose perspective does not always prolong that of the anticipating project; in the best case, of successful adaptation to maturity, there is partial parallelism between the order of events and the activity of the subject. The subject organizes his relation to reality like a territory where all is not yet constructed, willed, premeditated, done according to plan, but where construction plans take account of the given. The image the subject has of his activity and even of his projects is the reflection of a situation, which implies a reference to the real and to a preponderance of cognitive elements. The twilight of life, when the subject partially renounces situated activity, foregrounds symbol-images, acquiring, in the form of honors and titles, a social dimension, but also a subjective resonance as well as a magical power of self-consciousness as a means of *post facto* communication and re-evocation of the fundamental actions of a life. To go to the end of the analogical hypothesis, we might say that old age corresponds to the possibility of invention and renewal. This is not the case in our societies; yet in antiquity the prophetic role of the older man or woman came in excess of the possession of wisdom, as fruit of a long experience. Patriarchs knew how to lead their tribe to the promised land. The ongoing devaluation of the status of the elderly correlates with a weakening of prophetic modes of collective thought and of the official and public uses of divination, replaced by a plurality of practical planning.

3. Imagination and the Seasons

In temperate regions, and even more so in circumpolar ones, collective life has been and continues to be affected by a reaction to the seasons either according to the rhythm of agricultural labor or the alternation of work and leisure. Mauss has shown the way in which Inuit life changes when the long polar night brings back collective life with its rites and ceremonies, while summer is the time of isolation and individual activity corresponding to a positive vision of the world. In our mythology, spring is the time of renewal, desire, energy, and projects; summer, that of the realism of work, of action being accomplished at the noontime of the year, when fields are at their fullest. Then with fall, action relaxes, the year gets old, work is totalized in the form of harvest: the year was good or it was bad but it has been consummated. And so the memory of the dead is evoked. Finally, winter's dormancy brings the expectation of a rebirth, like a night between two days. In the past, the year began with Easter, the morning of the annual cycle. In France, August 15 is comparable to noon, midlife in its full maturity: it is the culmination registered in the poetic image, "Noon, king of summers." The mythology of seasons recoups that of the ages of life and the hours of the day because all these cycles have more or less deeply synchronized the genesis of images and are seen through the temporary predominance of one of the three phases of the cycle of images.

4. The Cycle of Images and the Becoming of Civilizations

Taking another step toward the collective character of the genesis of images, we may wonder whether the notion of cycle might not allow us to account for the succession of stages manifested in the continuous development of the content of cultures. Expression such as "the dawn of Greek science," or "the twilight of the idols," appear to take for granted that analogical metaphors of day and night, youth and old age, apply to some degree to the historical succession of stages (archaic or primitive, classic, then decadent) through which various cultural modalities pass—without any necessary coincidence, moreover, between the evolving modalities (religions, arts, etc.). This probably means that the cultural forms subjected to cyclical becoming are those that imply a strong charge of mental images; the pure sciences do have a birth, but they are more progressive, cumulative, as Pascal indicates, when he compares humanity to a single person always learning and never forgetting. By contrast, processes of growth and maturity, then decline, correspond directly to the common trove of images that constitute cultures and serve as norms for individual knowledge and action.

In the succession of primitive, classic, and decadent phases, we find two dominant traits. The first is the predominance in the primitive phase of *a priori* images oriented towards action, celebrating the act, the feat, and leading to initiatory or esoteric knowledge, with elevated values, within a logic of participation; such a culture has aristocratic and sacred dominants, like the art of Pindar or Aeschylus or the medieval *chansons de gestes*; they consecrate the glory of heroes and inspire high deeds such as the poems of Tyrtaeus. Having become classical, a culture finds the images of legend in current and common situations, always present in life, as the sense of everyday human relationships; culture is desacralized and tends towards the deepened *hic et nunc* we call the universal; rather than celebrating great feats or the forces of action, that culture provides the spectacle of action as it unfolds; and it is realist because its modality is the fully actualized present. Finally, the postclassical period seeks intense and poignant emotive-affective images; art is no longer a spectacle but a substitute for reality in the form of symbols as pseudo-objects; cultural forms are decoupled from real life like a double that masks it. Aesthetic values become dominant and constitute a complete universe, a subjective achievement; it is the era of the novel, Romanticism, the imaginary as a second reality, according to a logic of identification. In other words, archaic cultures are centered on action in a perspective of projection into the future; classical cultures mold perceptions and are essentially plastic, builders of a real object; while cultures in decline, rather than inciting action or shaping perceptions of an ordered and arranged (but not doubled) reality, produce a universe of images that dress and mask the world without adhering to it; an aesthetics is thereby created, that is, not a way of perceiving but a manner of experiencing images brought about by art, or even a way of considering the world as a reservoir of images. Everything in the world that triggers a fissure—ruin, historical look *[allure historique]*—allows an escape from perception in order to enter into an emotive-affective universe; symbols acquire meaning within the perspective of an imaginary past life.

Aesthetic art, in contrast to the plastic arts, consigns what it produces to the past: it creates ruins. It is this image-producing art which Plato chased from the polis.

Action, perception, and symbolic memories are thus the three fundamental modalities of the content of images that constitute the basis of cultures, and therefore differ from the sciences, since the third stage is not that of positivity which Auguste Comte discovered in the law of the three stages; knowledge is progressive and continuous, whereas cultures, after each cycle, break apart, change structure, and re-emerge according to new principles.

PART I

The Motor Content of Images

The Image Prior to the Experience of the Object

A. Biological Givens: How Motricity Precedes Sensoriality

1. The Phylogenetic Aspect: The Development of Motricity Precedes that
of Sensoriality; Virtualization

To say that motricity precedes sensoriality amounts to affirming that the stimulus-response schema is not absolutely primary, that it refers to a situation, or a present relation between the organism and the milieu that has already been prepared by an activity of the organism during its growth. Herbert Spencer Jennings's work on the simplest organisms has shown that reactions (a behavior[1] in the presence of an object) are preceded by spontaneous motor activities that exist prior to the reception of the characteristic signals of an object.

In fact, the very notion of the object should be analyzed with precision. It corresponds to a mode in the organism's relation to its milieu, one that implies á highly organized reception of signals. Among the simplest species, the perception of an object can appear in the course of spontaneous, nonreactive activities. Responses [comportements de réponse] to an object might be more frequent than spontaneous activities in the more advanced species, but among the lowest species, the opposite is the case; spontaneous behaviors are necessary and permanent anticipations of perception. These behaviors reveal the existence of a local activity which, even if it ultimately disappears behind the finalized activities of object seeking, continue to provide the basis of anticipations. And we may conjecture that among higher organisms such anticipating spontaneity is preserved but integrated within the activity of the nervous system under the guise of a source of initiatives or a function of endogenous novelty that is the basis of invention and the engine of structural changes that the individual can effect on the inner organization of its analogical representation of the milieu. According to this hypothesis, the activity manifested in Brownian movements among lower organisms, or in trial-and-error behaviors, would provide the most primitive aspect of what will become the genesis of anticipating images among organisms endowed with a highly centralized and strongly telencephalized nervous system. Indeed, randomness or chance comes not only from the stimuli coming from the milieu, carrying information, it is efficaciously deployed from an endogenous source: that of the initiatives of the organism as it encounters the milieu. The perceptual-motor relation is already act two in the drama where two protagonists—organism and milieu—exist, each as a primordial source of novelty and chance. It is the encounter of these two novelties that generates the perceptual relation: to the bundle of signals— an exogenous novelty—corresponds the local activity of an endogenous anticipation coming from the organism, the first form of the *a priori* image whose content is essentially motor.

We must posit then that the first form of anticipation, before the organism's relation to the object, is the set of activities that make the organism an auto-kinetic system; without the pronounced directionality of Brownian movements (as Viaud has observed in the dispersion of a population in a homogenous milieu, the center of gravity remaining fixed), this activity is only slowed down or accelerated by conditions in the milieu (thermo-kinesis, photo-kinesis) but not polarized by it; Brownian movements and kinesis are more primary and more constant than tropisms; tropisms themselves, still very primitive, display an orientation but do not effect an adaptation. They represent a reaction to agents more than to true objects and thus preserve an important part of the auto-kinetic character of the primary behavior of the organism. Only with the "pathies," or the behaviors Jennings calls "avoidance reactions," does a true reaction to an object occur—an adapted reaction modeled on perceptual behaviors.

To state that motricity precedes sensoriality in the development of a species is to affirm that the most primitive living beings execute a great number of movements which come to nothing because their perceptual apparatus is too undeveloped to direct these movements and endow them with efficacy, finality, and economy; the motor apparatus is in advance of the sensorial apparatus. This leads us to believe that the priority of the motor apparatus is maintained in the development of the nervous system, but is integrated within the organism in the form of a capacity the nervous system has to constantly generate sketches of nascent movements which are not responses to stimuli, and which thus constitute the postulate of all new behaviors, all attempts coming from the organism and allowing it to actively confront the relation to the milieu with a complex series of possibilities and ready behaviors; images of movement would then be, in this sense, behavior schemas ready to be actualized but still contained within the nervous system rather than effected one after the other.

Of course, auto-kinetic behaviors can also be dangerous: they can bring an organism into contact with a predator, for instance; they represent an effective means of scouting only within a milieu that is homogenous for long stretches—as are, in general, the milieus of very rudimentary organisms of small size; as soon as discontinuities emerge, as soon as true objects appear, and not simple gradients, the spontaneous anticipations can be adaptive only if they remain virtual, in the form of an attempt that remains within the organism, a fictive assay leading to the action only after receiving perceptual references that ensure an adjustment to the actual milieu.

2. The Action System as Ontogenetic Basis of Motor Images

An anticipation cannot be merely an initiative; it is an organized initiative, with a structure, a consistency with respect to itself, a form. Is there a biological basis for these structures that bear on the anticipation of motor behaviors? Yes, under the guise of an action system that is the dynamic and kinematic equivalent of what is, as a structure, the anatomy of an organism. A species is recognizable not only through the shape of its organs, their relative size and mode of assembly, but also through behavior schemas: ways of drinking, manners of moving, leaping, crawling, seizing an object. The organism is a set of behavior schemas as clearly definable and with as sharp a taxonomic value as the shape of exoskeletal spurs, the number of claws, etc. Such action schemas thus exist in living beings as anticipations of possible behaviors, as partial programs of behavior, and, employed virtually, they can provide a content to anticipations in the guise of preparations for situations in which the object is encountered or the anticipation of responses; the organism can, more or less fully, rehearse its comportments before applying them to a real object; getting up, attacking, fleeing, or confronting: these are sequences whose program a living being possesses in itself the way it possesses its own body; this, then, forms a basis for the local activity of anticipation—and may go as far as gratuitous motor play in improvised situations—but the foundation of the activity is provided by those schemes the being possesses and can elicit at any time as if it were a real situation. Such motor schemas undergird dreaming, during which, in particular, eye movements should be noted. Lucretius noticed them in sleeping dogs. Even while awake, a forcefully imagined action is accompanied by motor anticipations as its most constant organic content: nascent voicing, muscular contractions, walking, making a fist, etc. Emotions, which are not only repercussions but also preparations for action, include motor anticipations that put the elements of the action system in play, as Darwin has shown: in anger, the pulling back of lips uncovering teeth ready to bite, etc. There is then a semiology of corporeal postures specific to each species according to its action system.

3. Hereditary Coordinations of Actions in Motor Images

To the elementary sequences of action systems, we can also add the hereditary coordinations which are a part of instinctual activity—as common observation and ethological studies have both discovered. While the elements of an action system, specific to each species, cannot provide a basis for one species to grasp the sense of a behavior of another species, hereditary coordinations often exceed, in their generality, the species displaying it, so that they can not only feed anticipations, they can also serve as a mode of primitive communication through movement, a sort of natural, interspecific language. A warning cry, an aggressive gathering, mating rituals, or behaviors towards the young contain an action coordination that forms an image and may be understood by other species.

Moreover, such processes foreground the spontaneity of the nervous system and the play of motivation. Lorenz and Tinbergen have shown that hereditary coordinations are not necessarily reactions to objects or real situations;

if motivation is intense, a weak external stimulation is enough, and if motivation is very intense, no stimulation is required for the instinctual program to unfold. Finally, after being triggered by a stimulus, instinctual actions may continue to unfold according to an entirely endogenous order. All that is missing from this action are the taxic components adapting it to the real object when present (like the rolling of eggs in the Greylag goose).

Such findings are important for research on the origins of movement images, for they show that the organism possesses a reservoir of complex schemas of behavior that can be endogenously activated when the motivations are sufficient; there is therefore a veritable biological basis to the imaginary which is prior to the experience of the object. Genz has observed young captive apivorous buzzards that, in the absence of bee nests to dig up, performed gestures of bee catching as if with an imaginary nest. Preadapted to an object, movement is truly a practical anticipation of its presence and even of its structure; it postulates the object. The modalities of the object corresponding to hereditary coordinations are not well defined; yet there exists a certain prefiguration of the specific object corresponding to the triggering of instinctual activities. Räber has studied it among male turkeys raised in isolation; a black cloth hung and fluttering in the wind triggers an aggressive behavior; a black cloth laying on the ground brings about a pre-copulating behavior. There are thus certain perceptual "patterns" playing the role of triggering stimuli. We need not undertake a full inventory for the analysis of motor images, but we may wonder whether in the case of a very intense motivation the endogenous activation of instinctual comportment in the absence of an adequate stimulus does not generate a hallucinatory representation of the specific stimulus induced by motor anticipation in a rough schematic way.

We know, however, that images of movement do not always have as content the anticipation of comportments inscribed in the specific program of hereditary coordination; in humans this is the case with images of flight. Jung provided an interpretation of such images by presuming that evolution left vestigial images in higher species coming from forms of life belonging to earlier stages of evolution (for instance, the dragon referring to a reptilian image). Such an interpretation is seductive and interesting while remaining conjectural. It might be partially confirmed by the fact that certain animals—

for instance, terrestrial mammals—spontaneously know how to swim even when their species has not lived near waterways for a very long time. But we might also wonder whether motor images of flying are truly anticipations or whether they come from the perception of birds via subjective transposition. The frame of hereditary coordination is likely too narrow to allow the explanation of the genesis and content of all images with a motor content. Yet it shows that these images may have a content that is prior to a defined perception, even if later this content is transformed by a complex elaboration. Concerning images of flight, we might note that in older narratives of actual attempts at flying motion schemas that are inessential for birds but very important for human locomotion (jumping and momentum) were integrated into these anticipations. The first attempts at flying were leaps into the air, after running, sustained by beating wings. This shows that humans partially imagine flying through the momentum of running and long jumping that is part of their action system and occurs in their hereditary coordination.

Hereditary coordination is all the more important given that the relation to a specific stimulus may be relatively random. Studies in ethology have described the phenomenon of *Prägung* (imprinting) in certain species; a given behavior is preformed, for instance, the set of behaviors of a fledgling to its mother; yet the perception of the stimulus "mother" is not at all selective; a human or a dog presented at a given number of hours or days from birth are taken by the fledglings as "the being to be followed"; later, the relation becomes more selective as the mother must respond to more specific signals. It is important to note, however, that the image of the mother, in this case, is above all the anticipation of a behavior; she is the being one can follow. Such learning, effected once and all at once, is called *Prägung* by the ethological school; its force and quickness illustrate the role of the image as an essentially motor anticipation of situations in the case of instinctual anticipation; a behavior is already virtually ready; all it needs is an objective support. We might wonder whether similar critical periods where *Prägung* occurs do not show up among humans in the context of instinctual behaviors (passions, being love struck, feeling the partner is a predestined choice). This would constitute the origin of individual differences in the primordial categories of representation of parents, educators, perhaps the *socius* in general—all consequences of primal experiences effected on the basis of instinctual anticipation.

4. Spontaneity of Motor Anticipations during Ontogenesis

Studies by embryologists (Coghill, Carmichael) show that motor development may be contemporary with perceptual development, but that it is neither posterior nor subordinated to it at every step; in other words, the putting in play of perceptual development through its exercise or through learning that implies a reference to objects is not necessary for the appearance of organized schemas in motor development; the motor anticipation of behavior occurs by way of endogenous development; the organization of movement during ontogenesis is not a sequence of reactions; it has its own laws that are not drawn from perception nor do they result from the influence of the milieu. This autonomous reality of virtual behaviors is an organic basis for anticipation and constitutes one of the bases for motor images.

Coghill has studied the ontogenesis of swimming behavior in the Urodela family (salamanders) which appears endogenously as a progressively developing and differentiating form. In a related experiment, Carmichael has shown that chemically induced immobilizations, lasting for several days, do not delay full access to motor capability. Weiss, still with Urodelas, has shown that organized schemas of movement inhere in nervous organization and the structure of the body: the transplanting of limbs perturbs acting reactions to the point that no learning, even after a year, can compensate the effects of limb inversion. Analogous results were obtained by Grohmann when studying the onset of flying movements in pigeons (by immobilizing a control group). In this line of research, that of Kortland is especially important, for it shows that in a complex behavior, the first sequences to appear during ontogenesis are the activities of execution that correspond to the phase of consummation which, within that behavior as a whole, comes last; thus young cormorants possess the motions used to fix twigs in the construction of a nest before they know how to carry, pick up, or look for those twigs; the most purely motor and most stereotyped activities of execution, then, cannot at first be exercised on an object, for the preparatory phases of seeking and transporting the object are missing; anticipation begins with the end of the complete actual behavior.

On the basis of this observation, which has a general reach, we can grasp one of the causes of the imaginary activity of anticipation; the organism possesses a know-how that would have meaning only if the problem of the search for the object was resolved; such operative power elicits a substitute as an objective support.

Play behaviors and vacuum activities may be interpreted at least partially through genesis that inverts the sequence of behaviors; when the execution phase of a behavior is ready it can be actualized in relation to a substitute object, that is, one endowed only with features supporting the motor activity. A young cat, capable of seizing with his claws and biting, but not of seeking and detecting prey, may take as prey substitute almost any kind of object: a bobbin with thread or a woolen ball; because the image of the prey remains, foremost, a bundle of capture motions; the same, almost random object may also occasion different motor "plays": capture, posturing, intimidation, etc. In humans, instinctual behaviors also show up in reverse order, recruiting substitutes for play as a preliminary exercise of execution activities when the activities of preparation and search are not yet possible. Hence, playing with dolls corresponds to the end of the sequence of reproductive behaviors at a time when sexual immaturity prevents the preliminary phase of that behavior; all that is required is a basic and almost random object: a teddy bear, a rag ball, a pet; what matters is that the object can be cradled, rocked, and carried along; it is the support and aim of preformed movements constituting a "pattern." Perceptual resemblance plays a much lesser role here than its motor adequacy as a substitute; whence the error of adults who, unmotivated, construct dolls for children that are art objects or automata perceptually mimicking an actual child, from the point of view of perception; for the purpose of playing, such constructions are worth no more than a rag doll, unformed by perceptual norms, but conforming to the motor *patterns* of the child. The essence of playing is pre-perceptual. Primary and instinctual play needs no perceptual figuration, only a great variety of random objects that can be recruited by motor tendencies grouped in configurations. If we add that motor capacities create a need when they reach full development, we can then understand the presence of specific powers of recruiting random objects as motor supports of motor tendencies in adults (aggression, protection) when such tendencies are not absorbed by situations integrated into daily life; for example, the adoption of pets treated maternally by adults or hunting and ritualized killing; in both cases the image devolves not from objective features of the substitute-objects but from the configuration of prior motor tendencies. Human beings may themselves be recruited as support for motor play, that is, become images of what must be fought against, rejected from the group, or sexually sought. Collective phenomena are grafted on this recruitment activity coming from pre-perceptual motor tendencies, but the first condition of possibility of such phenomena is the existence of prior motivations; one source of motivation is constituted by the inherence in the individual of organized motor sequences corresponding to a need to act according to an orientation defined by such motor sequence.

Such opportunities for separate or, in a way, insular functioning would not be produced if the ontogenetic development of behavior was accomplished according to a plan of absolute simultaneity in the growth of subsets. In fact, Gesell has shown that the ontogenesis of behavior is similar to growth: not only does it proceed according to principles of polarity, orientation, and according to gradients—and not homogenous, like the inflation of a ball— but it is effectuated in successive cycles separated by de-differentiations that prepare new structurations. Each stage ends its cycle with a defined behavior that might suffice unto itself were it not a phase of a broader genesis (cf. "Prone Progression in Human Infant");[2] temporarily abandoned, this behavior will be reincorporated in its essential axes within the final, more complex and synthetic "pattern." Such essential axes within a behavior may be considered to provide the content of behavior-anticipating motor images. These axes also allow for play, not merely as a non-coordinated motor expenditure, but as a "gestaltized" organization of movements generally focalized on an objective support (ball, doll, etc.).

The role played by learning in definitive conduct may be considerable without taking anything away from the primitive aspect of motor images corresponding to partial systematizations of behavior; in humans, learning can modify sensory-motor adaptations in important ways and with great plasticity (as demonstrated by experiments on the effects of wearing prismatic deforming glasses), but such learning intervenes mostly in the context of motor-perceptual relations and not in the reorganization of the motor "*Gestalt*"; it is the availability of the motor *Gestalt*, with the needs corresponding to the exercise of this constituted availability, that forms the basis for the recruitment of random objects as image supports. Indeed, the phenomena of learning aids, aiming to insert a configuration of movements in the real and concrete motor-perceptual milieu, also exist among animals in connection with the most stable and clear motor stereotypes: the flight schema is innate in birds, but this *a priori* schema does not take into account the angle of flight, the necessity of compensating for wind speed when landing, etc. The insertion of the schema in the milieu requires an apprenticeship of a different kind than playing, and it implies recourse to perceptual data rather than to images.

These remarks are not meant to solve the problem mentioned above of the origin of (apparently) *a priori* motor schemas like those that trigger flight images in humans, with rather strong motivations. Perhaps these are extremely primitive motor schemas, like the reactions or free motions of the fetus floating in amniotic fluid, which liberates it from the constraining effects of gravity through the effects of hydrostatic pressure; the primitive and broad character of such a motor schema may well animate images all the way to the intuition of orbital flight with a relative freedom in relation to the cockpit; but this is only a possible conjecture among others regarding the origin of movement images.

5. Motor Images and Imitation: Phenomena of Sympathetic Induction

So-called "imitation" phenomena would seem to suggest that the perception of a movement is necessary in order for another individual of the same species to reproduce it; there would then be a kind of learning that presupposed neither spontaneity nor the preexistence of a motor image in the subject that reproduced a movement or characteristic posture. In fact, notions such as "monkeying" that presume the possibility of a servile imitation of perceived movements among animals are devoid of serious foundation. Certain factual imitations exist among birds (words of human language, musical tunes, perfecting of specific song); but such facts are rare and belong rather to the general category of perfecting innate schemas than to pure imitation. It was not possible to teach monkeys to write by guiding their hands for many hours. They are also unable to learn the use of a device such as the lock on a box, by observing another member of their species that knows how to use it.

Phenomena taken to be instances of imitation are generally cases of sympathetic induction: Katz and Revesz discovered this phenomenon in studying chickens that were fed in isolation until they refused food; placed among fasting chickens and the same kind of food, the former, however satiated, started eating again as soon as the latter began; the motions and sounds of pecking exerted a sympathetic induction equivalent to the reemergence of the motivation that had vanished; it is not a case of imitation, because pecking is entirely innate in chickens: as soon as it leaves the egg the chick knows how to peck; sympathetic induction implies the preexistence of a motor image functioning as a motivation. Such induction effects occur among humans particularly for the most instinctual activities; detecting the various types of sympathetic induction might serve as a way to investigate instinctual behaviors; this effect is observable in eating and behaviors such as gathering, fleeing, entering a hall, getting up from a chair, and leaving a room. It is even more notable in pairing rites (so-called erotic films) and in exhibitions of violence (the so-called "crowd" phenomena Le Bon studied) used in the propaganda of totalitarian regimes. All modes of reproduction and transmission of temporal sequences may evince sympathetic induction: TV, films, but also speeches, music and singing (Hitler's speeches, revolutionary singing, military marches); the "force of the example" is exerted through the effects of sympathetic induction; it intervenes essentially in domains where instinctual conducts exist, that is, in primary categories of behavior.

6. Inherence of Motor Images in the Body Schema

We call "body schema" the representation that each of us makes of their own body and serves as a reference in space.[3] This schematic representation, which is constant and necessary for normal life, may undergo alterations as a result either of brain lesions (parietal lobe), amputations, or various motor incapacities; the corporeal schema likely integrates sensorial data of various kinds—exteroceptive and proprioceptive—but motor anticipations play a considerable part in the organization of the body schema. Taking up the notion of an action system developed above, we might say that the body schema contains the intuition of the action system of each individual. It corresponds to the fact that an individual immediately knows how to use his set of organs, not only when the whole body is intact, but also following an amputation. In *The Organism,* Goldstein gives particular importance to the recovery of functions through a reorganization of the whole following a lesion. Goldstein cites an experiment in which all four limbs of anesthetized guinea pigs are amputated ; when the anesthesia wanes, these badly mutilated animals do not try to walk on their stumps; instead they immediately adopt a mode of writhing, comparable to that of limbless animals; motricity is reorganized as a whole on the basis of the remaining functional possibilities of the whole organism; it effectuates a complete restructuring. Of course, such an interpretation conforms with Goldstein's holism developed into a general theory of the organism and its functions, according to the doctrine which generalizes the figure-ground relation posited by gestalt psychology; but in this particular case, the organism does indeed translate the correspondence between motor intuition, a semi-concrete image of the body's possibilities, and the organization of the body. The primordial basis for the various motor images is the intuition of possible movements in their organization and succession. The modality of motor images is the possible, because they devolve from an action system that is initially experienced as the organized network of the movements of the body proper [du corps propre].[4]

Indeed, a concrete image of movement always implies, to some extent, a reference to the subject's body schema. To have a concrete intuition of an object's movement means, to some extent, putting oneself in its place and situation, as if our body were that very object. For instance, to imagine a plane taking off through motor intuition means developing in oneself the progressive application of forces to the takeoff, ever faster, with the feeling that one is expending one's energy without reserve, risking it all, without hesitation or slowdown, without turning back or any possible deviation, because at the end of the runway one must, by sheer force of speed, fly up and over the obstacles at which one is flinging oneself. This motor image develops itself with a relatively strong analogical precision because it is of the same order as running fast to jump over an obstacle such a hedge or a brook, which does correspond to the use of human motor possibilities. Conversely, it is much harder to imagine a plane landing, because the slowing down during the approach to the landing strip at a specific angle does not correspond to any use of the human body schema. The body schema acts as a selector in the imaginative anticipation of different movements. The movements that can be imagined are those that correspond to a possible implementation of the human body schema as an exhaustive and organized abstract of motor intuitions.

It is likely that cultural pressures limit the use of motor images as means of intuiting reality in human adults; moreover, the complete development of behaviors integrates motor spontaneities into organized sequences, which reduces their availability for play, though it is noteworthy that the motor use of the body schema is widespread among children for miming moving objects; a child playing is not merely a driver or a rider, but also simultaneously car and a horse; the body schema is extended to the internal animation of those objects of use most immediately connected to the behavior. Motor intuition, in the guise of behavior anticipation, practices an implicit animism. Later, the categories of perception will progressively overlay those of the motor image; gesticulation as a mode of expression will recede in favor of the use of speech and writing. But a study of the origin of the modes of verbal expression would very likely need to restore the primitive conditions of the semantics of gesture, which implies the projection of images of movement onto reality according to the logic of the human body schema and the activity sequences of which it is the principle.

To summarize, the primordial source of the *a priori* appears to be, in the form of anticipations of movement, the organism. Such anticipations take the form of a projection of motor images into the milieu coming from this unique and primary source that is the organism with its motor schemas radiating out of the body schema.

B. Images in States of Expectation and Anticipation

The preceding description of the organic conditions of the anticipation of perception and action shows that, for behavior as a whole, the perspectives of an expected future are as important as present givens or the repercussions of experience in the form of memory. The same character of a projective logic of anticipation shows up in the dynamic of states of expectation and anticipation in the subject, at a level that can be called psychic. The use of the word "psychic" to characterize a level is a delicate one; perhaps it would be better to call it "secondary," in opposition to primary. To avoid confusion, we will say that the psychic level corresponds to a mode of functioning of the organism that does not involve the organism as a whole in a situation but primarily calls upon the nervous system and the sensory organs; as such, the psychic level of activity refers to a milieu already explored and organized in a biological mode, that is to say, it refers to a territory; psychic categories and activities are not in opposition to primary activities: they follow them and presuppose that the milieu has been inventoried and classified according to primary categories (defense, attack, prey, predator, etc.) in order to be exercised. Confronted by an unknown situation, the subject first falls back on an activity from the primary level; then, when the milieu has become a territory, the organized environment is processed in the secondary, psychic mode, which means that the subject has passed from situations to objects; finally, the logical (or formal) mode appears when objects are taken to be the frames or supports for relations, which implies they were identified at the secondary level according to the perceptual-motor categories of common action.

1. Phobias and Compulsive Exaggerations: The Amplifying Character of States of Expectation

A phobia, properly speaking, is a morbid fear of certain objects, actions, or situations (agoraphobia, claustrophobia). This phenomenon occurs in attenuated fashion in ordinary psychic life: during ontogenesis, the hereditary coordinations of action, like flight, disgust, rejection, or avoidance movements, recruit objects that may be selected either by certain conditions of individual experience or by cultural modalities. Hence for our ancestors, snakes and toads occasioned acute exhibitions of disgust; in "Sleeping Beauty," Perrault imagines a torture ordained by an ogress: throwing the queen and her children into a vat full of "toads, vipers, snakes and serpents." Because of a fortunate twist—the arrival of the king—the ogress, enraged her vengeance cannot be carried out, throws herself head first into the vat, and is "devoured in an instant by the evil beasts she had placed there." Such beliefs obviously cannot rest on perceptual experience. They can only result from a mental activity of pre-perceptual anticipation prolonging the primary categories of hereditary coordination, deploying themselves in a vacuum, with no perceptual limits or controls coming from a real object. Psychic elaboration follows the axes of the organism's action system here; in the imaginary bestiary there are not only repulsive animals (corresponding to disgust and vomiting), but also aggressive and devouring animals (corresponding to avoidance reactions), and others like the imaginary salamander called "breath" that suffocates whoever breathes its toxic exhalations (corresponding to suffocation and breathlessness); there is also, in the same imaginary categories, a large caterpillar called "breath" that hides in the grass and kills cattle. Such beliefs are probably not gratuitous: toads do have venom in their epidermis but mostly as a defensive, passive, and rather inefficacious means of warding off aggressors; the imaginary activity reveals itself here through a veritable amplificatory projection of this property of having venom; imaginary toads are also endowed with poisonous spit and ejections of urine burning the eyes of those who get too close. What we have here is amplification through projection, in various directions and modalities, of venomous actions. As for the "breath" of salamanders and caterpillars, it too may be based on actual incidents; some caterpillars can cause venomous burns in the esophagus when ingested by ruminants, and the swelling may disrupt breathing; the great fear of cattle keepers, though, is bloating, which has a very different origin; the imaginary malfeasance of "breaths," then, results from the amplification and projection, in various directions, of the capacity to bloat and to suffocate. Motor images as body schemas or as intuitions of the inner unfolding of phenomena are amplified by psychic activity which aggrandizes, systematizes, and especially projects them onto things supposed to be objective and real. These things, in fact, are foremost the results of activities of amplificatory projection that characterize psychic functioning as an *a priori,* which is unlimited and without objective restraint, and stimulated endogenously by the force of motivations.

These automatisms of amplification and projection could be uncovered, perhaps, in different aspects of collective myth and individual belief; objects offered by the world as a screen for this amplificatory projection differ in time and space; but the fundamental dimensions of the activity it projects remain the same because the network of motivations barely changes. At the very least, this network of motivations expresses conditions that are modified only slowly over time; in today's societies, the myth of man-eaters and children devourers tend to disappear as the fear of hunger as basic motivation tends to wane. The ogre, the carnivorous monster or the Beast eating flocks and shepherds—like the Beast of Gévaudan—are images of the past.

To fully imagine an ogre, one must feel hunger and be haunted by the desire to eat one's neighbors—as happened in the sieges of certain cities during the wars. However objectionable such a feeling may be, this tendency serves as a seed for the image of the ogre when it is amplified and projected outside, on a being with a human form and an insatiable hunger whose object of choice is human flesh. The Minotaur, the Morhout of the Tristan and Yseult legend, ghouls, etc., represent the result of the same projection in different eras and in different cultural contexts.

In other cases, the process of amplification continues to be exercised without producing a projection; in other words, no myth surfaces, there are neither man-eating toads nor devouring ogres, only a compulsive exaggeration of certain aspects of protection, preparation, and precautions. Ombredane analyzes a number of cases of compulsive exaggerations in his course on motivation and the problem of needs. A compulsion is a behavior undertaken by an individual without any other motivation than warding off the anxiety or guilt that would arise in the absence of the action; compulsive exaggeration is the disproportional amplification of an activity that may originally have been a reasonable precaution. Exaggeration translates this effect of amplification, linked to the *a priori* aspect of motor anticipations an imagination in action; the fear of lacking food, instead of being projected through ogre or images of monsters, may be expressed in the indefinite hoarding of food supplies (sugar, salt); certain aspects of greed may be interpreted as compulsive exaggerations; Ombredane points to people who never leave home without taking along "a just in case" [en-cas], a small portable meal for mitigating the sudden deprivation of food, even if urban travel renders such precautions entirely futile; Ombredane also cites exaggerations in personal hygiene, the fight against microbes, etc. Certainly, such behaviors have been noticed in mental illnesses, but they exist as well in non-pathological life and may take on a collective turn, to the point of becoming veritable "patterns of culture":[5] each civilization amplifies certain defensive modes with corresponding exaggerations: against poverty, disease, the transgression of certain norms, etc. This amounts to a collective imaginary projection in the form of mythical images complementing such exaggerated anticipation behaviors (the Wandering Jew, the Devil as tempter and seducer . . .). Phenomena such as the arms race are, at least partially, of the order of amplification through compulsive exaggeration; they are correlated to mythical images of the enemy: the Yellow or Red Peril, etc. In his film *Neighbors,* McLaren has translated this phenomena of amplification and acceleration of rival and oppositional conducts.[6]

Ombredane indicates furthermore how rising anxiety recruits with increasing prematureness cues from an objective situation that might lead to a lack, much earlier than the moment at which the lack becomes real: the fear of lacking air in a tunnel, connected to claustrophobia, accentuates the feel of traces of smoke or dust which indicate the confined character of a place's airflow; a psychosis of "poor people deprived of clean air" is starting to develop in large cities where the composition of the atmosphere is far from indicating a danger of asphyxia. Could certain allergies be considered comparable to the amplificatory processes of defense activities? Certainly, this is the case with regard to the effects, although the psychic aspect of the activity is veiled in the case of allergies, while it is clear and conscious for compulsive exaggerations which are accompanied by a plethora of justifications and reasons.

2. Particular Aspects of Images in a State of Fear; Doubling

Negative expectation—fear—has its own mode of image organization. It was carefully studied and described by Lucretius, who sought to use philosophical thought and the critical spirit as a means of delivering humanity from the effects of fear, that is, the images it engenders and the exaggerations it produces. According to Lucretius, the fundamental fear afflicting humans is that of death. All related fears, for instance of disease and poverty, are but indirect and minor aspects of the reaction towards the threat of death. The essential character of the fear of death lies in its effect on the imagination: the doubling *[dédouble]* of the self; a person sees himself standing next to his own corpse, lamenting the poor dead person, almost as though we see a dead friend. This imaginary and illusory doubling leads to a feeling of great sorrow by anticipation, for we presume that a time will come when we will be a corpse, one in which consciousness and sensibility will be preserved. Lucretius opposes and denounces such doubling since, according to strict atomistic materialism, as soon as humans die, the atoms (molecules) that composed them disperse; the soul, which exists only as the gathering of lighter atoms within the corporeal envelope, disperses and consciousness disappears; because the connective forces that made the living compound have ceased to exist, nothing remains of this compound but components as scattered after death as they were before birth; the nothingness after is perfectly analogous to the nothingness before; before our birth we neither felt nor were conscious; after our death we will neither feel nor be conscious. But it is not enough to describe the illusion of imagination stimulated by fear; it is necessary to analyze its effects to combat them.

When an animal feels fear, it absorbs its fear in a flight reaction. Humans know in advance the uselessness of flight when danger is omnipresent, such as in a storm. Deprived of refuge in the physical world, humans then invent a transcendent alternative, in a more powerful being: they forge the image of gods so that they may then petition them. In reality, it is still from out of themselves that humans operate this doubling by positing outside of themselves the image of an analogous but more powerful being. The trouble is that, after the danger has passed, the doubled, actualized, and materialized image remains, threatening humans from the heavens: to appease its wrath, it must be worshipped, honored, it must be offered wretched, bloody, and criminal sacrifices like that of Iphigenia. In sum, with this doubling that allows them temporarily to appease their fear, humans have lost their freedom. They have become alienated, to use the expression Feuerbach would later take up. Religion is the superstitious fear linked to this actualized and ritualized image, and the rituals connected to it. The analysis of Lucretius (echoed by Horace) leads to seeing the supernatural as a set of images drawn from reality and human life, illusorily aggrandized and severed, in order to serve as support to the act of supplication, of the sacrifices and rituals to which humans are led by fear.

As a complement, Lucretius proposes methods aimed at countervailing the power of the imagination with its miracles and illusions robbing humans of freedom, especially in the amorous passions; there is a kind of medicine of the passions that is sketched through the intermediary of an objective representation of nature. Epicurean wisdom aims to provide the individual with an exact knowledge of his own limits and also real but very modest needs: all that is required is to avoid pain and to satisfy natural and necessary needs. We might say that Epicurean wisdom consists in giving to the present its full plenitude by not allowing it to be devoured by the forces of the imagination which constantly anticipate and wrench humans from the present in order to launch them on a quest for all that is not given in actuality. Instead of being at rest in the limits of their present, humans explore the seas, vie for power, and desire wealth, thereby depleting their only wealth: the short time they have for living. Imagination is a force that wrenches one from the present, prevents rest in the state of ataraxia, and pulls one towards the anticipated future and realities that present sensations do not give. The imagination has the power to make humans strangers to the present situation and indifferent to what they are actually given, as if it wasn't really theirs. In contemporary, or at least recent, terms, we might say that the image alters sensation, denatures it, diminishing the force of the present that is the basis of wisdom.

To fight against the image as a power of anticipation, Lucretius was in fact led to recognize the projection effect that characterizes it. Yet doubling seems very specifically linked to negative states of expectation, implying fear; the apparent independence of the image, severed from the subject while expressing the subject, corresponds to a barrier the subject constructs between himself and the reality posited by doubling. With fear, the subject installs himself inside a retrenched camp erected with the means at his disposal; the future is foreign because it is outside; the world is dichotomized into inside and outside because the emergence of the barrier results from a defensive and expulsive movement; even the gods, imagined to fight threatening realities, are foreign to the present human order of the subject since they lie beyond the defensive barrier. The point of departure is the defensive gesture separating the near from the far, installing defenses to preserve the near, doubling in some fashion the subject in order to send an emissary of himself in the guise of a more powerful god to fight the threatening adversity in the outside camp. To fight outside of the retrenched camp, the subject has sent out another self that takes away some of its reality, thus creating the beginning of alienation which is, at base, dualization.

3. The Image in Positive States of Expectation

When states of expectation are positive, implying desire and active seeking, the image still corresponds to an amplifying projection, but no doubling occurs here because the dichotomy of the near and far is no longer postulated; the positive state of expectation acts through the suppression of obstacles and real distances. Positive desire constitutes images according to a relation of immanence, an inversion of the transcendence produced by fear.

Lucretius' analysis may not apply to all the gods of the ancients: not all were, to the same degree, those that were invoked out of fear and to whom bloody sacrifices were offered; beneath the distant, official religion of the polis, initiation cults developed, providing more meaning for the inner reflective life in quotidian thought than for collective ceremonies. Moreover, fear is not the only potent motivation that can stimulate the desire to address an image; sorrow over one's lost ones, the wish of being reunited with them and living among them was an equally powerful motivation; to pass from the state of present separation to a new, future meeting amounts to finding the way that leads to Hell in order, like Orpheus, to seek Eurydice and bring her back to the light. Voyages, paths, passages, purifications, and expectations draw their meaning from relinking what was severed and finding a mediation where death has severed the link. Hope seeks passages and prepares a voyage; the images of hope do not seek rupture as a mode of defense; they do not posit a transcendence, but rather trace the path of a continuity between the shores of the living and the dead; it is the subject who must transform and purify himself to be worthy of the voyage; the beyond begins in the now and with the first steps.

Mediation, the immanence of revelation, the fate of the divine through the human and in the form of human existence, this is what is found in early Christianity, as a religion of hope. The very idea of incarnation and the image of nativity summarize this movement which is the opposite of alienation: the divinity may be here, *hic et nunc,* in the straw and on the wood, like this board on which we place our hands. Nativity is the image of the absence of distance of the divine: like the life of a child, the divinity begins there. The word "immanence" in fact is not quite suitable to express this genesis without hiatus, for immanence seems to lock up and contain what is immanent. Anticipation through hope brings a continuity with regard to the present that is like a birth.

The dimension of eternity too takes on a different sense, as anticipation of a personal future, in individual religions of hope; personal eternity is a new life, a resurrection, symbolized by morning and the flame as we see in the lanterns for the dead topped with a rooster (in the Germigny cemetery near Orléans). Palingenesis and resurrection belong to modes of anticipation where present reality is never defined, never irreversible—even death is not an absolute boundary or barrier; the anticipation of reincarnation or resurrection goes beyond death, reconnecting temporal continuity to one's first existence.

It is impossible to sketch, even summarily, the richness and diversity of the images through which various peoples have invoked a future life; there is, however, concerning the beliefs of antiquity, a beautiful and wise book by Franz Cumont, *Lux perpetua*.

4. Anticipation Images in Mixed States: The Marvelous as Category of Mixed Anticipation

Amplificatory projection always appears in the work of the anticipatory image, either through the centrifugal gesture of pushing away to ward off, in transcendentalizing fear, or in the immediate quest of initiatory communication, of communion, characterizing the anticipation of renewal in hope. Doubling followed by alienation is the opposite of the initiatory introduction.

But such pure cases, visible particularly in religious images, are rare; the mixed case, states of expectation where fear and hope intermix in variable proportions, is much more frequent. Love, Plato says, is the son of Poros and Penia (Abundance and Privation); and by the same token he is the son of mixed fears and hopes. In this case, the amplificatory projection continues to exist but it has neither the exclusive sense of a movement towards the outside, positing the transcendence of the doubled image as an idol, nor that of inner participation according to the world of birth in the immediate *hic et nunc*: in the encounter of these two movements, one tending towards transcendence and the other towards immanence, there occurs a kind of stilling of images, projected midway between the movement of true transcendence and the immanence in relation to the subject: an imaginary world of anticipatory images is thereby created, floating between extreme distance and immediate proximity, still, like a rainbow which always remains between ourselves and the horizon. We are dealing with a "third reality," to invoke the expression Edgar Morin used to characterize certain cultural phenomena and the transmission of information.[7]

One example of such third reality is the marvelous *[le merveilleux]* surrounding princes, artists, and actresses: these figures do not occupy the highest ranks, but they surround those that do, and commerce with them: they are the court rather than the sovereign; the court is akin to the city, it is close to the everyday, like a mediation stopping midway; in the warp and woof of the contemporary marvelous, princesses become superior to queens because they are less firmly installed, less distant—and more virtual since they can become queen. Participation in this marvelous is made possible by the media, especially weeklies with the largest photos, but also radio and television; such media represent precisely an intermediary screen floating between background reality and the reality of the subject. The time for accessing these screens is leisure time which belongs to an intermediary category between the insertion in the present of situations and absence, travel.

Let us note that participation in this intermediary world is made possible by the fact that these marvelous figures are described, photographed, and filmed in the relatively common circumstances of their life, comparable to the common, everyday existence we lead; this creates the effect of a subjective *rapprochement*; on the other hand, these figures bear signs of belonging to a faraway, superior, and inaccessible world, due to differences of birth, etiquette, extreme wealth, or even spatial distance. Participation in the historical marvelous as an intermediary world arises in the same way, through the description of the everyday aspects of the most prestigious historical figures: the loves of kings and the chronicles of lowercase history.

The outpouring of desires into the intermediary world of the marvelous is correlated to an impoverished horizon of the real; the recourse to the marvelous, born from limits experienced in everyday life, results in depriving real life, integrated to the social body, of a part of its motivations; the recourse to the marvelous translates the existence of powerful limits and the monotony of situations or tasks, like those of a housewife or a typist harboring no great hopes to see their condition, experienced as limited and determined, ever change. The novel was long the support for the activity of the imagination as a power of escape: it operates an imaginary deployment of personal power through the participation in the acts of the protagonist. Serialized, the novel directly feeds states of expectation and anticipation through the suspense it creates between installments. This temporal modality, which is essential here, translates into a loss of interest caused by the premature revelation of the end. The preservation of the state of expectation after the end of the novel may lead to multiple sequels, unlimited continuations of episodes, as we see in nineteenth-century novels.

Each type of expectation state evinces a corresponding kind of marvelous: Cinderella dreams of the Prince, while warriors, amidst insecurity and danger, and the confusion of threats of battles, think about the great, manifest, and illustrious deeds in which one can count on the clarity of a just cause and on supernatural aid. The qualities of the marvelous are the antitypes of those of lived reality.

In other instances, this complementary aspect of the imaginary with respect to the real resides in the object, rather than being figured in the unfolding of a hero's action (which permits the participation of the subject); freighted with expectation, the bearer of the outcomes of desire, the object is endowed with a metamorphic power as in the Golden Age or in tales and myths. Often, the animal is in fact a disgraced human who must be redeemed and saved with love and courage, even through a real sacrifice; the key for the future lies in the intensity of the present state of desire bearing on an object of ignoble but transfigurable appearance: the toad can become a prince again but only for her who has the courage to allow him in her bed. The Blue Bird too is a prince chained by a spell to his animal state. Other times, the object has not undergone metamorphosis but is in a state close to death, and only the intensity of desire can bring it back to life: Sleeping Beauty, wounded by the shuttle, kept her golden colors but lay in a castle surrounded with thorns and brush said to be haunted by an ogre; only the ardor of a prince "afire" is needed for all the trees, thorn, and brush to retreat on their own, closing back as soon as the prince has passed. The extreme desire is projected in the object which it seeks and transfigures: the princess too was waiting: "Is it you, my prince?" she says to him, "For so long I have been awaiting you."

There is an important difference between the object susceptible to metamorphosis, as base of expectation laden with desire and fear, and the symbolobject which does not undergo metamorphosis but remains the *analogon* of another reality; Cinderella's lost zibeline slipper is an *analogon*, a symbol that allows the young woman to be found again. In another tale by Perrault,

The Skilled Princess, the glass distaff of Finette, Nonchalante, and Babillarde are *analogon* of their virginity, only Finette keeping her distaff intact. The gold ring of Donkey Skin, which the prince finds in the cake, plays the role of an *analogon* allowing him to find the true princess under the tramp everyone despises. In this last tale, the symbol-ring functions as trigger of the metamorphosis of the tramp into a princess, at the same time that it exacerbates desire through waiting: the ring was tried out by all women of the country from the higher to the lower classes, from city to countryside, when at last the turkey-keeper is brought in. The symbolic link that exists between objects, according to the categories of anticipation, is not the expression of a perceptual communication between two realities; the slipper or the ring are not perceptually linked to the woman desired; they are modes of becoming that found the analogy, because the symbol-object elicits, in miniature, the same desires and fears that symbolized it; the gold-and-diamond ring is precious; it can be lost; it is hidden in flour and is discovered suddenly, like Donkey Skin, who, hidden under her rags and the soot covering her cheeks, reveals the splendor of her white dress as the donkey skin falls off when she tries on the ring. The glass distaff is a symbol of virginity because it breaks all at once, irreversibly. There are also perceptual symbols that psychoanalysis has studied, but those of the marvelous exist in the dimension of the modes of anticipatory becoming—they are ante-perceptual, implying the categories of action rather than perception.

Access to the marvelous may sometimes be tinted by the supernatural when the metamorphosis of objects requires the intervention of a supernatural power; in such a case a conversion occurs, the object becoming a reality out of a figuration, or a living being from a corpse. Such a change of nature prolongs and amplifies the movement of human feelings that then manifest as a call to a supernatural power that might effectuate what human beings can only wish and wait for. It is a miracle that comes after an intense longing. This transpires in the legend "Of the Child a Woman Offered to the Virgin Mary out of Love of the One She Had Lost." Here the strongest of human feelings—maternal love—crosses the boundary of the sacred to call for a miracle. We might also allude to *The Tidings Brought to Mary* by Paul Claudel, where the child of Mara, dead and cold, comes back to life, through a metamorphosis, when Violaine breastfeeds him; this is indeed a multiple miracle, since it is also the metamorphosis of the young woman, leprous, alone, and abandoned, into a mother breastfeeding her child, and into the spiritual wife of Pierre de Craon, whom she faithfully loved. In a simpler yet more general way, legends imply the presence of the supernatural in metamorphoses we might call amplificatory: where there was nothing, something becomes manifest, a ground that has turned arid becomes fertile once again, or a corpse is replaced by a living being resuscitated; hence the Knight with the small cask, unable to bring a single drop of water from a well in his cask, feels his heart break and cries at the remembrance of his past faults: a tear falls on the cask's hole and instantly it multiplies and stirs, the cask overflowing into a lively stream. After Penia comes Poros, out of the very excess of Penia. The same goes for the hagiographic legends in which pilgrims' staffs, hard and knotty, sprout roots, leaves, and flowers to revert to living trees. In metamorphosis, the presence of the supernatural allows the irreversible to be unbound from its irreversibility, and what is lifeless to find life again. The saint is the one who inverts the course of the irreversible: thanks to her the irremediable no longer exists. One evening, upon entering into the shop of a butcher who killed three small children, Saint Nicholas places his hand on the salting barrel where they lie, and the children come back to life. Thanks to the supernatural, remorse and regret may be transmuted into repentance because there is a renewal of the sense of openness and the dimension of the future according to which no specific action can create the irremissible "nevermore." In this sense, the coherent image of the possible as an anticipation framed by the future and fear intervenes in what was called in philosophy "the moral life," and we might wonder whether it does not play as essential a role as that granted to obligation. Bergson deeply felt this necessity of openness for moral life, and he linked it to the intuition of movement (while obligation proceeds *vis a tergo*), to a force that was determining and necessitating in the order of causes exerted upon the subject by social life.

When becoming is not conceived as amplificatory—either through the intervention of grace as a supernatural amplificatory power, or through the movement of life and creative evolution—the image of the future as individual or collective destiny encounters limits and undergoes a relative closure; the image may be judged and found to be predeterminable, like lives choosing their souls in the Platonic myth, at the moment when the messenger

announces that "the god declines any responsibility"; then, it is only in relation to the desires and pains felt in the course of previous lives that most of
the souls reincarnate in the body of a wrestler, a tyrant, or a peacock.

These images of the future, precisely because the god declines responsibility, contain no creative element; they are merely the countertype of situations actually experienced or perceived. The very image of the ideal city
is fully determined and limited in a cyclical conception of time that starts
again at the end of the Great Year.

The recourse to the marvelous or supernatural is not the only path allowing the imaginary anticipation of the future to exercise its amplificatory
power as a factor of reality within projected time. Within individual humans
there are also productive forces which, more modestly, may construct an
exclusive world in which the motor schema exerts itself and becomes concretized: it is the work of the amateur, that is, those who act out of love for
what they do. The initial postulate of amateurism is a relative dichotomy
that separates the theatre and object of constructive passion from the time
and place of collective obligation. At times, nonetheless, the lineaments of
the imaginary world arise in the moments of lesser tension of obligatory
collective activity; Ferdinand Cheval, who built for many years his Ideal Palace in Hauterives, would find on his rounds the stones with singular features
that he organized into fantastical assemblages; if they were light enough,
he would pick the stones on the spot; the heavier ones were collected later
with a wheelbarrow. Working alone for years, this man gave shape, as he
tells it, to a dream he had had. Among the shapes he created, several (such
as the great statues) belong to the category of the "reproductive imagination," inspired by the Cambodian temples Cheval had seen during his military service; but others, especially the non-figurative assemblages of stones,
truly express this amplificatory and proliferating power of the gesture of
construction that is diversified by going forward, directed only by the primordial intuition of a line or a motor theme. The Surrealists accorded great
importance to the manifestation of human imagination exercised outside of
the path of imitation. The film *Ingres' Violin* presents Cheval's Ideal Palace
together with other, similar productions by other amateurs.[8]

The development of DIY in contemporary industrial societies does not
correspond only to certain socioeconomic necessities (the disappearance of

household staff, high cost of repair, and upkeep of main appliances) or the use of complex devices in a decentralized habitat; the imperative to DIY also emerges from the organization of a permanent operative availability of tools and materials in a regime of leisure and freedom for the individual; it is the return of honorable and disinterested artisanship in the framework of leisure granted by the occupations of industrial society; the home workshop restitutes the local and independent dimension of production that belonged to the domanial, manorial economy; thanks to it, the worker, the salaried professional, the shop or public employee, has immediate access to the tools of production, and they become the boss of the whole project, from the first sketch belonging to the intuition of the image to the concrete completion of the project. The imagination as anticipation is thus no longer a function severed from reality and deployed in unreality and in fiction; it triggers an effective activity of realization because the subject who projects the image is the owner of the tools of production and the workable materials needed. The modality of the imaginary is that of potentiality; it only becomes the modality of unreality if the individual is deprived of access to the conditions of realization. Through a close analysis of the characteristics of the appliances required for DIY, we reencounter the preoccupation with the availability of the fabricating operation in relation to the imagining intention, sometimes taken to a non-functional excess; the machines made for amateurs present themselves willfully and systematically as entirely convertible or adaptable to all tasks, all materials, all sources of electrical power . . . In actuality, this flexibility is often more apparent than real, and the impression of freedom may be only apparent, too, or compensated by a loss of time when, from one task to another, one must change the assembly or combination of tools; such appliances appear to have been conceived so as to tailor themselves to the feeling of unlimited freedom for virtual uses (thus in the logic of the project in a pure perspective of the future) rather than with the concern for functional use. These all-purpose machines abstractly guarantee a full freedom according to long-term anticipation, but they then require the non-simultaneity of the various operations of use, detrimental to the short-term anticipation and adaptation to the present characterizing the intra-perceptual organization of tasks for execution. The rhetoric of virtuality is the index of imaginary anticipation characterizing the activity of DIY, partially born as a mode of compensation of the constraining regularity, the lack of autonomy, and the fragmented aspect of the tasks of everyday life—"work in pieces," in Friedmann's expression.[9] We may note the importance of the development of this kind of activity in a society like the United States, with a high economic level, with an important participation by upper classes, with no direct connection with the "dark work" of working classes, a vestigial form of the "*factotum*" in which there is an independence of conception and execution, since the *factotum* must at all times answer, according to the randomness of emergencies, to unpredictable demands unforeseen by the project.

To summarize, we can say that the image as motor anticipation is deployed according to different cultural contexts by bringing about an amplificatory metamorphosis of the object, either through identification with an imaginary world where others act in lieu of the subject, in a landscape where the splendor of the real is multiplied, or through a true action on a raw material in the situation of leisure; but in all cases, the effect of anticipation as *a priori* image is an amplificatory proliferation from a single origin located in the subject; this proliferation multiplies paths and forms in the future; it is the analog of a growth, a maturation, or a development comprising both differentiation and supplemental being [*supplément d'être*]; it enacts, towards the future, the amplificatory projection of the potentialities of the subject's present.

C. Intuition as Pure *a priori* Image, Principle of Reflective Knowledge

1. The Projection Schema in Platonism; the Role of Intuition

The intuition of amplificatory projection from current potentialities may serve as basis for a reflective operation whereby the subject is installed in the unicity of the source-movement in order to intuitively accompany the differentiation in the multiple and in the successive becoming of this intention or initial force. Such a vision is, at least partially, initiatory or mystical, even if it uses the power of conceptual structures as a relay. As principle of philosophical thought, the *a priori* image is the idea rather than the concept; it is even more purely unconditional and more thoroughly unique than ideas; ideas, which are multiple in a certain aspect, play a role in amplificatory projection which is not that of the source of the projection; behind ideas, as primordial origin of projection, there exists, beyond essence and existence, the one source of all projections, analogous to the sun, which, in the sensible world, lights up objects, allowing them to bear a shadow, which amplifies them, multiplies them, but also degrades them.

In the Platonic doctrine, the excellence and superiority of the Good with respect to becoming and the multiple cannot be understood without an essential postulate: the Good is the source of intelligibility and participation in the intelligible world; it is the Sun of the intelligible world; it lights up archetype-ideas; existence is a direct projection of essences in the intelligible world, a demiurge for the passage of the intelligible into the sensible; knowledge retraces the steps followed by projection or demiurgic imitation. This is what provides the full meaning of the Myth of the Cave: from the shadows and reflections of the world of *genesis* and *phtora,* which is to say, from the most multiplied and inconsistent images of projection, it is possible to behold the models themselves and the source of projection, granted one turn around, forcefully; this method of conversion, used analogically in the paradigm of the sensible, also applies to the path of knowledge in the intelligible world, where it allows one to reach, through successive stages of purification and initiation, the end of a dialectic in the antechamber of the Good. Knowledge moves upstream from this projection through successive degrees which gives sensorially perceptible existence.

It may seem paradoxical to consider the Platonic theory of participation as expressing a primordial image of pure movement, since it presents itself foremost as an example of a contemplative theory. However, we must grasp this theory of knowledge from the purview of an experience of progressive degradation of an original model (archetype) through the more or less distant and various images that may represent that model, becoming more indistinct the more distant they are from the primordial reality, like copies of copies, or reflections of reflections. In shadow projection (thaumaturgy) the shadow becomes larger the more distant it is from the model casting the shadow, but it also becomes fuzzier because projection from a light source proceeds according to the principle of proportional triangles; the ancients did not know optical systems allowing the production of punctuality; nor did they know a light source small enough to be treated as a geometrical point, which would have rendered sharpness independently of the magnifying relation. The relation of model to copy is the basis of participation; this relation is akin to that of being to becoming, of the One to the multiple, and finally of essence to existence within the sensible. The sensible, the indistinct, and the multiple are on the side of the copy, while the model possesses the unity of uniqueness and the perfection of intelligible essence; the passage from the perfect, intelligible essence to existence through generation and corruption is analogous, as demiurgic copy, to the projection that degrades and distances. The philosophical dialectic which leads back up to the intelligible allows one to become a spectator of the demiurgy that projects existences, instead of staying between the thaumaturges and the screen, eyes turned towards the wall where the shadows are cast, it places us between the light source and the stage where the thaumaturges brandish the silhouettes that cast the shadows. Philosophical knowledge is a gaze that accompanies the projection in the process of making itself and the demiurgy in the process of occurring, by no longer staying among the copies and existences in becoming, but very close to the source itself whence come light rays in their unity. Philosophical contemplation is not a participation in the demiurgic activity, it is the intuition of the movement of the rays being projected; it thereby installs the mind [*l'esprit*], as it is said of the Good, beyond essence and existence, that is to say at the source, well before the cast shadows (existences) and before even the models (essences); in illuminism, the contemplative gaze goes in the direction of the light-rays projecting existence; the subject of the gaze coincides with the unity out of which they emanate.

The highest philosophical initiation is thus not only a knowledge of the models (Ideas) but a mode of being that makes the philosopher coincide with the absolute source of forms and existences; it is indeed the intuition of anticipation in a pure state that is sought in this turn back towards the most unconditional principle, the most complete and radical *a priori*—the most anterior to any mode of being. It is not movement, but the intuition of all projections towards existence and the multiple.

2. Procession and Conversion

A second path is possible in the use of the intuition of anticipation: that which Plotinus uses to rise towards the One, superior to all hypostases; contemplation is prepared by exercises (reading texts, conversation) but it is conducted in reflection and silence; after contemplation, which is like an ecstasy, the mind [*l'esprit*] expresses what it has seen in words and discourse. Plotinus compares contemplation to the moment when geometers, after having sought, can see; and after seeing, they write or trace the figure of the solution. In other words, revelatory contemplation is the starting point of speech, of explanation, and the gesture of communication. Knowledge is a conversion that leads to the point where one can seize the procession that organizes existences from the One. In this doctrine too, intuition provides knowledge because it is effectuated at the end of an ascent that allows an absolute anticipation to be recovered, and the world to be grasped as a procession, in a state that is a complete *a priori* in relation to any deployment of sensorial experience and temporal existence.

3. The Intuition of the Moving and the Knowledge of Creative Evolution

A pure intuition of the moving [*le mouvant*], according to Bergson, allows us to grasp life in its most profound nature without the obstacle of concepts, which play a pragmatic and utilitarian role but pluralize and immobilize the real; logical and conceptual thought corresponds to a knowledge of what is *partes extra partes*, in the order of the quantitative and the static. Through a forceful turning back on himself, the philosopher can detach from the habits of language and the mechanized servitude of conceptual thought in order to grasp, through intuition, the qualitative and dynamic continuities of the deeper self, its freedom and unity. In this sense, we find in Bergson a dualist attitude closely reflecting those of Plato and Plotinus. Yet it is not the whole of existence and temporality that are rejected in favor of the unique source known through intuition and participation. The equivalent to participation and procession for Bergson is no longer a degradation compelling the philosopher to attach himself to the contemplation of unity and its origin; the unity of the primordial upswelling is preserved in the continuity of life's movement that becomes diversified through matter; matter itself is like a movement that comes undone; the intuition of the moving is no longer constrained by being absorbed in the pure anticipation of the *a priori* creative gesture; leaving the source, intuition accompanies the river's coursing, follows evolution in its development, since the *élan vital* is a perpetual *a priori* that remains a source throughout existence; creation is not localized at the origin, it remains present throughout the stages of becoming, for intuition allows us to grasp evolution as creative. Automatisms and kinds of closure are ordered according to this unique movement that deposits them along its course: instincts and closed societies are like waters that eddy while the rush of the river's waters continues on. The origin is ever-present. Movement does not produce distance from the origin, it is never cut off from its past, since there is no degradation. In such a doctrine, intuition is a participation in the creative movement of evolution; knowledge is rendered possible because the subject is the recipient of the *élan vital*: he finds within himself what exists outside; what is in him is nothing other than the original *élan*, now running through the subject, like a single sentence begun long ago which, always interrupted by new additions, still remains the same in its lasting duration. At whatever stage of its development movement is always inchoate; we could say that movement is a perpetual origin that is prolonged, a permanent anticipation of itself. Similarly, the image, in this case, is not a simple metaphor; nor is intuition pure subjectivity; as the subject discovers the way in which he participates, he prolongs and continues his participation; he continues evolution, anticipates. Teilhard de Chardin added to the individual or personal dimension of this participation in a creative becoming that of the collective, since he considers the goal of personal flourishing to be an arbitrary limit reflecting a certain aspect of civilization.

The philosophical doctrines of intuition differ over time if we take into account normative ideals: that of Plato proposes stable structures in relation to which amplificatory projection's only role is to multiply and cause to exist; that of Plotinus is an invitation to ecstasy in the mystical seizure of the One, via the principle of procession; conversion is not necessarily followed by a fallback to temporal existence, as in Plato, who wants the philosopher to be the magistrate of a city with fixed laws, images of numbers; in contrast, Bergson and even more so Teilhard de Chardin, take intuition as the starting point for a real participation in the becoming of life through humanity. And yet, the primordial character of the motor content of any *a priori* image of anticipation, in spite of the fixity of the archetypes, was already latent in Plato; philosophy is also the knowledge of mixed things, of the indefinite dyad, of the *génésis eis ousian,* according to the philosophical *metretike* of number-ideas. Hence this philosophical doctrine, replete with *a priori* images, was able to become, quite naturally, the inspiration for the highest school of political philosophy of the ancient world, and the model for the most audacious reformers. *A priori* images are fecund, even and especially when they are reinserted in the world as long-term anticipations, after the long road—*tèn makran hodon*—of philosophical thought.

PART II

The Cognitive Content of Images

Image and Perception

A. Biological Givens of Perceptual Functions

1. Primary Biological Categories and Secondary Psychical Categories:
   The Role of the Milieu Organized as Territory

We may consider the relation to the milieu that takes place according to primary categories of valence and signification to be biological; the first gathering of data that a living being must conduct is that which provides answers to questions such as: "is it a predator, a prey, a sexual partner, an offspring of the same species . . . ?" To each of these categories of a situation there corresponds a definite mobilization of the action system of the organism, which bestows a global adaptation to the given situation; here the object is not yet identified as individual, recognized as this object, already captured in experience; the informational category of the biological is that of a first adaptation in a milieu that is not yet organized, recognized and classified, and thus where anything can appear at any time anywhere; it is the state of alertness and vigilance a living being is forced to maintain outside of its territory.

Within the territory, in a world where there is no longer any novelty with regard to vital categories of attack, defense, etc., a living being can deploy a properly psychical activity, one posterior to the identification of the object following the first sifting or classification according to vital categories. The issue is not to oppose the animal to the human but to situate the frequency of behaviors of a biological or psychical type; the more the milieu is organized, the less it is necessary to conduct a preliminary sifting of signals according to the primary categories; after a cursory categorical scouting, the field is freed up for psychical activity because the class of the object is no longer in doubt. When the nervous system is less developed and possibilities of multisensorial concentration of information weaker, the activity of primary organization takes more room; we must ultimately suppose that animals can only have a properly psychical activity within their territory, and that this territory's size and organization is proportional to the animal's capacities of perception and integration. The consequence, specifically, is that resolving problems involving the inventive imagination humans deploy (detours, instruments) succeeds much better when an animal is in its territory than when it is in a situation where it could not organize its milieu. It has been noted that jaguars, capable of taking long detours when hunting, display great inertia in captivity when confronted with a problem easily resolved by taking a simple detour. The reason is that in this new unorganized world it lives in a biological regime of perception expecting to find enemies or prey, or even partners, but does not see things as objects that would induce intelligent conducts. Humans act the same way, and what used to be called regression may be understood as implementing perceptual categories of biological type, due to the novelty or emotional aspect of the situation. Any entirely new situation, any intense rupture in a normal situation, represents an opportunity to start perceptual classification anew, beginning with sifting through primary valences.

2. The Image as Immediate Anticipation in the Identification of the Object: Image and Concept

On the basis of experiments and observations, ethologists have rigorously defined conducts of the primary perceptual type in which positioning towards the milieu cannot wait for information to be complete; one must speak, begin to act, take an active attitude and get nearer, which is a genuine operative conjecture on the possible nature of the object as belonging to one of the categories to which the individual's action system applies. Hence, the bee-eating wasp chasing domesticated bees does not have sufficient capacity for sensorial synthesis and integration of remote information to group all of the information before launching towards his prey; if he waited to have enough information to succeed with certainty, he would miss every opportunity. Here, conduct is perceptual-motor in the sense that it is composed of successive waves of information gathering and motor reactions that modify the relationship between the organism and the milieu, pulling the wasp closer to the bee and allowing it to implement a different sense than the one before. Each wave of sensorial data is the *"releaser"*[1] or trigger *[déclencheur]* for a defined reaction allowing the reception of a new wave of information provided by another sense. At the close of the action, enough information is gathered to identify the object, as though the sensorial synthesis had been possible from the position of primitive observation, but with this progressive perceptual-motor conduct, error cannot be avoided, for the insufficiency of mono-sensorial information in the first stages—especially the first stage— leaves large chances of error, for instance 9 out of 10. Such conducts are nonetheless possible and productive according to their logic of increasingly committed trial and error, on the basis of errors avoided, since the first tries engage relatively little activity and are totally reversible; getting randomly closer to a possible prey, hiding for no real reason in one's burrow at the slightest alarm—these are conducts as easily undone as they are accomplished, in contrast to the consummating operations at the close of actions and in direct contact with the prey, following the grouped perception or the successive stages of approach behavior.

In fact, in progressive perceptual-motor behaviors, the role of intra-perceptual images is primordial: since perception is given only at the end of the activity, at the moment of consummation, each preceding stage is founded on a sketch of perception that is, precisely, the image; the image is the anticipation of the object through potential characters that are richer than the capture of the identified object; the flying object that triggers the approach of the wasp may be a domestic bee, a bumblebee or a wild bee . . . It is an entire class that triggers a pursuit; posteriorly, the contributions of other senses will reduce this anticipation rich with possibilities, and only presupposing the necessary primordial compatibility to trigger an effective response attitude allowing a continuation of the approach. In the case of the human, we can give examples of those images presupposing a vast compossibility and bringing a defined attitude; something terrible or threatening, even before one sees what it is, comprises a vast compossibility and generates an attitude of flight, defense, or circumspect information gathering. The impression that something is happening, that an important event has just occurred, is the richest of all, even though it contains no informational precision. This interest of novelty, causing a high level of vigilance, may then become diversified according to definite categories: arrival of friends or foes, bad or good news, or sudden obligation; through successive waves, the situation closes around the identification of an object, with which a properly psychical activity begins. A gathering around an accident, a riot, the scramble of people fleeing, are first perceived in a primitive manner even by humans when the subject is in a situation where sensorial data arrive in a new and unexpected way.

Images appear, then, in the form of perceptual anticipations of potentialities, as more general than individual objects. Should we consider them as analogs to concepts and as bases for concepts? They differ from concepts in that they are *a priori* allowing the insertion of the living being in its milieu, and are not the results of an inductive experience, thereby *a posteriori* constructions summarizing experience. Yet we may consider them as the basis of certain concepts which are in fact images enriched and focalized by experience, at times in a single image (*Prägung*). In reality these *a priori* categories of perception are one basis for spontaneous associations and evocations taking place after perception; they prolong images of long-term anticipation and insert themselves in the relations to the milieu, even if motivations are less strong than those allowing entirely pre-perceptual images to be expressed. Class images are gestaltized, as experiments of the school of ethology on the perception of birds of prey by domestic fowls have demonstrated; in order for the alarm reaction to take place, not only must the lure present the "short neck" stimulus but the beak must be pointing forward in the direction of motion: there is then an *a priori* conjunction of form and motion in this configuration. In other configurations there are *a priori* linkages of color and movement "pattern," for instance, in the reactions of sexual pursuit in the male butterfly *(Eumenis semele)*. We might also cite the gestaltized combination of attitude (raised head), form (inflated abdomen), and color (grey but not red) that is the *a priori* perceptual image the female stickleback has of the male, triggering the characteristic mating swim. Such gestaltized *a priori* are usually organized in more or less complex series with each configuration during a conduct, like pre-mating exhibition, forming the trigger for the subsequent series; but what matters here is the *a priori* gestaltized character of each of the images allowing an action sequence; it is this configuration that collects sensorial data and constitutes the neuro-physiological key of the reaction; if incident stimuli do not display features corresponding to the image, the reaction does not occur. While they are not concepts, these stable configurations allow perception to be effective and followed by a selective action even when it is not addressed to a specific individual but merely to a specimen of the species presenting the requisite features (see the *Cours sur l'instinct, 1964–1965*).[2] These configurations are thus, for instinctual conducts, analogs to concepts for more elaborated conducts based on learning.

3. The Particular Characters of Images in Instinctual Perceptions Depending on Species: Social Aspects

Ethology has analyzed "releasers" in animal conducts better than in human ones since residues of learning play a masking role in human behavior. The type of figurations varies according to the dominant sense of each species; for birds, these are often sets of visual stimuli so specific that in the guise of feather appendages they guarantee against crossbreeding of different varie-ties of the same species (this is the case of the set of colored feathers on the underside of duck wings which males display by beating their wings during mating behavior); songs and movements may also play the role of behav-ioral stimuli-keys; in a large number of species, predators, prey, and relatives correspond to intra-perceptual images. Tinbergen speculates that a similar function exists among humans who perceive certain *allures* and configura-tions that have a meaning for their instinctual conducts. Hence there exists a characteristic configuration of the infant perceived by parents (convex fore-head, chinless); this image reappears in ersatz animals that fulfill the need for instinctual satisfaction; a childless woman adopting pets chooses those that have the characteristics of the image of the infant; dolls made by adults are ersatz of children; the optimal child selected for the needs of the film indus-try (Shirley Temple of yore) incarnates the image as "releaser" for instinctual conducts. A bird with a long pointy beak does not elicit maternal feelings, while a sparrow or red robin does. We should note too that the film indus-try sometimes constructs groupings or condensations of perceptual con-figurations, such as the image of the child-woman *[femme-enfant]* with, on one hand, aspects corresponding to sexual "releasers" and, on the other, to children's features. Such condensations are possible because each image, being merely a configuration or grouping of features rather than a determined object, does not present the problem of the excluded middle. Shirley Temple, beyond her optimal babyish appearance, was sexualized through dancing, singing, and situations in which she was the partner of adult males. Brigitte Bardot, corresponding to the optimal feminine appearance was also, in some of her parts, if not a child at least a *gamine*. Finally, certain collective circumstances produce other groupings such as the "toy soldier" who is both the child to be protected and the virile hero—the soldier at the front.

Are biological images corresponding to instinctual conducts constant over time for a given species? This is a delicate question especially for the human species; the "schematic idols" from Cycladic or Minoan cultures present an appearance for women that does not conform to the canons of modern European societies. Prehistoric steatopygous figurines are even more surprising; we must therefore presume that images intervening in perception are either subject to evolution or sufficiently indeterminate to receive different formulations when they show up in art forms or magical and religious representations.

Finally, Tinbergen considers that the triggers of instinctual conduct can only act in a concrete perceptual situation; in particular, a regulation of conducts takes place through changes in the configuration of the concrete and complete situation; a fight might be stimulated at the onset by the sight of the opponent, but it is conversely deescalated as soon as the opponent is viewed on the ground, wounded or bleeding; the perception of spilled blood forcefully inhibits aggressiveness; it corresponds to an instinctual image. (Indeed, we note the existence during fights among animals of submission or retreat inhibiting the opponent's aggressiveness, even before any wound). Tinbergen suggests that contemporary wars have become particularly lethal not only by way of an increase in weaponry power, but also because weapons hit remotely, without any possibility of seeing the image of dead or wounded enemies; the situation has become all the more ambiguous since the stimulation of aggressive conducts takes place as much or even more than before through the image of the opponent, while the instinctive de-escalation of the deployment of aggressive conduct—the image of a corpse—no longer exists. Sometimes, photojournalists and war correspondents act as channels for the inhibiting image; during the Korean War, newspapers across the world printed the photo of a four-or-five-year-old Korean girl crying on the battlefield over her dead parents, alone amidst a chaotic landscape. A similar event occurred recently in France when a little girl named Delphine was the victim of a terrorist attack.

In relation to the development of each individual, elementary intra-perceptual images emerge one after the other to make possible the perception of reality with a defined meaning; we could call this the "possible consciousness" of the individual; it is not a matter of global perceptual or intellectual development, but of the capacity for perceptually processing the meaning of a situation; hence a child non-sexually aware might perceive the mating behavior of animals as a fight. In the performance of a play from classical theater a child scarcely perceives the situations having to do with amorous feelings; such scenes are for him without structure and empty; by contrast, a dispute over an injustice, like the one with which Corneille opens *Le Cid,* is clearly perceived by a young child, since situations of competition correspond to his own relation with the milieu.

The notion of possible consciousness is indeed related to the perception of situations in a primitive mode, yet it is difficult to account for it with the notions of gestaltization defined by ethology since it implies a collective aspect: at a certain time and in a given situation, a given group is able to grasp the meaning of a situation while other situations do not have any meaning for it. For instance, during the Russian Revolution peasants immediately grasped that land ownership had changed, but not that political authority no longer belonged to the Tsar; possible consciousness acts as a selector of incident information, welcoming certain traits and refusing others; in the genesis of myths and the deformation of news and the spread of rumors, possible consciousness plays a central role; hence Christianity was seen in Rome as an initiatory religion conducting the human sacrifice of small children, since such a conception corresponded to the representation of actual initiatory cults in some religions from distant lands; here possible consciousness amounts to the "non-Roman," as compounding all that is exotic and barbarous. Of course, since these are conscious representations belonging partly to cultural contents, we might say that there is nothing biological in such ways of perceiving. Still they are primary, but at the level of the collective; they are modified according to collective conditions (feeling of danger, pressure towards conformity) and constitute the basis for psychosocial regulations; the representation of the foreigner or the deviant is in reality a perception; the *socius* is perceived without mediation in a way that is as primary and as gestaltized way as the partner or nurturing parent is; the idea that the domain of social reality is that of learned behaviors while the directly biological categories devolving from instincts would be spontaneous is very much theoretical. On the plane of phenomena, intra-perceptual images have meaning for psychosocial situations; they are no less spontaneous or less primary than those that allow for a primordial adaptation to dangerous situations, or the relationships between parents and their young; the human face, seen frontally, whether familiar or unknown, is probably one of the first gestaltized perceptions of the infant; the valence of familiarity or foreignness is part of perceptual processing as is that of predator or prey. This foreshadows the importance of the perceptual and primary character of cultural stereotypes (clichés) with their attendant reactions. Humans are *zoon politikon*.

The existence of images constituting the primitive categories of perception, before being affirmed in a definite and universal way, deserves more pointed research. Indeed, it is beyond doubt that there exists possibilities of qualifying, at the onset, groups of stimuli according to instinctual categories across many species, especially in the register of the dominant sensibility of each species; for example, minnows have a substance in their blood that spreads in water when an individual in the group is wounded; this substance provokes fright in the entire group; as soon as other individuals detect its presence in water they adopt an immediate reaction of flight; it is neither a matter of training nor of learning. The sense of sight being dominant among primates, psychologists (particularly those of the Gestalt School) have sought to find visual structures acting as similar alarm signals or having the power to attract; a young chimpanzee is scared by a doll whose eyes are made of shoe buttons; this would be a "pithecophobogenic" visual structure; yet Guiraud critiques this interpretation by stating that the doll scares the young primate because it is new and unexpected in its experience; for Guiraud the innate structures serving as a basis for perception could not have reached such a degree of selectiveness and precision, if they exist at all. It is indeed very difficult to establish the degree of generality (hence the richness in compossible forms) that a primary perception may harbor. Is there either a primary response, a primordial perception for that which is scary or dangerous, or are there two primary categories: attraction and repulsion? And is novelty attractive or repulsive? It is repulsive as possible danger, as presence of a putative predator, but it is also attractive as the possible presence of some object that may be a prey or a partner; it is not easy, then, to affirm that novelty in itself is either repulsive or attractive; novelty is a category that contains all possibilities of reaction; the prior mobilization of reactions is a state of heightened vigilance; after the first wave of information gathering this state may be channeled towards inducing an action system to either flight or approach; however, this absolutely primary state exists only when the flow of information is too thin to trigger the dichotomization into reactions of flight or approach; this is often the case for the young, who have imperfect sensorial adaptations; the response is then vigilance and curiosity. Yet in certain cases the orientation of reactions seems to be forced on the organism by the immediate meaning of the structure of the stimulus; a dove that has always lived in a cage will react by fleeing when presented with a snake, without any prior reaction of vigilance or curiosity. Young monkeys display fear reactions to a human being dressed in large black veils corresponding to the image of a ghost. On this basis, it is difficult to say whether all perceptions begin with very general stages such as a reaction to novelty before splitting into a dichotomy scheme of flight or approach attitudes, continuing until the activity of consummation-execution, or whether some perceptions begin immediately with the reception of an already strongly orienting signal that is selectively received without learning and that triggers a definite appropriate reaction as in an automatic function. It is likely that both perceptual modalities exist, that their relative importance depends on the species, and that they have different consequences for the introduction of learning processes, since the stereotypical response to a stimulus-key lacks plasticity and adaptability because it is not progressive.

4. The Role of the Intra-perceptual Image in Choice; Victimology and Depth Psychology

We might summarize by saying that the image acts as an attitude trigger and an information selector with respect to primary perceptions of a progressive type, those comprising successive dichotomies, but it is not a trigger for an activity of consummation or execution; this would explain the broad compatibility of images that do not entail a logic of the excluded middle: these are principles of a logic of classes as a system of compossibility. But besides this image of compossibilities in a regime of progressive perception, this system needs to make room for specific configurations endowed with a predetermined meaning, capable of directly triggering an activity of consummation or execution, such as the sight of a snake by a bird.

This function of directly triggering an execution response is bracketed the more behaviors based on learning replace autonomous instinctual behaviors; nonetheless, the coexistence within one living being of two uses of the intra-perceptual image (as potential class or as trigger) may be the occasion of changes in the regime of correlation between perception and activity which bring, after a reception of information in the progressive regime, a direct and abrupt passage to an execution activity; such a reaction has, formally, the characters of an instinctual reaction (the direct and immediate response to a configurative stimulus), but it is not a true instinctual reaction, since it began as a perception in the progressive regime and was diverted toward a spontaneous reaction, as if the image of compossibilities had been mistaken for a specific trigger. Certain actions of delinquents seem to lend themselves to an interpretation according to this schema of a sudden passage to an execution activity, in particular in cases where premeditation is low; by analogy with the studies of the processes of expression, we might say they are behavioral anacolutha; hence, to see a woman, as first perception in the progressive regime means to direct one's self towards a progressive identification leading to the recognition of the person, or at least a social or collective type of differentiation (a young middle-class woman, an elegant woman, an employee); possible attitudes (greeting, indifference) appear only as a conclusion to progressive perception; conversely, the mobilization of a sequence of instinctual conduct such as seduction, based simply on the initial perception of class, marks a sudden leap in the regime of perception and does not conform to collective norms; such a leap is not merely untoward but criminal if it jumps over the stages of the instinctual sequences themselves, reversible at first, and leads directly to a consummation activity (attempted rape). Disputes and fistfights belong to the same type and signal a bifurcation of the progressive sequences of behavior towards instinctual reactions.

Yet this general schema of behavioral anacoluthon remains too summary; the bifurcation towards sudden activities of execution is likely not entirely random; it cannot be accounted for solely by invoking the impulsiveness of the subject or his lack of emotional control; we must also take into account the presence of configurative stimuli that trigger an operative short-circuit and induce, at least partially, the subject's behavior; in other words, victims are in some cases the bearers of perceptual "patterns" that stimulate various categories of instinctual reactions, as if there was in the victim a certain power of appeal of criminal gestures. According to Mendelsohn, from Jerusalem, it is the structure of the aggressor-victim that explains criminal acts rather than the delinquent alone; this author recommends preventive and healing measures to victims, because in some cases victims are endowed with a "victim potential" that stimulate possible aggressors. Indeed, there is a concentration of similar crimes against certain persons (for instance, attempted rapes) leading to the idea that victims emit a certain information that directs criminal acts. Nevertheless more research and a rigorous methodology are required to validate the basic hypothesis of victimology.[3]

Szondi, in a similar area of equally conjectural research, that deserves nonetheless to be cited, thinks that perception permits choices corresponding to very selective impulses [pulsions] in the subject which predispose him to certain categories of acts (for instance, a tendency towards strangling); the theoretical interpretation of Szondi rests on the distinction of dominant and recessive characters; it leads in practice to using tests to choose photographs of various categories of criminals; the non-indifference to this or that category of photographs would selectively indicate the existence in the subject of an impulse that selectively directs them towards a definite category of acts, while preserving the freedom of the various socially accepted sublimations.

Szondi's theory is contested, but it is interesting formally as presenting an audacious hypothesis attributing the determinism of deep personal choices to complex perceptions that detect tendencies in other subjects that are not expressed in everyday activity; this hypothesis can be better understood if we accept that personality is structured in layers and levels (depth psychology);

projective perception testing becomes very much relevant in the context of Szondi's impulse theory.

B. The Role of the Intra-perceptual Image in Information Gathering

When perceptions of the instinctual type do not arise, for instance, when reception of information takes place in a territory in which the object is identified and the domains of appearance of each category of data are already classified and ordered, the subject's activity is primarily differential in the sense that the useful signal is an index of difference between what is already known about the object (quiddity, form, dimensions, colors) and what is actually new with regard to that knowledge. In this case information is no longer relative to the class or identity of the object, which represents both the end term of information gathering according to classes and the shift to differential processing, which may be called a secondary and properly psychical level.

The intra-perceptual image still plays the role of a model, a *"pattern"* of the greatest generality to which the set of incident signals may be connected; but in a perception of the secondary type, the difference between sensorial data and the image is interpreted as a state of the object; the image is the system of the compossibility of states. Incident information acts as an element of decision in that compossibility. Finally, as the object may evolve during the perception itself, local activity allows for a selection of information relative to this current variation; this function may be called derivation. We must study successively the identification of the object, differential information gathering, and finally derivation. These three activities are progressively finer and prolong information gathering of the primary regime.

1. The Role of the Intra-perceptual Image in Object Identification: Perceptual Constancy and Adaptation

Constancy is the name of a general effect of perception which ensures that objects are grasped as sheaves of absolute properties despite their variable and changing relations with the subject during their movements, and despite changes of the milieu (lighting, proximity of other objects, angle of view). The constancy principle may be decomposed in several particular aspects, into for instance, the constancy of forms; a circular object continues to be perceived as circular even if the circle's plane is not perpendicular to the visual angle; form constancy has limits, however; when the circle's plane is almost parallel to the visual angle, constancy may fail; there is a constancy of colors, of sizes, of hues of grey, etc. In each category constancy has limits; for instance, color constancy is maintained in spite of changes in the chromatic composition of lighting so long as there is a continuous spectrum of visible radiations, even when the color temperature of the source varies within broad limits (from that of the sun, around 6,500 degrees K, to that of the flame of a candle). Conversely, colors are altered if the structure of the radiation spectrum becomes discontinuous, as is the case with electroluminescent sources of mercury vapor. More generally, to study perceptual constancy, we call upon the reduced perception, that is, a situation of the object in which the dimensional (or qualitative) field is limited; for instance, perception through a field glass that cuts off a small section with no surroundings allows the grasping of an object in reduced perception. Relative to constancy, perceptual activity is comparable to an implicit quick calculation of the dimensional or chromatic scale of a known object, thus of the situation in a continuum. The information gathered is compared to that situation "pattern" on a continuum; it is in relation to this predetermined mask, anticipated in real time, that incident signals are received and interpreted as providing the knowledge of a person—tall or short—as a function of distance and surrounding objects. If conditions spontaneously impose reduced perception (for instance, a person appearing at the top of a cliff, without objects of known dimension in close proximity) size perception remains uncertain; we cannot tell if it is an adult or a child, without the intrinsic size ratio of head-to-body. The image is here like a virtual object whose appearance in this or that a place is anticipated from the surroundings and from the continuum of size, color, and form; when the object appears it is in relation to these images that it is grasped; reception is then already in this case differential and comparative. In the case of a single object in motion, the imaginary anticipation of its dimensional and aspectual changes allows the grasping of the object as constant if perceptual data agree with these anticipations.

Constancy, which implies an anticipation activity and the production of images, contains a reference to experience and is not universal; there are

universes of constancy for a determinate object, that is, types of surroundings allowing for dimensional anticipation and comparative activity. Between
two universes of this kind there can be a discontinuity in magnitude producing an impression of non-constancy when the object is outside its usual surroundings (larger or smaller size, color changes). The universe of roofs is
not that of living interiors; a pottery chimney tube decoratively placed on
stairs seems enormous and much taller than those belonging to rows on top
of Parisian roofs; the reason is that there is no image of pottery chimney
tubes within interiors. A phone line insulator placed on a table seems much
larger than when it's on the top of a pole, and a section of rail used as an anvil
in a workshop seems larger than actual rails on the ground. Conversely, household items placed outdoors seem smaller; during the war, the inside of evis-
cerated houses was visible from outside, and pieces of furniture or wallpaper
seemed different than what we see when entering a flat—and quite dirty in
the sunlight.

The perceptual function of constancy involves the deployment of an activity of short-term anticipation akin to that of servomechanisms and [motion]
predictors ensuring the automatic tracking of objects; this function includes
postulates relative to a determinate type of object that may be modified by
training; hence for almost all mobile objects first detected by sound, visual
scanning is directed to the point of space from where the object appears
to be producing the sound; the sonic object and the visual object are presumed to coincide spatially; yet with fast planes this short-term anticipation
is deceived: visually, the plane is ahead of where the sound comes from since
the sound arriving now is that which it emitted one or two seconds ago; after
a few attempts one's anticipation is readapted: upon hearing a jet flying overhead, one looks for it farther ahead; the intra-perceptual image of the jet
takes into account the lag between sound and visual identification. Constancy
in the usual sense of the term is a particular case of short-term anticipation
activity that allows for the identification of the object and the permanent
reception of signals which allow for its tracking; the image thus presupposes
a code of transformation of the object, a formula of potentiality allowing
the prediction of the transformation of received signals on the basis of surroundings and the ongoing action.

2. The Image in Differential Perception

When sensorial data are received in a stable and normalized manner through the process of constancy, the schema of the object, constituting its image as a system of intrinsic compossibilities, allows the perception of the present state as a figure against the ground of intrinsic compossibilities. Hence, somebody we know, identified in spite of distance, movement, surroundings, lighting, etc., appears, secondarily, as tired, joyful, or tense. Awareness of the current state calls for a rich and precise perceptual image. What we designate as "intuition" or "foreboding," like that of a mother who knows before the doctor that her child is sick, that "something is the matter," may be attributed to the richness of the image of compossible states of the child that only the mother possesses; all the doctor can do is compare the child to other children of the same age: the inductively derived image of the experience of same-age children (which is, rather, a concept) cannot be as well adapted to differential perception as that coming from the various states of the child, organized as a system of "masks," of snapshots [clichés], to which the child's present way of being is compared. People who have long cared for a patient perceive in subtle ways the moment when the patient's state improves, or to the contrary, deteriorates; they have formed an inner schema helping them perceive the present state in comparison to the particular model of the patient. This dimension of the individual as a system of compossibility of a certain number of linked states is illustrated and highlighted by the method of clinical observation, whose essence lies in developing in the observer a concrete representation of the subject that is sufficiently fine-grained to serve as a basis for the perception of the present state in the signification it has for the subject. This concrete representation is an image.

The differential perception of the states of an object does not concern human beings alone; it also appears in technics and more generally in the intuition of a knower sufficiently familiar with an organized reality to know concretely the compossibility of all its states; this perception at times overflows into the present state, like the mother's intuition that her child is becoming sick; a mountaineer can better perceive the state that precedes a storm or a snowfall; even the presentiment of an avalanche may precede the seemingly random and unpredictable event. This kind of perception of a state requires a special knowledge of all the details of a place; the place needs to have become a territory rather than a mere field of activity; this is why animals living in a definite territory are often the first to perceive an irreversible change or an alarming state; before the eruption of Mount Pelée in Guadeloupe, snakes were seen leaving the epicenter of the cataclysm *en masse,* drowning in the sea. The reactions of birds or insects are often used to forecast weather by people who have long observed them; such reactions are linked to the perceived state of the atmosphere, humidity, and light.

In the case of differential perception, the image used as the ground for perception is comparable to that which a shepherd has of its flock; without counting them, he sees that one or two animals are missing; he could not possibly count his sheep through the image, however; the image only plays its role in the perception, and it is the misalignment between the image and the data of perception that appears with clarity; there is no independent representation of the image as a numerable and manipulable reality. For instance, one case often cited is that of the image of the columns of the Pantheon; a mental image would not allow the columns to be counted, yet it would render sensible an alteration in the number of columns were they changed overnight; a great number of mental images, particularly those of clairvoyants, present this aspect of a mask that precludes details or manipulation, and which is, as such, non-describable; outside of the presence of the perceived object, these images remain schemas, tendencies providing the subject with a definite impression, yet they cannot replace the object; in reality, they are a mode of receiving the object, a short-term anticipation of its possible states allowing the subject, after identification of the object, to have a perception of its state.

The word "intuition" is often used when the perception of a state entails a large number of data to be held together by the subject without recourse to any discursive operation or exploration; this is what Pascal calls the heart in response to problems whose solutions draw on a large number of very subtle principles; the places where various people stand in a hall, their different social status, the need to greet one without offending another and without forgetting to greet the most important people first—these are examples of the *esprit de finesse; the esprit de géométrie* could not resolve these problems in a sufficiently short time since putting into equation such preferential sequences, which interfere with a complex topology, would be too difficult. In truth it has to do with the perception of a state. To solve the problem of the *esprit de finesse,* one must have a rather precise image of this society so that it is seen not as a plurality of discrete persons, but as a veritable organism in such or such a pose (contracted, drawn out, spread out, etc.). The operational mode naturally devolves from this perception of a state; the *esprit de finesse* inhabits those who already possess an image of the organism they are approaching. The perceptive chair of a meeting is attuned to the states of the participants in the way one grasps the successive comportments of a wild animal; an orator also possesses an accurate perception of the state of his audience when he knows it well; yet the image allowing such a perception to occur is not sufficiently malleable so as to take roll of the participants after the meeting; an image by itself is as obscure as a perception lacking the support of the image.

This role played by the intra-perceptual image can account for the enormous capacity of the sensorial reception of information, while the faculty of attentive apprehension of discrete and new elements is limited to a few binary units per second; what use is vision's ability to quickly gather millions of distinct points?—precisely to feed this differential perceptual activity that receives outside data the way coded responses are corrected through a grid; only errors, that is, non-coincidences between the image (playing the normative role of the grid) and actual incident data (responses) are transmitted to the true receptor, the subject of perception.

If the sensorial data are too poor to calibrate the image, but still sufficient to elicit it, then it is the image that structures the message received by the subject; this is the phenomenon of the crystal ball in which reflections evoke images without saturating them, since reflections are poorer and less precise than images; a person seen through the fog or penumbra is "like a ghost" because sensorial data are barely sufficient to evoke images; a photograph out of focus or a painting that is but a sketch may have a greater force of evocation than sharper or more complete works; could the mysterious character of the Mona Lisa, and all of the paintings that seem to be gazing at the viewer, come from a certain fuzziness mixed in with features that recall mental images? A large number of arts use suggestion, which is essentially a call to images with incomplete perceptual data, less rich than actual images.

3. The Role of the Image in Adaptation to Change:
Perception of Derivation

During the course of perception itself, we can observe the focusing of the receptive activity when data brought by incident signals display regularity, for instance, a law of iterative recurrence; in this case, after a few seconds of adaptation, the continuous rhythms and variations become components of the reception system of incident signals, and only discrepancies from these models are actually perceived in the proper sense of the word, grasped as new and capable of triggering a new attitude or action in the subject. We might say that the internal image of rhythms and regularities neutralizes the signals as carriers of possible novelty, as content of psychic reception. A whole set of phenomena of habits—in the sense of 'habit' as an adaptation that reduces the vigilance of perceptual events—belongs to this genesis of neutralization models of perceptual events; one adapts to the regular passage of trains at night, to the noise of machines, etc.; by contrast, an irregularity in the regime of incident signals triggers a true psychic reception, whether it be a supernumerary event or a lack sufficiently strong to awaken a sleeping subject. (We might also cite the old example of the ticktock of a windmill.) The efficacy of this subjective mask of incidences is such that, when misperceived, it can create intense perceptual illusions; in the experience of consecutive visual motion, if a striped belt or a disk bearing a spiral stops, it generates a subsequent effect of illusory movement going in reverse to the primary motion; such an effect can occur on any background (a human face, for instance) so long at it carries the lineaments or even a few details of a structure. In such a case, the internal image of the received movement, acting as a cinematic negative of perceptual events, is endowed with some inertia; approximately twenty seconds are required to constitute it in full, and, when the primary movement stops, the negative of external signals continues to act for several seconds; since nothing balances it out, it generates through differential effect and derivation an illusory impression of reverse motion compared to the primary motion. The same images of regular incidence allow the *reception* of accelerations and decelerations as a new reality against the background of an already given motion; the perception in this case functions as a comparator that sends the derivation signals to the properly psychic reception. The image is yoked to incidences but with a delay that is necessary and essential for the comparison to be effected. It is this delay that allows the image to emerge as a differential signal sent as illusion to the psychic reception when the variation of perceptual events is too rapid; a sudden stoppage of noise causes silence to be perceived as a truly positive signal, in the form of a noise-ending blow. Completely random events alone cannot be neutralized by the image as an auxiliary of perception.

C. The Intra-perceptual Image in the Perception of Shapes: Geometrical Images

1. Subjective Contour and Associated Image

The existence of intra-perceptual images was discovered during studies of the visual perception of shapes, particularly by Schumann, in the experiment of subjective contour (see the course on *Perception* in the May 1965 *Bulletin de Psychologie*, p. 1184ff).[4] To designate this category of perceptual phenomena, Woodworth uses the expression of "attached image," connoting a purely central origin.

The central, psychological and non-peripheral effects that act as a power of modification of the dimensions and relations of perceptual subsets do indeed correspond to the dynamic theory of Lipps (1897) which calls such introduction of a tendency into the perceived object *Einfühlung* (empathy), a tendency felt by the subject in the presence of the spectacle of the world and introduced into objects where it generates enlargement, narrowing, elevation, contraction, or expansion of one of the parts relative to the others. The object is modified in perceptual representation in a manner that conforms to a tendency implicitly introduced by the subject. Architects who build large monuments (temples, theaters) correct, at the outset, lines, spacings and dimensions so that the deformations induced by the subject are harmoniously compensated for; it is for this reason that the columns in temples are neither parallel nor equally spaced out and that large horizontal layout displays a certain curvature that compensates in advance the perceptual deformation that might make them look awkward. According to Lipps, a standalone square, when inserted into a vertical superposition of rectangles and squares where it appears to be supporting the weight of the whole edifice, displays a deformation that exaggerates its vertical dimension so that it will appear as a rectangle when seen in the position of a stone supporting

a great weight; according to the *Einfühlung* theory, this effects results from
the vertical force of elastic reaction the subject imagines within the stone.

If the perceptual deformations are caused by the introduction of imaginary forces in the configuration of objects rather than from properly optico-
geometrical effects, there must exist a difference between perceptual illusions
produced with a non-signifying material and those produced with a signifying material having the same geometrical properties. This is how Poggendorf's illusion was shown in its signifying version by Filehne: within a décor
of ruins a vertical band with parallel edges becomes the body of an ancient
column, while an intercepted oblique becomes a rope between two devils.
Éliane Vurpillot has also compared different montages of the Poggendorf
illusion in both signifying and non-signifying versions; there too the oblique
becomes a rope or cable tensed on a pulley by a worker lifting up a bag.
Piéron has proposed that this configuration be staged not only in a signifying set but in one that is concrete and real, for example, with a man drawing water from a well with a cord going behind a plank. Indeed, it is in this
direction that research should be oriented in order to detect and measure
precisely and objectively the influence of present imagination on perception; in a large number of experiments on geometrical representations or
realist miniature models, there is a change in the order of magnitude of
the perceived object when going from the non-signifying version—a "mute
painting on a canvas"—to the signifying version, a graphic symbol of large-
scale actualities like as a monument or a human being; it is difficult in such
cases to avoid the interferences coming from the perceptual adaptation to
the scale of the perceived phenomenon (perspectival effects, representation
of the situated corporeal schema, etc.). In order to conduct conclusive experiments on these effects of intra-perceptual images, the non-signifying geometrical figures must have the same size as the real signifying figures, that is
to say, that of the doors, barriers, and columns that constitute signifying elements. We might be able to show that the effects of *Einfühlung* are neither
exceptional nor rare, and that there exists if not an implicit animism, at least
a latent organicism in perception that posits tensions, forces, resistances, and
actions in the shape of things.

We might indeed be able to summarize the phenomena of subjective contours as well as those of *Einfühlung* by saying that the subject of perception

is prone to capturing, within the configurations of reality, subsets having not only the average size of the human organism but also the basic properties of all organisms, that is, the capacity of locomotion, polarity, and the orientation of movements and of the body schema. Perceptual groupings do not proceed from chance, nor only as a result of symmetries and geometrical equilibria; a contour delineates a subset that might be a living organism, moving as a whole, oriented as a whole in the same direction; there are no subjective contours when the details to be gathered do not exist or are not manifest. Contrary to the common error of amateurs of photographic techniques using broad, violent, and contrasted compositions, it is not simply the black-white opposition that cuts out regions within a whole, there has to be precision, a nuancing in the shot so that sets can detach themselves; a totalitarian art of violent oppositions annihilating details through sharp contrast developing and printing creates the impression of a Chinese ink drawing, but does not really generate the effect of the composition of reality. A contour is the active frontier of a population of elements, a republic of details; it has a functional meaning like the tegument of an organism in relation to the organs it covers up and whose coordinated plurality it makes manifest. The *Einfühlung* may be assimilated to those effects of seizing organized and organic subsets as intermediaries between the elementary order of microstructures and the order of configurations of the whole; to perceive a rope as straight because it is pulled by a force means to place oneself as an organism in the place of this rope, to make the rope an extension of the arm, or to imagine it as the body stretching out through the effort of tension, elongating as it lifts a burden. The order of magnitude of contours and attached images is the same as that through which the common effects of *Einfühlung* reveal themselves because it corresponds to one of the most primary categories of perception, the encounter with living retorts to the subject in the universe. Similar groupings in organic units are possible with sounds, for example, in white noise, which, because of its random character, offers multiple opportunities of subjective structuring.

2. Reversibilities

A second important argument in favor of the metastable character of perceptual equilibria is the existence of reversibilities; the effects of reversibility would not be conceivable if we presumed that definitive perception corresponds to the most probable state, to the minimum of potential energy of the system, thus to a degraded state. If reversibilities, implying spontaneous changes during perception as it is prolonged, may appear, it is because potentialization continues to be accomplished during perception itself; in other words, the regime of perception comprising reversible configurations is formally similar to that of a switch, switching on its own when the condenser governing the inactive element reaches the difference of potential needed for that element to become a conductor.

Reversibilities are especially evident for geometrical figures that can be seen in spatial perspective such as Schröder's stairs; since there is no vanishing point, the subjective viewpoint is alternatively above and below the stairs; when perceptual toggling occurs, a sudden leap flips from one configuration to the other. The same phenomenon takes place with Rubin's cross, made of two imbricated Maltese crosses, one with arc circles, the other with spokes; when one acts as figure, the other becomes ground and seems to extend underneath the figure. Inversions occur spontaneously but may also be induced by willful attention, at least to some extent, which shows that the figure-ground equilibrium is not akin to a stable equilibrium. What might correspond here to a stable equilibrium would be the degraded state of a disorderly configuration in which various possible types of perceptual configurations would simultaneously mix together by superimposition.

3. The Image as Singularity or Privileged System of Perceptual Compatibility among Orders of Magnitude

It is possible to restore a meaning to the principle of isomorphism of Gestalt psychology by applying it to the intermediary level, the middle order of magnitude of perceived realities; what *constitutes the image [fait image]* in a perceptual whole is neither microstructures nor whole configurations, as perfect and geometrical as they may be, but the always precarious and tense correspondence or compatibility between the molecular and solar order of realities. Hence, the "good form" of bees' nests corresponds to a rare and precious system of compatibility between individual honeycombs and the row grouping them, partly due to the hexagonal structure, and partly to the back-to-back imbrication of cells sharing a common wall; it is the formula for the maximum of capacity and solidity with the minimum of wax; it is a matter of equilibrium in a certain sense, yet a kind of particular and rare equilibrium that human inventions realize, or the compatibilities of organs in a living body, or again works of art that institute a harmony between the structures of each of the elements and that of the whole; this equilibrium, obtained against the threat of disorder and chaos, is clearly not the same as that which, at the end of the leveling of all the oscillations through the degradation of energy, produces the flat and horizontal surface of water or the spherical surface of a drop suspended in an isotonic liquid; what, however, connects such structures of stable state systems to pregnant forms (such as a straight line or a sphere) is that under certain aspects they attain dimensional minima, like the straight line that is the shortest line between two points, or the sphere that is the smallest surface enveloping a given volume; such minima become optima not as systems whose energy is degraded but when considered as solution to a problem, thus when, instead of being the formula for the whole system, they are means, subsets seemingly playing the role of mediators and intermediaries between a larger configuration and an elementary matter; the spherical form is a good form when it is an intermediary structure such as a cistern or a balloon, the thin glass bulb protecting a filament from the action of the atmosphere, or a submersible enveloping a universe amidst another universe, as a functional system of compatibility between two milieus embedded one in the other; the case of geometrical figures as pregnant images therefore does not mean that pregnancy is attached to stable equilibrium states or to the most likely shapes according to chance, for there are cases when geometrical shapes are solutions of exception to the problem of maxima and minima posed by the relation between two orders of magnitude of reality.

a. Singularities Are More Pregnant Than Regularities

In the most common perception, what becomes an image and pops out is not regularity, a pure and constant geometrical character. On a perfectly flat and straight road, what jumps out at the viewer is the pothole, the irregularity, the beginning of a curve after the monotony of a featureless straightaway;

what is pregnant on a smooth and regular face is a scar or birthmark. In a general way, information brings the knowledge of novelty, thus of the unpredictable, the accidental, the singular. One person can be differentiated from another because regularities and symmetries of the organism organize according to a singular formula that characterizes that person by accounting for certain accidental aspects. In ordinary existence and various situations, what is pregnant is the source of novelty that traps a continuous action (scandal means "trap"); it is the unexpected that imposes itself and becomes figural against the ground of regularities.

It is true, however, that in some cases regularities are eminently remarkable and become pregnant, but such cases are precisely those when the appearance of a regularity on a background of chaos or random confusion is a singularity indicating a change of domain; it triggers a state of alarm and a surge of vigilance which are real signals of a change in regime or an imminent encounter; perfect circles, squares, and triangles are rare in wild nature. If, in the middle of a moor or uninhabited lands, one suddenly comes upon a perfectly drawn circle on the ground, this form is pregnant and leaps to one's attention; it is viewed as something new, rare, and unpredictable within the landscape: it indicates humans have passed through this place and that we have come across the foundation of a prehistoric dwelling or more recent traces of human activity such as the foundations of a watchtower. Geometrical shapes are usually artificial; they become pregnant when they are encountered in the wild; it is not forms themselves that are pregnant, it is their incongruous presence as a signal, a possible source of information, the occurrence of originality. Even when they are produced naturally, such as a mushroom circle, they are interpreted through legendary beliefs and become fairy circles or dancing grounds for witches; because of erosion, the "fairy chimneys" erected on friable ground topped by large flagstones are surprising because of the finesse of their vertical thin lines amidst a chaotic landscape of ravines. In a milieu of random configurations a geometrical form is pregnant because it is necessarily potentialized as a virtual signal. Behind it arise prohibitions, dangers, the foreclosure of laws and human institutions; the simplest of all geometrical shapes, the straight line, is already the sign of a frontier, the ditch that must not be crossed under penalty of fratricide as in the classical and brutal legend of the foundation of Rome.

b. Geometrical Shapes May Become Pregnant through Their Mutual Relationships

A rounded arch in a monument built in a completely homogeneous style is not particularly pregnant; this reduced pregnancy is not due to the intrinsic characteristics of an arch that is a perfect semicircle since, if we make a geometrical drawing of this type of arch, it is not particularly pregnant; however, it may become so if it mediates other shapes which, compared to the rounded arch, deviate on both sides of this average proportion. This is the case for the Cathedral of Orléans (Saint-Croix) seen from the cloister, that is, from the south: the full semicircular arch is topped by a flattened arch and flanked by two lancet windows, when the whole vista is taken at a glance; in this construction, which is like a dialogue between three shapes, the rounded arch plays an acutely mediating role; it is like the active center through which the extreme aspects of the flattened and pointed shapes double up and oppose each other. It would likely be possible to find similar examples in the acoustic arts in which pregnant forms are not necessarily the most singular ones, but are those playing the role of mediator within the whole between extreme terms of pitch and timber; in this case, the pregnant character is connected to average qualities not because they are the result of a degradation tending towards homogeneity, but because they are like a unique measure that makes extreme terms compatible with each other: they represent the successful singularity of this compatibility.

c. The Intra-perceptual Image Is the Style Common to Texture and Configuration

Such a mediation is a rare and tensed encounter that cannot take place in common occurrences. The relation between matter and form can be a violent and arbitrary relation, where the form carves out and masters matter in a way that is as artificially normative and unyielding as geometry in nature, like bushes a gardener prunes to obey the fantasies, poor in form, of the estate owner; the natural shape of the tree is replaced by the monstrosity of vegetal cubes or balls (Musset described the shorn yews of Versailles "in onion rows"; today we can see this in the garden of the Villandry castle). In fact, there are elementary shapes in matter like the grain of wood; each type of wood has its particular grain, and the fibers of an oak have a different pattern than those of a chestnut-tree or a maple. A violent geometrical shape, like that produced by a lathe, imposing a revolving figure on the wood, does not respect, support, or prolong the implicit and mute forms of raw matter transformed into workable matter. The more primitive the tool, the better we can follow the real lines of matter; such is the case with the two-handed curved draw shave used by barrel-makers, which is guided by the wood fiber, in contrast to the scratching stock, an instrument of torture for implicit forms; the latter planer traces trim lines, as thin and numerous as the woodworker wishes, with no definite relation to the material structure.

For a long time, art was of a synthetic type, adding more objects to objects, like a painting placed on a wall when a house is built. Yet there has arisen an analytical art that does not produce supplemental and secondary objects masking the base or primitive objects; this art consists in addressing matter from the outset in such a way that its texture and aspect are directly integrated in the configuration without paint or plaster. A wall built with well-fitted and well-cut blocks of granite or porphyry needs no plaster or paint. Each material already possesses the microstructures and original texture that cutting, polishing, or sandblasting can reveal without adding or hiding anything.

Textures may also be produced in an artificial manner, voluntarily or involuntarily; hence, a newly forged metal plate folds differently according to the direction of the fold in relation to the direction of deformation given by the rolling mill; more conspicuously, grooved sheet metal meant to resist deformation, such as those in cars of high-speed trains or in modern apartment buildings (rue Croulebarbe in Paris) cannot be mounted arbitrarily in relation to the configuration of the whole in which they play a part; we would not accept a car in which the grooves would be vertical rather than horizontal, that is, in the direction of the car's length, of the train's length which fits the horizontality of the tracks, the overhead lines, railway architecture and, more generally, the movement of the train which amounts to the perceptual essence of the configuration. In the same way, it would run against perceptual harmony to affix grooved metal sheets horizontally on an apartment building when it—as that of rue Croulebarbe—is a trim and high tower. We may note also that such analytical aesthetics corresponds to an implicit perception of the working of things: vertical grooves on a train would trigger a multitude of small turbulence countering the aerodynamics of surfaces; a horizontal arrangement on a building would not favor the optimal flow of water; finally, in all these cases, grooves parallel to the greatest dimension of an object correspond to optimal resistance to torsion and buckling, when surfaces themselves, now multifunctional, are not just siding or facing but play a role in the rigidity of the whole (construction technique of body-less vehicles according to the beam principle as used in some buses). In this last case, the meaning of "intra-perceptual rationality" requires the direction of grooves to be parallel to the greatest dimension of each sheet of metal when they are rectangular. We may call this style, common to the whole configuration as well as the component, *the image*; the image is not given by the components alone which merely generate the subject's need for it; nor is it imposed by the lines of the whole, which are only able to create, through a totalitarian effect, false windows; the image is the actual encounter of the postulate of the components and the postulate of the whole within a perceptual axiomatic of compatibility.

The Baroque, at least in its most automatized and vulgarized developments, might be defined by the independence of microstructures in relation to configurations, leaving the intra-perceptual image afloat and indeterminate; any detail might be added to the whole configuration, and this addition of fruits, flowers, or rocks has no limit in load or complexity. A contemporary Baroque has emerged with the proliferating automatisms or Op Art, with microstructural, geometrical, and contrasting motifs developed for themselves and serving to dress objects already endowed with a shape and a meaning; for instance, rolls of "opticalized" adhesive tape can be glued on cars, furniture, and various objects. The human body itself can be "opticalized," that is, overloaded in a Baroque mode with jewelry or painted or glued patterns; chessboard cameos and earrings reproducing in black-and-white the railway signal of complete stop (a square made of four red-and-white squares); and paintings and tattoos of various kinds showing clothing to be exchangeable in its perceptual functions by adding microstructures superimposed on the human form in a relatively arbitrary way, acting like masks. Of course, this automatic proliferation of microstructures should not be confused with research in which perceptual microstructures are integrated to the configuration in such a way as to underline its articulations or to exalt their perceptivity through networked highlighting (white shoes or hems in vivid colors); indeed it is not impossible that the fashion of opticalization draws its inspiration from signaling techniques (runways, roads, targets, test patterns, or flags in car races); yet it repurposed these high perceptivity patterns for a rhetorical usage detached from functionality and arbitrary in relation to the configuration, in a way that is irritating and vain in the literal meaning of these two terms.

Cesar Jannello has conducted in Buenos Aires logical and mathematical research on textures by using a point, a rectangle, or a line that can be developed according to the formula of a predefined progression in a multidimensional network creating impressions of incurving, inflating, or hollowing of surfaces. Such formulas are of interest for architecture, particularly for arranging vast surfaces or volumes by organizing in defined progressions the networks of windows, chimneys, or floor plans and levels. Le Corbusier was very sensitive to the relation of microstructures to configuration. This architect did not conceal his materials nor use plaster; concrete shows up as concrete and tubes and cables, rather than being hidden in corners or sunk under wall coverings, form lines, or bifurcations, gather and progress along prolonged vanishing lines in hallways, geometrically suspended to upturned T-brackets. As in living beings, every line of the whole configuration is multifunctional; a hallway is a place of passage, a collective locus that collects and distributes not only human beings in different rooms, but energy, air, water, and information; what is multifunctional remains open and unsaturated; on the T-brackets of the hallways of the Dominican convent of l'Arbresle other canalizations may be run if yet unknown forms of energy should one day be distributed. Thanks to its modular concept, we might also prolong the convent without rupture to augment its size, unlike the chapel. Finally, we should note that this analytical art is the most welcoming, the most able to integrate new realities, precisely because its unity is that of the image, which is not material and which bridges textures and the configuration. There are probably few convents in the world whose style could support the siting of a large propane tank so near buildings—fifteen meters from the chapel; this is possible with Le Corbusier's style. Finally, the non-dissimulation of materials allows for a conversation, in the image, of textures and configurations; in the convent of L'Arbresle, the cells were coated with a hard concrete finish blown laterally on the walls to form waves and hollows; in these long cells, light accentuates the relief in the coating to produce the impression we are in a long cave of sheer rock as though there was a profound and substantial link unifying nature and technicity.

In analytical art, the link between nature and technicity appears when the configuration is related to the geographical reality upon which the built work was constructed; a waterway to be crossed or a hill to be vanquished may be enough to create this linkage (which is the intra-perceptual image) between the dimension of the whole integrated to the world and the micro-structures of human building; this is the case for the segment of the highway coming from Paris to Clermont, near Montferrand, with high road lights and thick-grained roadway coating against the background of mountains and cityscape, and also for the segment of the new road traversing Châtellerault through its newly built neighborhood.

This stability of the image as an operation common to texture and configuration is not limited to a perceptual effect closed on itself; it triggers the concrete expression of forces, tendencies, and significations that devolve from the perceptual action and bestow its scope to a monument. That is the meaning of the memorial to the Resistance erected on Mount Mouchet. This massive and simple stone block before a vast unobstructed horizon is like an extension of the rock of the mountain; it is surrounded with no boundaries and no other embellishments; in a way it is the last of the tumulus mounds scattered by the roadway leading to this harsh and wild plateau. Driving down towards Saugues, we find this same quartz-rich granite—the main local rock—cut in large chunks and serving as support for posts or boundary stones. Born from the ground and bound to this place like the memory it perpetuates, the monument draws its meaning from being the structure of singularity that gathers and focuses the force of things.

To summarize, the pregnancy of forms expresses the inherence of the intra-perceptual image; this image is neither given, nor results from a stable state of equilibrium. It is the act of a subject who finds meaning at all orders of magnitude of perceived reality in the tensed and thought compatibility of the most elementary materials and the vast configurations inserting this portion of reality into the world. The equilibrium expressed in the intra-perceptual image is that of the living in relation to its milieu, rather than that of the lowest level of energy in a system; it is not the resting state of a single equilibrium but the linkage of two systems, the subject and the world; the intraperceptual image is the nodal point of insertion of this linkage into the world; it stands in a symmetrical relation with the existence of the subject as organism in relation to the limit separating the subject and the world.

PART III

The Affective-Emotional Content of Images

The *a posteriori* Image, or Symbol

A. The Level of Elementary Conditionings: *Prägung* and Critical Periods

1. Imprinting *(Prägung, Prégnation)*

In 1935, Lorenz described a mode of acquisition consisting of a very short and very early kind of impregnation.[1] Such a mode of acquisition produces modes of activity and reactions to stimuli taken to be congenital instincts which are in fact a particular type of learning. Lorenz discovered this mode of conditioning because he thought that the categorical imperative of researchers in ethology was to live with animals in their natural environment, leaving them free to retain the *tempo* of their spontaneous existence. Moreover, Lorenz perfected this method of observation through participation by learning gestures, vocal expressions, and attitudes allowing a human being to intervene by forming a natural group with the animal; hence, for a bird born in an incubator a human may play the role of mother if he or she can answer the cries of a young bird as its mother would do. Lorenz studied the complete set of behaviors of a chick named Martina by learning the meaning of the chick's "wiwiwiwi" ("I'm here, where are you?), its "wirrrr, wirrrr," etc., and the various cries of the adult, "gangangangang," or "gangingang," or "ran." By thus instituting a very early relation between the young animal and the observer, Lorenz noted that learning processes occur over a very short time; a certain number of hours or days after its birth, a young bird (grey goose or duck) is imprinted with the image of its parent-being, whether its

93

natural parent or an adopted parent, a human or an animal of another species; to achieve this, a certain number of signals and responses are required. Imprinting occurs or at least takes hold within a regime of exchanges between the young and its surroundings; accordingly, a chick may start by following a dog yet soon abandon this adoptive parent that does not answer its characteristic signals, while a relation with a nurturing human parent can become lasting if the human has learned to respond according to the semantics of the species.

These observations are far from isolated and may be associated with several categories of facts whether among animals or humans. It has been noticed in particular that the parasitic varieties of the cuckoo species, laying their eggs in the nests of other species, are endowed with the capacity of recognizing their nurturing parents; the young cuckoo, once adult, is able to recognize the nest of its host species and, by preference, will lay eggs in this species' nest; learning here amounts here to a "second nature," since the offspring of a cuckoo born in a warbler's nest, for instance, will go on laying eggs in warblers' nests. Without making hypotheses on representation among birds, we can say that, practically speaking, being born in a given milieu allows the recognition of this milieu through certain characteristic stimuli and generates a tendency to choose this milieu over others. Among humans, observed cases of wild children have shown their predilection for food (for instance, raw meat) they had to eat among their nurturing parents; these are remarkable facts because they appear to be an interference of the non-human in the human and have drawn attention to the irreversibility of such fundamental learning. Yet a great number of other learning processes that seem to be traits of character and innate characteristics of personality are probably also forms of learning acquired early on: food habits, habitat preference, and perhaps reactions of sympathy or antipathy to persons having a specific look, or corresponding to a specific image; defense or sympathy reactions may bear the determining mark of early and irreversible learning experiences, as much as food preferences or other choice reactions; learning processes are not solely representational or motor; they imply an association between modalities of comportment and a characteristic set of stimuli coming from the milieu having acquired a determinate valence.

We can even go further; according to some research, it appears that choice reactions to configurations of a milieu occasion not only individual learning processes but hereditary conditionings transmissible to offspring. American researchers have captured rodents of the same species in a wild treeless environment and in a forest. They were then raised in a laboratory under identical conditions; the offspring of both groups were then led to an experimental apparatus with a tunnel opening onto the boundary between two environments, one with and the other without trees, the subjects having the possibility of opting for either; among offspring from the forest environment the proportion of those opting for the same environment as their parents was higher than those that did not. Of course, this general experiment does not allow us to say where this transmitted principle of choice might be located; it could be, for instance, an organic disposition (an uneven development of adrenal glands) altering the regime of needs, thermal equilibrium, or light sensitivity, and the differential choice may result from a search for a *preferendum*. However, the fact remains; the valence of various stimuli configurations may be altered by early individual learning experiences, and perhaps in some cases through transmitted hereditary experience. Indeed, the support for information in organisms may not be exclusively cerebral, which would explain why the replacement of one nervous system by another (hereditary transmission solely of the species' structures), while erasing neural memory "traces," could give way to a transmission of information or reactive dispositions through a non-neural chemical pathway (experiment on planarians); reactive modalities of the affective-emotional type, which play such a large role in choices, define and fix the valence of images which are one of the bases of the organization of comportment.

2. The Human Aspects of Elementary Conditionings

Psychoanalytical studies have insisted on the importance of the early experience of children around their mother, then educators, then broader circles. Moreover, the process of introjection—the imaginary incorporation of an object or a beloved or hated person within the subject's ego or superego— represents a lasting basis for affective-emotional reactions in given situations; these are complete images introduced in the primary psychism (see Melanie Klein's studies) serving as models for the subject's choice and subsequent reactions. Yet we might expand this interpretation to consider that this acquisition of affective-emotional valences may be instituted every time the subject encounters a new situation, when the awakening of motivation is intense, and the lack of previous structures affords a margin of indetermination to the behavior. Stekel has studied human sexuality in this purview in two books titled *Impotence in the Male* and *Frigidity in Women,* in which the author analyzes the causes of a large number of dyspareunia. The comportment of an entire life appears to be directed by the affective-emotional components of fundamental moments in a subject's history that are not necessarily connected to childhood.

The necessity, in the course of ontogenesis, of constituting definite affective-emotional reactions discloses privileged periods that may be termed critical periods; hence, an abandoned child needs to constitute in himself the image of his mother at a given age, and when older, even if the child is well treated in his adopted family, he can continue to display features of abandonment behavior (affective indifference, constant testing of the affection of his circle) rendering adaptation difficult and often provoking rejection; what is lacking is a complete image of the mother that includes an affective-emotional response to a definite grouping of images, attitudes, and perceptions offered by adults.

But not all images concern human beings; they include also a primitive relation to objects, and one's social circle contains privileged objects as well as privileged beings like the mother.

3. Images of the Object

It is quite probable that early experiences do not sharply differentiate between the images of living beings (parents and peers) and objects; later, though, a splitting takes place whereby images of the relation with living beings become separated from images representing the milieu as the basis for the gradual organization of the territory. Both ethology and psychoanalysis have emphasized phenomena of irreversible learning devolving from the primitive relation to parents and other living beings. The other category, that of objects, has occasioned much less attention; often it is approached only through symbolic linkage to the first. But we might wonder whether this is not a rather anthropocentric vision of various situations. Even in the case of humans, reality is probably less simple and less homogenous.

With regard to animals, the very precocious character of their relation to objects without direct connection to the parent is beyond doubt, at least for certain species. Among nest-dwelling birds, for instance, parents are the necessary intermediaries between the world and their chicks, who remain entirely dependent on them for food; the nest alone is a non-living reality with the status of object; while for non-nest-dwelling birds, the parent's valence is foremost that of a protector and guide; food is sought and absorbed as soon as birth, the chick already having the sensorial adaptations and coordinated automatism of the action system that makes this activity autonomous (pecking, scratching the ground, or digging up insect nests among buzzards); the relation to the object is as primitive as the relationship to the *socius* or to the parents; finally, in some categories, the parent is absent or already dead (reptiles, insects) when the offspring is born. In all cases, imprinting concerns the milieu, and we can suppose that the election of privileged objects having the same valence as parents takes place in cases cited by Lorenz. Food is not the only type of function that can trigger imprinting that defines primordial images; shelter is an equally primordial reality since reactions of flight at the signal indicating the approach of a specific predator may be as precocious as those towards the search for food; this domain could open new research towards a more general ethology, perhaps less interesting for a comparison with humans, but allowing the analysis of determining factors of the conduct of species that are lower on the ladder of living beings.

For people too, it is not only other humans that are real. A brilliant educator, Maria Montessori, has understood the importance of the direct relation between the child and objects; she has sought to compose a "revelatory milieu" of objects around the child because she believed that the child needs to encounter stable objects that can be manipulated and seized as much as it needs to encounter loving and generous human presences. The Casa dei Bambini is a milieu filled with objects that are stimulating, never misleading or deceitful, and which do not trigger negative affective-emotional experiences. To borrow a metaphor from ornithology, we might say that Maria Montessori has sought not so much to make the child into an artificial nest-dweller, or at least an artificially prolonged nest-dweller; rather she placed within reach of the child objects that serve as key points within their material universe: sinks that are not sized for adults, door knobs that obey the force and prehensile capacity of young children, and horizontal switches that can be palm-activated (digital prehensile capacity comes later and lacks strength for a long time). Maria Montessori's pedagogy artfully grasps the physiology of perceptual-motor functions of the child, allowing the child to organize his own territory of objects without having constant recourse to the adult as caregiver for dressing, washing, or bodily needs. The American civilization of the time, very open to objects and developing in a low-density country with little available personnel, widely welcomed the Montessori method. We will not develop here other aspects of this pedagogical method, but it is clear that with such bases an important place is reserved for spontaneous discovery through manipulation and observation, and that the didactic and authoritarian aspect is all the more reduced; yet it is not enough to say it is an active method, since a method may be active by calling on essentially human realities, while here activities are centered on objects.

Besides this systematic and coherent aspect, we may consider the toy (or the familiar object recruited by the child without adult intervention) as corresponding to imprintings related to things. Indeed, a toy is the correlate [*répondant*] of the ego in the milieu, for better or worse; it forms a couple with the child, like the *symbolon* with the other *symbolon,* half of the primal whole from whence come *symbola* in a random division. This is what causes the child's deep and essential bond with the elected object that we may call a toy, although it is not always what the adult means by this word. For it can be an animal, a tree, rocks, an old clock . . . ; the *symbolon* lends itself to replacements; a yellow hen, elected as favorite toy and named "Little Yellow" may be replaced by another yellow hen considered to be the daughter of the former, whether that is the case or not, and named "Little Yellow 2." A whole dynasty of elected objects may come in succession, like a car series from which a buyer chooses—carmakers know how to produce successions and filiations through names and shapes so that the new models continue the older ones. This does not mean—in spite of a psychoanalytic interpretation—that the object is the symbol of the Ego in the sense of a representative of the Ego, an image of the Ego. Rather the object is the Ego's correlate and associate, without any confusion with the Ego (apart from extreme cases in which belonging becomes an envelope—an Ego-skin); the object is the other in relation to the Ego, and not the same, but an other tightly bound to the Ego, its best friend.

In this sense, and to this extent, we can clearly understand the normative and pedagogical importance of the design of toys, which represent for children living in large cities a major source of elected objects; such toys— prompts for the formation of images—are prototypes for the relation to the object, and their characteristics facilitate imprinting in the child. We shall leave aside dolls (as an arsenal of role-play) as false objects through which a child finds a smaller being than himself and which allows him to act as an adult in a world of norms and artifice; in fact, doll play takes place partially in the presence of the adult, and more specifically of the mother, when we are dealing with true instances of role-play rather than the first manifestations of the child's parental instinct.

Adult norms remain outside the object of election: the miniature model, a scaled reproduction of vehicles or machines, is also an occurrence of role-play through which the child can play at being an adult—the captain attacking the Alamo, the head of the team launching missiles or satellites, or more simply a railway station master; these are accessory toys unless they become more like instruments (miniature toy cars launched by hand for races). These adult norms, besides the fact they curtail the freedom of choice in electing a symbol-object, impose an already socialized character on this choice, which passes through the intermediary of a sale, and thus through obstacles that are economic, ritual (Christmas present, gifting), that involve relations with representative adults or bartering with peers, or forms of imagination translating the traditions and tastes of a given population (such as the Mickey Mouse toy series). Moreover, because adults misunderstand toys, they often overlook norms of reliability: a toy is not a serious thing, it only needs to work during the sale, on the store counter. This leads to a cruel and bitter disappointment when the object that was self-chosen breaks apart in the child's hands, instead of staying with him as he grows, resisting wear and tear and not disintegrating as soon as it is disassembled. A large number of toys are like the tureen in the tale from Auvergne where the guests of the Dauphin of Auvergne are instructed not to open it under punishment of exile. The symbol-object, this perfect associate of the ego, must not be a reserve of secrets, a mysterious receptacle not to be opened, like the doors in Bluebeard's

Castle, for parents who never open the objects they themselves use, even when it would be helpful. I am not proposing an analysis of the impact on the child of the avatars of the toy once it has become a self-chosen object, yet the very fact that the toy can become such an object underlines the importance of its construction according to a high standard of reliability; in order to fully ensure and fulfill its elementary role as a key point in the object world, a toy should last an entire childhood, perhaps an entire life-time, and have neither secrets nor weaknesses; for the child, it is the proto-type of the world.

There remains the question of the perceptual-motor characters behind irreversible learning experiences in the child-object relation; some observa-tions on the marked preference among young children for objects with bright and saturated colors, rather than subdued and desaturated colors, seem to indicate that the clarity of sensorial categories intervenes in imprinting. This effect may be associated with the role played in imprinting in animals by intense, contrasted, and brightly colored "patterns" serving as specific stim-uli and intervening as veritable keys for imprinting; these are the patterns found in the inside of the beak and throat of young birds opening their beaks in expectation of food; the opening of the chick's beak at the approach of parents is a selective stimulus-key that conditions the gift of food. In this particular case, we might say that imprinting is not needed, the image of the youth asking for food being specifically predetermined; yet there is a con-tinuity between this case of extreme selectivity and other cases in which imprinting can occur within a margin of indetermination. For instance, the great plover in a situation of choice between its normal clutch and a "super-normal" brood with more or larger eggs, or eggs with a sharper and more contrasted speckled pattern, opts for the supernormal clutch, whether artifi-cial or from another species, and abandons its own clutch; the supernormal stimulus thus plays a role in some cases in choices followed by imprintings.

The election of objects may have effects among adult humans in multiple forms regarding choice. In some civilizations where there subsists a continu-ity between childhood and adulthood, such as in the contemporary American civilization, the conditioning (packaging) of products of common consump-tion shows a search for bright colors and contrasts; civilizations that place values of childhood and adulthood in opposition do not proceed this way;

for products of quality, the latter offer a discreet packaging in halftones aimed at connoisseurs with a rhetoric of signs of recognition or the signature of the maker.

In short, the various aspects of the election of objects as a form of imprinting remain to be studied in a methodical and objective manner, but there are strong indications regarding the existence of such effects.

B. The Level of Psychic Processes: The Mental Image, the Symbol

1. The Consecutive Image

If by "image" we mean a concrete representation with a sensorial content built in the absence of sensory stimulations—or appearing in the absence of such stimulations—the phenomenon of the "consecutive image" only partially deserves its name, since sensorial stimulation plays a role in it, even when the object is no longer present. However, since there is an almost constant transition between the effects of consecutive images and true memory-images implying no recent peripheral stimulation, we need to consider the consecutive image.

The sense of sight in humans is that which is able to convey (at least in peripheral receptors) the most information; to this preeminence corresponds a high aptitude of organs or nerve pathways, perhaps of nerve centers too, to make a real stimulation caused by objects reappear after a short interval; this reappearance, halfway between perception and memory, is called the "consecutive image"; it can occur in waves and through various modalities, hence the terms of primary, secondary, or tertiary consecutive images.

The primary consecutive visual image is called the Hering afterimage: it is produced after the stimulation of the eye by a bright area; when the stimulation ends and is replaced by darkness, the bright area seems to reappear after a short interval and that impression subsists for several hundredths of a second; if the area is very bright (a white area) a color bleed may be observed in the consecutive image (green, yellow, red, purple, blue, green, etc.). After a second interval, the image reappears again, generally with a complementary coloration if the stimulating area was colored. This secondary image is known as the Purkinje's afterimage, Hamaker's satellite, or Bidwell's "ghost image"; this secondary image has a short duration; finally, after a rather long interval, the third image—the Hess image—appears for several seconds, with sometimes a quaternary image or negative Hamaker image. We can obtain some of these effects (at least the first two) by quickly closing our eyes after having looked at a colored or white array, a window for instance; but eyelids are translucent and light continues to pass through the skin, colored in transmission by blood, which generally produces a persisting purple hue superimposed on the properly consecutive effects and thus interfering with them.

The interference of consecutive effects with a luminous stimulation diffused through eyelids produces results that have a high aesthetic richness. We can obtain them by staring at a lit part of the sky (not the sun itself, which could damage retinal components) then by closing one's eyelids still facing the sky, contracting them to a greater or lesser extent, which causes both the amount of transmitted light and the chromatic composition to vary.

Consecutive images may in fact superimpose themselves on perceptions if the stimulation was sufficiently strong. If, after having stared at a bright figure, we turn our gaze on a white screen, the consecutive image can be seen in the guise of a similarly shaped figure with a complementary color. This phenomenon occurs also for figures with black-and-white contrast, in which case superimposed consecutive images appear grey or slightly colored.

The first consecutive images are likely due to retinal phenomena, since they follow the motions of the eyes and change size according to the distance of the screen on which eyes fixate (Cuvillier, *Manuel de philosophie*, vol. 1, p. 190); this is why Cuvillier does not call these phenomena images, proposing instead to call them "consecutive sensations." However, we cannot affirm that they are only phenomena of fatigue in various parts of the retina; the oscillations of positive-negative phases in consecutive images (the Hess phases) may be associated with pre-equilibrium waves observed by Broca and Sulzer; nonetheless, these phenomena belong to the category of active adaptive inhibition rather than that of fatigue.

Do consecutive images belong solely to vision, or can we speak by extension of consecutive images that are aural, tactile, and olfactory? Theoretically, if consecutive images are linked to phenomena of active sensorial adaptation, we may expect to encounter consecutive images that are sharper the more a sense is broadly adaptable; hearing, while less broadly adaptable than vision, which has several regimes (photopic, mesopic, scotopic), covers nonetheless a considerable span in terms of energy ratios (120 to 130 decibels) and frequency ratios (12 octaves); indeed, after hearing an intense sound, a consecutive sound may be observed if receptors were strongly stimulated outside of the possibility of prior adaptation, for instance, with an explosion; but the image-sound is not the repetition of the stimulus; whether the stimulus is continuous or transitory, the image-sound presents itself as a weak continuous sound generally at higher frequencies (we say that one's ears are "ringing"). Consecutive effects seem to be less marked when the adaptation capabilities and the capabilities of information reception of a sense are themselves lower.

In summary, it seems judicious to accept the distinction established by Yves Le Grand in *Optique physiologique*, vol. 2, p. 313, where he writes that the effects of consecutive (or successive) contrast are wrongly called consecutive images: these are consecutive images due to fatigue, that is to say, effects of adaptation which, according to Yves Le Grand, have nothing to do with consecutive images *per se*; true consecutive images are phenomena of persistence, even if in practice the "fatigued" image resulting from a phenomenon of adaptation may be superimposed on a true persistence image and cancel it; in the case of intense luminous stimulation, according to the research of Robertson and Fry, the equilibrium between successive contrast and the image takes place after approximately two minutes with an initial stimulation of $10^4 \text{cd}/\text{m}^2$ and a field of posterior observation of $100 \text{ cd}/\text{m}^2$.

2. Immediate Images and Eidetic Images

We give the name of immediate images to a more complex mode of persistence, one with a longer delay than the sensorial persistence of a peripheral character and manifested as the persistence or repetition of an already structured datum, thus of a perception rather than a simple sensorial datum—so long as we adopt a distinction between sensation and perception as designating in practice a more integrated central activity. Egger's *La parole intérieure*, p. 106 (cited by Cuvillier) described the case of hearing a bell or a clock at a distance: "Many times, it happened that I heard the distant sounds of a bell or a clock. I soon noticed that they repeated indefinitely, and this seemed unbelievable to me. My imagination was prolonging the series after my ear had stopped perceiving it. Since the sounds perceived were very weak and as delocalized as can be, the last one I heard and the first one I imagined presented the same characteristics, and I could not distinguish between them at the time."

Immediate images are those which, for a normal subject, are most prone to be confused with the actual perception of the object when receptor organs are stimulated almost to their threshold; furthermore, such threshold stimulation may take place in various ways, either due to the low energy of the signals, or because the "background noise" of receptors and centers is in itself a source of signals (if we accept that there can be a "background noise" in nervous pathways and centers).

The case of weak external signals, which Egger cites, is found in the visual register and in the tactile register; if a light is projected on a screen, then progressively lowered, a moment comes when the subject can no longer tell whether the screen is still barely lit or only appears to be lit; the more the subject is motivated, the more he exerts efforts, and the more images can be taken for real and objective stimulations: this happens in a progressive manner from an initial condition of correct sighting (tachistoscopic vision experiments); in fact, not only does the immediate image arise, but also older memories and ultimately collective norms. In the case of the perception of autokinetic motion (Charpentier, Aubert), suggestions coming from third parties are also very efficacious. In the tactile register, we may cite the following experiment among others: a small disk such as a coin is shown to the subject, and it lightly adheres to the skin when applied against it with pressure, although it comes off at the slightest movement; then, a similar disk is pressed against the subject's forehead but removed when pressure stops, and the subject is asked to make the disk fall without use of the hands: the subject indeed attempts to make the imaginary disk fall, since he continues to feel it stuck to his forehead, which of course it is not. A large number of magic tricks or casual tricks use this confusion between the immediate image and sensorial data.

The background noise of sensory organs brings about a stimulation that interferes with the signals actually coming from the milieu and may feed the immediate image; if this background noise were a white noise, it would trigger only a rise in thresholds; but generally, it is not equienergetic; the more it is selective (or "colored"), the more it can sustain a confusion between immediate images and objective perceptions. Within the register of hearing, the curve of lower thresholds indicates that, for faint sounds, the sensitivity of receptors is greater between 600 and 3,000 Hz, which is precisely the span of the human voice and its harmonics; the weaker the sound, the more the ear functions as a selector and ultimately a selective generator of endogenous sounds; this selectivity disappears at higher energies (Fletcher's curve); hence, the most common immediate auditory images come from speech, singing and those sounds belonging to the frequency band selected by auditory receptors when they receive faint sounds. Visual receptors among humans do not display a similar change of selectivity in relation to the signal level, in spite of the Purkinje phenomenon, which is rather faint and does not predetermine the visual "background fog" to feed a certain category of immediate images rather than another.

What is the degree of precision of the immediate image? It appears to vary widely according to subjects, to the meaning under scrutiny, and to age; we will call *eidetic image* a predominantly visual image that has a degree of precision comparable to direct perception and lends itself to mental examination; for instance, a word that was seen in writing may be spelled backwards; numbers may be subjected to operations as if they were written on a blackboard; the development of eidetism is at a maximum among children aged 10 to 14; it allows for the rapid learning of information in concrete form such as geography maps, diagrams, and schemas. We should note that this faculty coincides with the maximum of perceptual activity (producing the maximum of optico-geometrical illusions for ages 10 to 14). In his *On Intelligence* (vol. 1, p. 80), Taine examines the case of young calculating prodigies, in particular that of Colburn, who could neither read nor write, yet could "clearly see in front of him" his computations. In the same book, Taine cites the case of chess players who can play a chess game with their eyes closed and their head facing towards the wall: "They have numbered the squares and pieces; at each move of their opponent, they are told the piece moved and the new square it occupies; they give directions themselves for the movement of their own pieces, and go on in this way for many hours. They often win, even when opposed to skillful players. Evidently the figure of the whole chess-board, with the different pieces in order, presents itself to them at each move, as in an internal mirror, for without this they would be unable to foresee the probable consequences of their adversary's and their own moves."

For Taine, and according to the description of one of his American friends who has this faculty, the subject sees the whole chessboard *simultaneously,* with all the pieces as they were in actuality after the last move. "As each piece is moved, I see the whole chess-board with the new change effected. If I am in doubt in my mind as to the exact position of a piece, I play over, mentally, the whole game from the beginning, attending carefully to the successive movements of that piece. It is far easier for me to make a mistake when I look at the board than when I don't. . . . I see the piece, the square, and the color *exactly* as the workman made them—that is I see the chess-board standing before my adversary, or at all events I have an exact representation of it, and not that of another chess-board" (op. cit. 81).[2] This player affirms that before starting to play he begins by looking carefully at the position of the pieces on the chessboard in order to have an anchor and come back mentally to that first impression; in practice he does not see the green-and-white board nor the shadow of the pieces nor other small details in their structure, but if he wants to see them he can. Taine adds that such representations repeat or return involuntarily, arising back into one's mind, for instance, during a bout of insomnia.

Is such an aptitude advanced or primitive? Taine affirms that "the first players are not the most skillful at this artifice"; some players are able to conduct simultaneous games in eidetic vision with a power of imagination whose extent and lucidity are truly prodigious; but the truly great players such as La Bourdonnais can only mentally play two games at once; this remark points in the direction of young savants who are sometimes quite unknowledgeable and have difficulty furthering their study of mathematics. Confronted with such cases, Essertier (in *Les Formes inférieures de l'explication,* p. 83) hypothesized the primitive nature of eidetic images: they would represent the vestige of "this prodigious memory encountered among primitive people . . . the last witnesses of a mental universe now bygone." This hypothesis displays an excessive agreement with a monolinear theory of evolution accounting for mental as well as social forms. It is interesting insofar as the phenomenon of eidetic images may be linked to a definite regime of mental activity and to a level of awareness distinct from that which produces reflexive thought and a critical attitude; any subject in fact may experience eidetic images when faced with a situation of violent emotional stimulation; some concrete features of the situation may register deeply and make the same scene reappear later in a quasi-hallucinatory manner and with a very intense pregnancy of detail.

Even if it should be admitted that eidetism is one aspect of the savage mind [*la pensée sauvage*], it would not be a sufficient reason to consider this mental activity as simply vestigial or a sign of "regression." To the contrary, an eidetism may well appear to be one of the roots of artistic imagination and perhaps inventive imagination in general; an activity of a rather primitive kind, integrated in the development of intellectual symbolism, would provide a basis for creativity, which implies all at once a direct, new, and concrete view of reality, and a highly developed abstract symbolic aptitude which is required for the ordered and organized construction of a new work; creativity, as a set of aptitudes combined in the subject, implies the extreme terms of the old and the new, of the savage mind and abstract symbolism.

In this sense, Taine notes that a concrete memory rich in images that are comparable to eidetic images exists among many artists: some images that are more irregular, more nuanced, more difficult to remember than those of chess players present themselves with equal precision to certain painters, draughtsmen, or sculptors who, after having attentively beheld a model, may make a portrait from memory. "Gustave Doré has this faculty; Horace Vernet had it; Abercrombie cites a painter who, from memory and without the aid of any illustration, copied a canvas of the martyrdom of Saint-Peter from Rubens, with such a perfect imitation that, the two paintings being placed side by side, a great attention was needed to distinguish the copy from the original." Taine also cites the case of Mozart who, having heard Allegri's *Miserere* twice in the Sistine Chapel wrote it down in entirety from memory. "As it was forbidden to copy, the fidelity of the Kapellmeister suspected, on account of the difficulty of the exploit."[3] Similarly, Balzac could see objects in his head, lit and colored as in the moment when he had gazed upon them; Testut, an anatomist, would give his courses with "the imaginary sight of the region of the body to be described" before his very eyes. These last two cases cited by Cuvillier may be associated with a learning experience of Brière de Boismont, cited by Taine; Brière de Boismont conducted the exercise of imprinting in himself the face of one of his friends and succeeded in having a visible mental impression that seemed external and "placed in the direction of the visual ray" with the dimensions and attributes of the model; "The image is vaporous and of another nature than objective sensation . . . yet bounded and colored." Taine maintains that some drawing schools in Paris train their students to reproduce from memory a set of objects after glancing at them for a moment; over time, their aptitude for such practices increases; at first the students experience difficulties; the image vanishes as soon as the setup is covered over; but later the image comes back and may be sustained for a long enough span for drawing it. We might add that presti-digitators develop this mode of memory through eidetic images; seeing the audience for only a few seconds before being blindfolded, some of them can describe audience members as if endowed with extra-sensorial perception; in reality, they make use of an eidetic image.

The immediate image is distinct from the eidetic image because, very much akin to sensation and perception, it preserves concrete characteristics devoid of signification; in the eidetic image, while characteristics remain concrete, they are already selected in the direction (*sens*) of their typical and significative function (the absence of shadows or sculptural details in chess pieces, but conservation of the rules for movement, direction and position); the characteristics preserved by the eidetic image represent so many anchor points between the subject and his environment; these anchor points secure ulterior paths of access to the objects of the milieu for the subject; they also offer elements for a combinatory activity. Indeed, several authors who observed eidetism have noted the plasticity of these images; the starting point is provided by the initial state of a situation perceived effec-tively; yet the subject may later act mentally on the eidetic image to impose transformations of it as though he were acting effectively on objects (writ-ing a number in chalk on an imaginary blackboard, modifying the position of the pieces of an imagined chessboard through eidetic vision); when the representation becomes uncertain, according to the testimony of chess play-ers studied by Taine, the eidetic image may be restored through a recapitula-tion of the different successive modifications taking place during the game. Woodworth cites the research of Urbantschitsch (1907) on eidetic images, as well as those of Jaensch, and considers, in opposition to Taine's opinion, that the eidetic image differs notably from perception; it does not resemble a photograph, since its details are not all simultaneously present; it develops progressively; when a question relating to a detail is asked, some amount of time may elapse before the detail is sufficiently clarified to provide an answer. "Small details reveal themselves while adjacent parts of the image remain blank. The quantity of details described in no way corresponds to the sum of what might be found in an actual image" (Klüver 1930). The plasticity of the eidetic image is such that some subjects can modify it willfully or under the influence of suggestion; objects may change form or color and move within the image. Finally, among children we can note that subjects obtain good images only of scenes of interest to them; eidetic images register the significant objects of a situation and the significant traits of these particular objects; in this way, they are quite different from photographs or paintings by artists who are interested in the relationship of light and shadow without emphasizing the salient lines of remarkable objects (Woodworth, *Psychologie expérimentale,* pp. 62–63).

For Woodworth, the eidetic image is a phenomenon of memory rather than of perception; it displays the characteristics of mnesic images, not those of perception. This conclusion is rather close to Binet's study of the memory of chess players which discovered that it contains the representation of the moves the pieces can make ("the bishop is not a baroquely shaped piece, it is essentially a piece that moves obliquely," *Travaux du laboratoire de psychologie de la Sorbonne,* 1892, p. 44). We might say that the eidetic image is already, in a very elementary sense, a symbol, since it outlines perception and stylizes it according to the subject preserving the memory. The fact that the eidetic image deserves to be studied as a mnesic phenomenon removes nothing from the particular character of its acquisition. We might perhaps note—while waiting for further research—the continuity that exists between the phenomena of imprinting [*empreinte*] and those of eidetism.[4] Intense situations triggering a high degree of vigilance favor the acquisition of an eidetic image which, by the way, may not concern directly the object generating the emotion or the heightened vigilance. Hence, during a phone conversation bearing important news and necessitating precise and attentive answers, one may acquire through eidetic vision the memory of a visual detail without any logical connection with the content of the communication and which requires no active visual perception: the image of the threads of a screw on the phone receiver, a detail of a piece of furniture, etc. Most often, eidetic images acquired during an intense situation are linked to the central and significant object around which the situation is organized; but if the situation is abstract and symbolic, and concerns only one of the senses as in a phone conversation, the registered image may not be connected to the central and significant object, which demonstrates that the "hot" situation generates a state comparable to that of the critical periods favoring imprinting *[empreinte]* for the various forms of perceptual-sensorial activity.

3. Memory-Images; Notion of a Reproductive Imagination; "Imaginative Types"; Generic Images

The memory-image is that which may reappear at any time after the end of the perceptual situation to which it is related; the image is then the occasion of a representation or a revival *[reviviscence]* characterizing the secondary state and differentiating it from the primary state, the latter being extended in rather than represented by the consecutive image and the immediate image. A theoretical question arises: In what way is the memory-image different from the eidetic image? Practically speaking, the nucleus of the eidetic image may function as an active center for a complex memory-image. The famous example of Proust's madeleine could be analyzed within the purview of eidetism, for theoretically nothing prevents such perceptual-sensorial imprinting phenomena to extend beyond the visual category; moreover, other olfactory eidetic images can be found in Proust, such as the smell of gas for automobiles, which forms the nucleus of a multitude of visual and aural imprintings related to travel, the horizon of the road, and visited landscapes. According to Proust's description, revival occurs many years later through the intermediary of this smell in a very different situation than travel: the subject smells gas fumes rising from the street below while he wakes up in a Parisian hotel. (We are extending the use of the term "eidetic"; originally, it applied only to the visual category).

The existence of an active eidetic center within the memory-image faces an oft-repeated and now classic argument: that of the impossibility of enumerating the components of the represented object; more specifically, if a person claiming he "sees" the Pantheon in his imagination is asked to count the columns he "sees," such enumeration is generally impossible; on the basis of this incapacity, certain authors have contested the concrete character of memory-images, taking the descriptions of such images as sheer nonsense. Yet the demonstration is far from conclusive; researchers who have studied the various operations of perceptual analysis (particularly Professor Possel in building a reading machine) have recognized the importance of concrete supports, of arresting points that allow the analyzing gaze to secure reference points in the object. It is almost impossible to count the bars of a metal fence or the rows of a brick wall without reference points. When the natural heterogeneities of the object display such features in themselves (a rusty bar, a thinner bar, etc.) the perceptual analysis is easy. In a real object seen in a concrete situation, local heterogeneities may be important and progressive, accompanying and guiding perceptual activity: the columns of the Pantheon when placed in a circle are all lit in a different way; moreover, the apparent intervals separating them increase progressively because of perspective from the sides to the center from the viewpoint of the observer. The resistance offered by these reference points, anchors of an analyzing perceptual activity, is no longer present in the image, because the image is already abstract and "purer" than perception; in the mental image of the Pantheon there are no longer shadows and details of distinct hues that individualize each column, providing an internal structure to the series. By contrast, the enumeration of components in an eidetic image remains possible when these components are differentiated by their signifying functions, as in a written word (its letters considered as letters are different from each other not only in perception but in the image).

Researchers from the second half of the nineteenth century noticed individual differences with respect to the vividness and precision of memory-images; first, we may wonder whether everyone possesses this capacity of semi-concrete mental representation to the same degree; however, subjective descriptions and analyses require delicate interpretation if one seeks to use them as an absolute basis for the evaluation of the degree of "concreteness" of images within various subjects. On the other hand, a typology is likely to be less arbitrary when it is a matter of comparing in the same person the degree of vivacity and precision of images relating to various sensorial categories.

This differential aspect, long noted in literature and arts, was first signaled by Fechner in 1860 and studied by Galton (1880). Asking subjects to evoke the image of a specific object, Fechner registered variations of aptitude in the evocation. Galton devised a "breakfast table" questionnaire: subjects were invited to evoke the image of their table when they had their breakfast in the morning, noting the degree of definition of objects, the relative brightness of the scene, the character of colors (distinct, natural, etc.). The scholars and scientists interrogated by Galton tended to answer they had no mental image; yet other responses showed that certain objects (one or two, for instance, among those placed on the table) remained clear in the memory-image of several subjects; after having sought to establish an (inverse) correlation between the vivacity of imagination and intellectual abilities, investigators continuing Galton's research turned towards the study of imaginative types according to the various aptitudes of each subject for visual, aural, and other types of imagery. Charcot's studies of aphasia have shown that a given class of images is predominant depending on the various individuals examined; systematizing his observations, Charcot divided the imaginative types into four: the *visual* type, the *aural* type, the *motor* type, and the *mixed* type.

The "visual" type recalls a text by representing the page on which it is printed; in the process of learning, these types rely on spatial schematizations, using illustrations, colorful referents, and diagrams; moreover, they tend to convert the data coming from other senses into visual representations, and if they have a poetic bent, they invoke metaphors expressing this conversion (Hugo writes: "The laces of the sound chiseled by the fife"). Hugo used engravings and ink drawings, with strongly contrasting shadow and light, to translate his vision of complex scenes and situations with non-visual components (for instance, a storm around a castle nestled on the side of a craggy hill). He stated that abstract ideas evoked for him concrete images: the *law* gives the image of red robed judges; *color* is the opposition of the green of a plant with the red of a fabric; form is "a round block, a woman's shoulder" (quoted by Cuvillier after Ribot, *Idées générales*, p. 133). The visual type may become diversified according to the predominance of the concrete representations of forms, colors, geometrical relationships, or typographical signs. Almost blind, Michelangelo used touch to recognize and admire statues. A painter like Delacroix grants priority in his work to a search for colors acting not only as elements but as image because they provide the atmosphere for a scene (see, for instance, his *Femmes d'Alger* painting drenched in blonde light that showers objects and figures); another Delacroix is titled *Bataille entre un cheval bai et un cheval bai-brun dans une écurie.*[5] Of course, we must take into account the romantic culture of the time (color is a manifesto against the classicism of the line; Hugo writes: "I placed a red bonnet upon the old dictionary"), yet color has for Delacroix a signifying force that is not present among other painters of his era. Concrete visual geometric memory corresponds to the kind of feats found among chess players. As for the "visual typographic" type, it is found among people who see mentally each word uttered as if it were printed; Bourdon, in his *Intelligence*, p. 44, cites the case of a student who saw the words he spoke in written or printed form "generally in larger font than those of other people." Fernald (1912) showed that the properly "photographic" image of a word is very rare; during his experiments he never encountered a subject truly capable of reading the letters of a word backward out of a mental image; generally, subjects asked to do so complain that letters do not stay in place when they try reading backward; subjects with strong aptitude for evoking visual images succeed in reading backward after finding a process for decomposing a word into several groups of syllables and inverting each syllable separately. By contrast, subjects who do not have solid visual images ultimately rely on a less efficacious process such as spelling the word from beginning to end repeatedly, eliminating one letter each time (this sequential unidirectional method is comparable to that which could be used on an aural image, but sound sequences are very difficult to reverse by acting on a mental image, since it is only abstractly that the course of time may be reversed). Those rare cases where subjects, generally children, show themselves capable of reading a word backward in eidetic vision—a long and unfamiliar word, for instance, in a foreign tongue—can be seen as illustrations of the properties of the eidetic image as such. Such properties in ordinary mental images are limited—generally, but even for subjects gifted in visual imagery—to the clear view of a reversible group of two or three letters at the most.

We should note also that the superiority of the "visual" goes no further than the reversal of a left-to-right sequence into a right-to-left sequence; the visual image is not complete enough to allow reading in all directions even if the subject enjoys a very developed visual tendency; this is what the experiment of the *square of letters* made of 16 or 25 letters placed in a square that must be learned by reading in the usual manner. Binet, Fernald, and Müller have found that, after learning such a square, a subject has difficulty reciting it from bottom to top, and even more difficulty with diagonal lines.

According to Müller, the method used to overcome this difficulty is the same for a "visual" or "aural" type: it consists in using groupings and localizations, and all subjects work in the same way.

The "aural" type is described by Binet as corresponding to the translation in names and words of the signs used for a mental operation without graphic support: to add mentally, aural types repeat verbally the names of the numbers (*Psychologie du raisonnement,* p. 25, cited by Cuvillier). Binet also notes that, when learning a text, persons of this type engrave in their mind the sound of their words. There is a considerable set of mnemonic devices using sound images: the list of the names of Roman emperors, the list of pairs of cranial nerves, etc. The structuring of sequences (rhymes, assonances, rhythm) facilitates memorization and allows for evocation to be picked up at an articulation point (stanza, verse) without starting the recitation of the text from the beginning; the existence of inseparable blocks repeated in a text, like nouns with their natural qualifier, favors the fixation of sound images; It is found foremost in texts composed when writing was not widespread: this "pharmakon," as Plato says, that is, this drug against forgetting, caused the loss of use of memorization devices without material support, among which were all the recurrent aspects of sound sequences so evident in poetry and music. In fact, in a spoken text or a complex sound sequence, not everything gives rise equally to a mental image; there are privileged structures that even the subject less gifted for aural images retain without alterations, such as "Rodrigue, as-tu du coeur? / Tout autre que mon père l'éprouverait sur l'heure!";[6] this aptitude for becoming image is not directly linked to a theoretical, abstract, or conceptual meaning; the title of Hugo's poem "Oceano nox" easily forms an aural image without recourse to its signification: "Night on the Ocean."

In *La parole intérieure,* Egger affirms that any thought is accompanied by a kind of inner noise which is like a mental speech.

Without repeating the example of Mozart cited above, we can cite that of Beethoven, who, having become deaf, rehearsed, internally, enormous symphonies, or that of Mendelssohn, who was able from childhood to accompany by memory entire operas. In literature, the role of noises and sounds varies according to authors and schools. Daudet has much tenderness towards noises, sounds, and "picturesque" words that create images; onomatopoeias abound in his *Contes,* in which we find what the Gestalt School called "implicit meanings" integrated in the structure of protagonists' and topographical names: Tistet Védène, Pampérigouste, etc.

The imaginative "motor" type is sometimes associated, according to some researchers, with the "aural" type because there is a link between aural representation and the motions of pronouncing a word or emitting a sound; it should be noted, however, that the span of the register of the human voice is not as broad as that of hearing, even though the maximum of aural sensitivity corresponds to the sounds habitually present in verbal expression and singing; hence coupling between phonation and hearing is not total.

Stricker has studied in detail the "motor" type in his work titled *Du langage et de la musique.* Stricker himself claimed to be a typical case; his image-words, rather than being visual or aural, were almost all kinaesthetic, made of images and perhaps also of sensations of articulatory motions. Stricker devised a test showing the importance of the motor component of a verbal image by having subjects try to think of words that can be pronounced only with a relatively closed mouth (such as "bubble," "mutter," "wisp"), but constrained, in advance to keeping their mouth open, some subjects were unable to imagine these words, which proves that their verbal images are essentially motor. An "aural" type, to the contrary, can imagine these words while keeping their mouth open.

We should add that the motor part in certain images such as words or numbers may be substantial for some subjects; in order to recall how a word is spelled, some people need to write it down after having mobilized the concrete register of kinaesthetic representations through a few twists of the wrist, without actually writing, a bit like clearing one's voice before singing. Naturally, in such cases one can speak of a habit; yet how are we to distinguish exactly a motor habit from a motor image? The real question we should be asking, actually, is that of the legitimacy of a parallel established between the active content of images and the perceptual content; there are of course receptions linked to movement and allowing for its adaptation to objects, to the situation (motor and perceptual-motor control); yet perception in no way exhausts the reality of the motion of the body proper; perceived motion is, much more essentially, the motion of objects in the perceptual field; in this regard, there may be images of movement in the visual category, others in the sound category, and yet other in the tactile category. It is not solely the sensory organ receiving information that determines, on its own, a category of mental images, but rather other features related to the situation: stable and simultaneous configuration, irreversible sequence, and recurrences; it would be important to analyze the characteristics of the imagery in a less sensorial and more formalized way, and more logically, by treating images as groups of signals; we would then see that the index of movement (stability, duration, alteration, changes in the situation's configuration) affects a large number of images. Michotte's study of the perception of causality allows us to discern a few types of images of movement (slithering, shock, pursuit) that appear in perceptual categories and may also be preserved in mental representation. The kinaesthetic image of movement is nonetheless clear in the representation of certain objects whose use involves a highly defined gesture such as a faucet, a nut, a bolt, the rotating disk of a telephone, a doorbell button; the vividness of the images of movement linked to these objects shows up in the tendency to act on these objects without a real need, which prods children to touch faucets, phones, doorbells, etc.

Charcot adds a mixed type to these three pure types: depending on their origin and acquisition, images within the same subject are at various times motor, auditory, or visual. According to Woodworth, the mixed type is in fact the most common: pure types are rare. It is even possible that certain people present a tendency towards an olfactory or gustatory type. Zola, studied by Toulouse in 1897, would be of the olfactory type: the representation of people, streets, and houses evoked odors in him. In Baudelaire's work, olfactory notations are frequent and insistent without, however, presenting an endless variety comparable to sound or visual images; indeed, the most common phenomenon is the remarkable power of evoking images in other registers that display olfactory and gustatory stimulations: the smell of tar on roads, or the taste of the sap of a pine needle in the mouth . . . Cuvillier considers that for a gourmet such as Brillat-Savarin, the author of *The Physiology of Taste*, there must have existed powerful gustatory images. Finally, the register of tactile images seems not to have been deemed worthy by former researchers to constitute a type of imagination on its own. The reason is that our civilizations are scarcely manual; words of the tactile register are few aside from the category of fabrics and furnishings (silky, velvety). Yet tactile images exist, those that allow us to evoke a substance, sand, dust, wood, soil dirt and its consistency, and they constitute one of the aspects of the attachment to concrete details of the world and to certain modalities of work.

The dominance of a given type of imagery in a subject may be studied through "objective imagery tests" that were progressively perfected since Binet by Angell, Fernald, Müller, Davis and Bowers. Paul Fraisse's *Manuel pratique de psychologie expérimentale* presents the most complete and recent method, that of the systematic comparison by pairs of images of different registers; the subject must assess which image is the most clear and vivid. After their assessment, the ranking corresponding to all the subject's answers is compared to the way in which he thinks he belongs to this or that imaginative type, and rather notable divergences may surface, as Betts found in 1909 by studying Galton's questionnaire.

Are mental images generic or particular? This is a question which, by virtue of the role played in the theory of knowledge by the answers one gives, has longed deserved the attention and study of philosophy. To consider mental images as particular means to place the origin of their acquisition in a historically well-determined circumstance within the subject's life, as in the case of an imprint. To consider them as generic means affirming that "within memory" there is a work of condensation, summation, simplification, and organization that occurs between a plurality of perceptual circumstances of acquisition and the re-appearance of a unique memory-image, which gives the image a generic signification rendering compatible a plurality of concrete experiences; the image, in this case, results from a process of primary and concrete induction; the process does not stop at a first degree, and it is then possible to try to explain all of mental activity on the basis of this activity, of which the generic image is a first result. Taine, in the second volume of *On Intelligence*, studied the possibility of this general interpretation of mental activity. The problem is knowing whether we can pass gradually from perception to abstract ideas without a hiatus marking a difference of nature between the content of perceptions and that of ideas, or, to the contrary, whether abstract thought is radically different from "concrete thought" (with "abstract" meaning here not "resulting from a process of abstraction" but highly formalized as in scientific theories). That is the question opposing empiricism (which affirms continuity) to idealism which, even when it admits the perceptual origin of the content of images, refuses continuity between perceptual contents and highly formalized theoretical thought, for which a non-perceptual origin and source must then be sought (innateness, a vision of god). Descartes vigorously affirmed the discontinuity between perception and the principles of theoretical knowledge (innate ideas); and methodical doubt leads to dismissing equally adventitious and factitious ideas. Berkeley in *The Principles of Human Knowledge* also rejected continuity and declared himself not in possession of "the admirable faculty of abstracting ideas"; Berkeley admits for himself only the faculty to imagine, to represent the idea of particular things he has perceived, to compose them and divide them in various ways (the two-headed man, the centaur), but always endowed with a particular form and color; one can very well imagine a hand or nose detached from the body, but they are always a particular hand or nose with a particular color and shape; "likewise the Idea of man that I frame to myself, must be either of a white, or a black, or a tawny, a straight, or a crooked, a tall, or a low, or a middle-sized Man. I cannot by any effort of thought conceive the *abstract* Idea above described."[7] One cannot, according to Berkeley, imagine qualities that can only exist incarnated in an object separately from that object; the object cannot be imagined without its qualities. This affirmation contradicts the conception of induction in Aristotle; in the passage from particular senses to the common sense, a work of generalization and abstraction is already taking place, and this work continues in the shift from the passive intellect to the active intellect.

Taine shows how the passage from particular perceptions to generic images is effected through a process of fusion (*De l'intelligence*, vol. 2, p. 260). When a subject has seen twenty or thirty araucaria trees, none of the individual images entirely survives in his mind; "the twenty or thirty resurrections are blunted by one another; depleted and agglutinated by resemblance, they have thus merged together and my current representation is but their residue." Huxley believes generic images are formed like generic portraits obtained from composite photographs in the process deployed by Galton around 1880. Studying several members of the same family, Galton brought out their common features, constituting the recognizable family resemblance through a purely physical process of attenuating individual details and conserving traits displayed by a large number of subjects in the group considered. After having centered and framed the apparatus (so that the eyes and the nose ridge of all subjects coincide on the sensitive plate), each subject is photographed on the single plate for a fraction of the total time corresponding to the sum of all the successive snapshots; if there are ten subjects and if the shot, given the lighting conditions, should take one second, each subject is photographed for a tenth of a second, so that that the total exposure time of the sensitive plate is one second in all. After developing, fixing, and printing in positive, we can see that only the features present in seven, eight, or ten of the ten subjects appear, the other details remaining fuzzy—or, more precisely, having been photographed in conditions of overexposure, each appears only faintly, when randomly superimposed on other individual features, in such a way that the most strongly registered details are those that benefit from a physical process of adding quantities of light that are successively brought to bear on the same regions of the plate by the ten shots. At the time, the process was applied not only to the various members of the same family, but to ethnic groups (Jews, English), professional groups, etc. The process was not systematically exploited but could be perfected; it represents, through an analogical system, a mode of automatic calculus, albeit a bit rigid since it requires Euclidian coincidences, while living beings have a rather topological structure.

Before rejecting as a whole the empiricist thesis, we must understand its reach and see that Aristotle's affirmation that "the soul never thinks without images" is not merely the recognition of an infirmity implying the necessity to extract and to learn; it also contains the idea that knowledge progresses out of experience by totalizing itself. The image is already a process of partially formalized knowledge allowing generalization to occur through analogical systematization. When Aristotle audaciously states that a plant is comparable to an animal upside down, mouth in the ground the way a tree plants its roots, he makes perhaps a partial error about the trophic role of roots, but he energetically exploits the possibilities of systematization and discovery of the image by attempting to form through mental superimposition, after a 180-degree reversal, the generic image of animals and that of vegetables. In fact, empiricism contains and affirms, through the vehicle that is the image, the possibility of the infinite progress of thought.

We would still need to know whether induction takes place according to the process of totalizing by summation, to which composite portraits are a physical analog (akin to the physiological process of innervated paths invoked by Descartes to explain the formation of habits in a wholly mechanical way), or whether the dynamics of images are closer to the growth of living beings. In truth, in spite of Ribot's theory which adopts Taine and Huxley's conception of generic images, we may note that the number of presentations of the object only influences image formation indirectly; we may have seen thousands of trees without having any clear image of those trees, even if they belong to a single species whose various individuals are very similar. Conversely, falling once into stinging nettles is enough to retain a precise image of them, and, through this first imprinting, to instantly form a whole class of nettle-looking plants with or without poisonous hairs such as the red or white deadnettle, etc. Inductive classes proceed, practically, from a germ, an absolute origin in experience; the whole class is given in the first experience, and the path of concrete knowledge resembles more an arborescent structure with more and more complex ramifications than a structure of summation, that is, in the end, a structure of concentration of the multiple into a unity. This explains the common dichotomy of "good" and "bad" or true and false: subclasses had to be added, the tree had to ramify; when we know bolete mushrooms, the devil's bolete belongs to the "false"; dichotomies proceed from secondary imprintings [empreintes] that are not superimposed on the data of the primary imprinting, which is the origin of the class, yet they attach to this line of knowledge through a kind of graft; if it weren't for successive instances of imprinting branching out from a primordial experience, it would be difficult to explain the wide generality of dichotomy in concrete thought; a dichotomy devolves simply from having to add the input of a new knowledge on to an already constituted class; what makes a dichotomy is novelty in relation to the old: reality is usually much more complex and simultaneous, and the theoretical overhaul of knowledge rarely retains the dichotomic paths of discovery. It is the image which, from the primitive imprinting through successive stages, divides and subdivides a class into subclasses, like a tree which, restarting its original process of germination from its trunk each year, subdivides itself progressively from its main limbs up to the thinnest branches. Inductive knowledge through images was highly effective in ancient natural history, perhaps because of the connaturality of processes of growth or evolution of living beings with the modes of development of images.

We may note, rightfully, that the inductive knowledge which serves as a basis in Aristotle for its adequation with objective reality is that which bears on the living world considered as an object of taxonomic investigation; indeed, the different variations in a plant or animal species that stem from a primitive stock take place according to a process of adaptive reactions to new conditions (altitude, climate, interaction with other species), which displays a substantial formal analogy with the memory-image which is itself enhanced and differentiated on the basis of a primitive imprinting through successive experiences that bring new features. In other words, the branching structure is shared by the naturalist's taxonomy, working on the present result of an evolutionary process of living beings, and by the activity of the image which, through the subject's life, receives from the primordial stock (the initial imprinting) branches that manifest later imprintings arranged via successive inputs partially diverging from the primal trunk. Such a tree or branching structure is much less clear when processes of formation in nature involve multiple interactions in a mode of simultaneity rather than an evolution through successive stages from a stock; the classification of minerals, with all the metamorphic phenomena, is less permeable to taxonomic induction than species of animals or plants within which, prior to scientific research, common knowledge has already recognized families, varieties, groups, and lineages.

In seeking to explain the reasons for epistemological success of knowledge through images, still not fully formalized, one must also ask whether the schema of empiricism adequately accounts for the becoming of images, particularly in the case of the memory-image. The now-traditional empirical schema appears to presuppose that there is a progressive reduction of multiple cases to a more common and arbitrary concept (understanding of a class); the various concrete cases observed are thus theoretically simultaneous and equally important: they are equivalent with respect to their informational contribution to the understanding of the class towards which they converge; in order to abstract the definition of a dog through the different dogs actually encountered, a short reddish dog is just as important as a tall and white one; all are equally, to the same extent and simultaneously, dogs; all individuals are logically equivalent as sources of information; there is no privilege or authority with respect to other cases; induction erases the historicity of informational encounters, which can be successive only within the subject's experience. It is the same with the process of deduction that exploits the results of induction ("formal" deduction): consequences are on the same level; deductive divergences that go from the unity of principles to the multiplicity of consequences are symmetrical to inductive convergences. Yet we are dealing here with an ideal systematization that is perhaps true when we speak in terms of conceptual knowledge, but not when we seek to describe the genesis of the image and the mode of knowing it provides: the divergences and convergences of images are marginal and adventitious— they are asymmetrical. To return to the example of the araucaria chosen by Taine, all the araucarias we have seen are not on the same plane; there is a first araucaria, an original image of this symmetrical tree with green thick needles that remains the truest, the most authentic, the most prominent in memory, which will be the source of norms for all succeeding imprints. If the araucaria in our first experience were to be short and dark green against black dirt, another taller and yellower will be seen as "a tall yellow araucaria," and yet another as a smooth trunk araucaria or with crooked branches; in other words, successive experiences (as sources of memory-images) inscribe themselves as variants of a basic text whose anteriority is considered an absolute term of reference and an inexhaustible source of comparative norms. The origin of classes resides in an imprint acting as an archetypal first model—as principle. It is in this sense that the paternal home is the model of all houses, that one's Mother or Father are the models of authority or the source of goodness and the purveyors of assistance when help is needed. Later experiences may be defined through relationships of divergence that acquire meaning as secondary branches of the original archetypal source: the bad mother or the mother-in-law both acquire meaning in relation to the given original mother, who becomes the good mother explicitly only when later experiences have revealed the existence of bad mothers; yet in spite of the semblances of language there is no symmetry between the good mother and the bad mother with respect to images; the bad mother and the mother-in-law are less fundamental than the good mother—the mother with respect to the original imprint.

This way of presenting the path of the image within memory along asymmetrical branches strays significantly from an inductive line gathering together in the comprehension of a class the content common to different concrete individual cases previously encountered; with respect to the image, the class is already given with the first imprint; it is the stock for subsequent data that modify the extension of the class without entirely reshaping its comprehension, and in which primordial features continue playing a major role. To take an example that is easier to analyze than the good/bad mother, we know that swans were considered birds that were necessarily white until the day when black swans were found in Australia; logically, according to induction, the component of whiteness should have disappeared from the understanding of a swan; in actuality, and rather paradoxically, the extension did indeed occur, yet its comprehension did not shed the component of white plumage; within understanding, the content of the image of the swan retains whiteness, and the black swan of Australia is seen as marginal, somewhat aberrant—an exception with respect to color. In the same way, the bad mother goes "against nature" as a kind of monster or counterfeit version of the mother, which can be known and thought only by reference to the authentic original mother. The most important epistemological characteristic of the memory-image is the independence of its extension with respect to understanding; knowing through the image is thus different from the traditional description of inductive knowing.

We should also note that Taine, for whom the entire mental life springs from images and their relations, in fact relies on the idea of an analogical developmental process within natural phenomena and mental images (in vol. 2 of *On Intelligence*); it is closer to what was later called "isomorphism" in Gestalt theory rather than a true induction which requires the passive reception of data received by perception.

Finally, we can anticipate the processes for the saturation of the image and the formation of the symbol on the basis of this conception of the constitution of the memory-image, which proceeds by the branching out of successive imprints from a common and primitive trunk, which ultimately stems from the first imprint that founded the class; a "tree" of memory-images that developed from a first imprint tends to become a symbol when the opposite tendencies of subsequent imprints bring the primitively asymmetrical structure (the bad mother as aberrant case of the primitive mother) into a state of symmetry in which the image is a coupling of incompatible qualities which are, nonetheless, linked together (the mother that is both good and bad, nurturing and possessive, source of life and threat of absorption negating the child-individual). This coupling of incompatible yet linked qualities expresses the state of supersaturation of the memory-image—a metastable state that is the necessary condition for invention, that is, for a structural change restoring compatibility within a new system. The image having become a symbol condenses a contradictory experience; it presents itself in this form with the opacity of a real object that is irreducible to any "attitude of consciousness" and partially refractory even to an elucidation by consciousness; the symbol-image yokes the subject to events of which it retains a complex memory, and it makes the subject depend on these events of which it preserves a real and representative fragment that is the equivalent to the object as concrete and to the enveloping situations; conversely, the symbol opens a path towards the object in the sense that it is a means for conjuring it, restoring it, out of traces. And traces are effective in conjuring the object when all the various aspects of the object are simultaneously represented within the imprinting system concerning that object, with an inner equilibrium that constitutes both the coherence and at the same time the tension of the system.

Thus, in order for the memory-image to evolve to the point of becoming a symbol, it must condense an intense and heightened experience energetically tying the living being to its milieu, and it must develop through a series of qualitatively different and successive imprints irreducible to one another; it is the heterogeneity of imprints linked to a same source that gives to the symbol its inner tension and renders it different from a totalization comparable to that of a composite portrait. I am not arguing that the hypothesis of the constitution of generic images through a process of totalization does not account for a number of processes; totalization may occur in cases were no imprinting exists, that is, in cases where the acquisition of memories takes place through relatively weak motivations and remains close to the functioning of immediate memory; however, distant memories that are strongly emotionally heightened, but also relatively information poor, do not wait for all of the successive and partial snapshots to take place before finding their organization; to extend this photographic metaphor, we might say that the action of the developer occurs after each contribution of experience, and that memory, rather than remaining in a state of latent organization until the series' end, is corrected and amended with each new contribution of an intense experience, and is supercharged by successive imprints that consequently form a series in which new contributions may clash with older contributions without erasing them.

Lastly, the totalizing process described by Taine, Huxley, and Ribot may exist within the progressive constitution of the image as it progresses towards the state of symbol: after the main dichotomies have taken place, experiences that are homogeneous in relation to each other within one of the dichotomy's paths may overlap and thus partially erase their historical individuality: the list of a person's good deeds, on the one hand, and bad deeds on the other, opens the register of two separate generic totalizing images; if good and bad deeds interfered in a single regime, they would erase each other; yet the image of a person with a long list of good deeds and an equally long list of bad deeds is not at all the same as that of a person that does neither bad nor good and remains perpetually neutral; in order for totalizing to occur, previous dichotomies, constituting the classes of totalization, must have taken place in a more implicit and primitive mode of memory, which corresponds to imprinting; the processes described by empirical theories correspond to partial memories; the image is anterior to the distribution of tasks among these partial memories, and in the course of experience, the progressive transition from image to symbol happens through the interactions of these partial memories: the image is anterior to partial empiricisms and is developed by going further than their results.

C. The Imaginary as Organized World; Effigies and Symbol-Objects

The memory-image, in the perspective sketched above, may then have the properties of a generic image, and even of several generic images in a relation of interaction, without having to constitute the source of information as a plurality of individuals of a given class: it may be an individual, a plurality of individuals making up a family, an ethnic group or a nation; this is why the development of the image towards the symbol operates in the same way whether the image is of a single person or a group; knowledge through the image melds the individual and the group; the image of the English, of the American, or the Italian, for a given individual, has a mental content analogous to the image of a person: the generic dimension of the image's reach disappears once the image is constituted; hence knowledge according to images gives rise to the possible substitution of an individual by another as a substrate for responsibility (hostages, etc.).

The tendency of the symbol to develop through action reveals the internal tension contained in a grouping of divergent characteristics; but this action may either express itself directly, without an intermediary construction, through attitudes and conducts, or use the body as intermediary object (imitation, expressive mimicry), or else recruit or even construct new objects as analogs of the reality represented by the image.

1. The Notion of the Imago; In What Way the Imago Is a Symbol

For Lacan, *Imago* is the name given to a paradoxical entity, an unconscious representation that lies below the complex and constitutes one of the organizers of psychic development (vol. VIII of the *Encyclopédie française*): the Imago organizes images and thoughts; it accounts for attitudes displaying the nexus of contradictory forces any complex is made of, and is thus the basis of certain structures in which the complex is a concrete factor. That is, for example, and especially, the Imago of the maternal breast which is at the basis of the weaning complex. The original situation of the child is a relation of extreme dependency on the mother; weaning corresponds to the birth of autonomy, bringing new satisfactions but also a loss of security and the satisfactions linked to dependency. To echo expressions used above, we might say that a dichotomy occurs when the possibility of autonomy comes to be grafted onto the primitive relation to the mother; so long as the possibility of autonomy remains symmetrical, occasional, and truly marginal with respect to the relation to the mother, it does not create an Imago; the Imago is produced as a figure of tensed equilibrium which, revisiting the absolutely primary character of the relation to the mother, places that relation on the same plane and at the same level as independence; the Imago is a figure of equilibrium that renders independence and the relation to the mother symmetrical by transforming their relation after the fact, by reconsidering their relation as a dependency now felt as a threat, with the danger of absorption, a return to intrauterine existence; the unconscious representation that is the Imago of the maternal breast corresponds to the simultaneous duality of the narrow relation to the mother as object of aspiration, and of the wish for emancipation corresponding to the personal development of the child; the tensed simultaneity of this divergent pair of aspirations is symbolically expressed in a death wish linked to precocious forms of ties with others; the mother is represented as a kind of resting place, of nirvana, of a renunciation of separated individuality (see Ms. Favez-Boutonnier's course on *L'imagination*, pp. 88–89). The Imago thus brings together, in a tensed and symmetrical equilibrium, two situations which, in fact, manifested themselves in succession in their full expression, and in an asymmetrical way. The Imago is a symbol because it refers to a reality other than that of the ego, and it is able to refer to the other reality because instead of summarizing and linearly condensing successive experiences, it concretizes and condenses them into a paradoxical entity that is the disclosure, within the ego, of the real relation with others as a source of alterity. The symbol induces thoughts, images, and attitudes that reach others in an ambivalent way; the duality or ambivalence of the Imago expresses the real duality of the other and the subject because it summarizes the changes of situation triggered by the development of the subject in its relationship to a single person; the maternal Imago is the union in a simultaneous couple of the two successive perspectives of the relation to the mother from the point of view of the child. The Imago is a symbol because it points back to the object through the whole gamut of its possible manifestations contained within the extreme terms of the Imago (here, the mother as source of subsistence, and the mother as annihilation of the child's individuality); the Imago as a tension between these extreme terms virtually contains the spectrum of all possible situations with respect to a given person; it is in advance the exhaustive summary of concrete relations, and thus represents a mode of access to symbolized reality on the part of the subject. The Imago is not merely the summary of what is experienced; it marks the beginning of reversibility towards action.

Lacan cites other complexes and their corresponding Imago: the alter ego corresponds to the complex of intrusion, which is at once a highly attractive replica of the ego and a rival, and then there is the Oedipus complex. In Lacan's view, there is a difference between the image and the symbol, the latter appearing at the level of complexes where we find three terms (the Oedipus complex), whereas images express the duality of persons. However, even if we must admit that the reality of the symbol is more complex than that of the image, the Imago as organizer is already an elementary symbol since it contains in representation, whether conscious or nonconscious, a gamut of possibilities rendering it capable of corresponding to all real situations of a relationship to a reality: the mother, the intruder, etc.; thanks to the duality of extreme terms, the Imago deploys a wide spectrum [spectre] of possible relations marked by situations actually experienced. The Imago is a symbol because it allows the passage from the discontinuous spectrum of historical experience to the continuous spectrum of possibilities contained between antithetical extreme terms; it condenses and reorders experience to make it into a universal mode of access to a given reality. It formalizes the random series of imprints. Yet there does not appear to be a difference in nature between a primary type of formalization, such as that of the spectrum of qualities and attitudes between two opposite extreme terms (such as life and death, dependence and autonomy) and a more complex formalization mobilizing a ternary structure such as that of the Oedipus complex. A binary formalization simply opens up a wider set for the interpretation of experience than a ternary formalization; the binary mode responds to the temporal succession of the heterogeneity of attitudes and relations within a changing situation, while the ternary formalization implies an objective simultaneity and a plurality in the field of objects (for instance, mother and father simultaneously present in relation to the child and to each other as a couple while individually relating to the child). The more elementary a formalization, the more experiences it can host; the bipolar relation between life and death envelops everything, can contain everything, since it sets the extreme terms of experience.

Of course, it might seem odd to consider primary modes of thought as formalizations; however, we are indeed dealing with a formalization when it is a question of the images and symbols that make up the common background of a culture, especially from the perspective of Mircea Eliade's work. He roughly reprises Jung's idea of the archetype as a schema of the imagination, a mold for images belonging to humanity's past (perhaps even pre-human stages in the becoming of the species). For Eliade the symbol is foremost religious while images refer to individual existence; such a distinction all but amounts to saying that images are more primitive than symbols— symbols formalizing certain kinds of imprints involving, not only the formalization of the variations of the relation to others along a continuous spectrum, but the actual presence of a *tertium quid* (the Father, the Law, Society, Nature, etc.) which cannot be formalized by the simple polarity of a continuous qualitative spectrum, but requires at least a ternary structure. Indeed, ternary structures allow individuals of the same group to communicate, since they formalize the interactive experience and provide a terrain of universality corresponding to an intellectualized, adult, vigilant, conscious expression. But binary structures also allow communication according to less universally collective modalities, less well inserted into the action of the group, and implying a lower degree of vigilance: fairy tales and myths sometime display binary structures (the Ogress, the stepmother; wealth and poverty; pride and humility; the oscillations of a Nemesis). Finally, within a given culture, there is a certain linkage that connects individual binary structures to ternary structures that presuppose the presence of Society, Law, or Divinity: this is the case, in particular, of individual salvation in a religion; the dichotomy of an individual life and death is reframed within a supernatural context where it is a question of everlasting life and death; the conversion of a binary into a ternary structure is made possible by an intermediary structure (sacred-profane, creature-creator, temporal-eternal) that is, one might say, a dual inlet, since it is a dichotomy only at one of its extreme terms, that of the relation with the ego, but it participates in a more complex structure from the point of view of the privileged term (the sacred, the creator, the eternal) which is superior and anterior to the other; such retrofitting structures act equally as structures of conversion. Ethical-religious actions of passage and of the transformation of the self, like sacrifice, can receive their formalization only through such conversion structures between binary and more complex forms.

Whatever its reach, then, the memory-image can already receive a formalization, even when it concerns the sole individual or their very primitive relation to the parent; it might be better to speak of a "binary symbol," or "ternary symbol," rather than of an image in the former case and symbol in the latter, for there is a symbol as soon as there is a formalization of imprints; if binary symbols were not formed, would it even be possible to acquire the ternary symbols allowing communication with others in a universal mode? The world of the individual imaginary prepares access to the register usually called symbolic; the individual imaginary reflects the universal conditions of existence since it expresses life and death, health and sickness, joy and sadness, pleasure and pain; the register of the individual is binary yet it includes a formalization of experiences, a symmetrization of imprints, and thereby, a symbolic power.[8] In *The Imaginary*, Sartre denies any distinction between the imaginary and the symbolic function: they are both forms of unreflective thought, aiming at the possession of the object. While Sartre's definition of the "imaging consciousness" is debatable, his interpretation is extremely interesting because it emphasizes a relation of existence and of action between the object and the subject, one woven in images and symbols rather than, as in most other doctrines, including Husserl's, relations of signification which to a greater or lesser degree associate images and symbols with signs. Finally, we should point out the theory of Piaget who, in *La formation du symbole chez l'enfant*,[9] connects the distinction between image and symbol to his distinction between functions of accommodation and functions of assimilation; yet there already exists in the image a constructive activity which entails that it is not simply an extension of perception: "The pure image [*l'image simple*] is an interiorised imitation of the object it relates to, just as an exterior imitation is a direct copy of the model by means of the subject's own body or of actions that result in a material reproduction of the model (drawing or construction)." The distinction between simple image and symbol corresponds to access at the level of representation: when images let affective correspondence be established among them, the passage to the symbolic level takes place; play, in particular, uses symbols that manifest affectivity (intentions or desires); later, symbols stabilized by conventions, especially language, effect a transition towards concepts; the specificity of the symbolic function lies in the connection between signifiers and signifieds; according to Piaget, this function only truly appears at the stage when play allows for the assimilation of the real into the ego, as dreams do, and bestows signification. Piaget's theory, while maintaining the distinction between image and symbol within a genetic perspective, does not exclude the possibility of forms of transition between image and symbol— images being more primitive than symbols. What we would like to say is that a truly implicit formalization of images takes place according to the simplest dimensions, corresponding to individual life, that is, in the form of a continuous spectrum of the binary type that permits correspondences; such a formalization already bestows on images a symbolic signification and reach.

2. The Symbol-Object

The pure case of the image or symbol as mental realities can only be exhaustively studied in relation to the analysis of dreams and daydreams, which requires a specialized study that we must leave aside in this course for the sake of time. However, from the perspective of a future study of invention and creation, we must consider the role played by the objects used as supports or instruments of symbolic formalization. The appearance of invention within human activity is not an absolute and sudden novelty; it develops progressively, through the aid of objects which may at first be simple adjuncts, but which take on heightened prominences and autonomy by concretizing, condensing, and organizing a plurality of simultaneous and successive functions into a system of compatibility. We may call these objects intermediary or analog objects.

The first and easiest to use of all intermediary objects is the body in expressive imitation. When used in an intensive way, the symbolic function of imitation corresponds to the reenactment of a memory; it calls forth the mimed object and brings it to life by evocation, as though the mimed object took possession of the mime. During funerals in ancient Rome, the procession was headed by mimes evoking the memory of the deceased by reproducing his way of walking, his tics, everything that constituted the motor caricature and individual traits belonging to that person. This mime activity had the same meaning as portraits, statues, and the *imagines* of ancestors. Still today, the evocation of the dead comes with a certain induction of their habits, the choices they made, or the words they uttered in various circumstances; memory provides norms through images, and it induces mimetic imitation through the body as intermediary object. Our culture restricts mimetic activity that is considered vulgar; but, within the function of remembering and evocation, we can see the body proper *[le corps propre]* serving as intermediary object, for instance, when former students who had the same professor recall not only the professor's teaching, but the whole atmosphere of the time when that cohort attended his courses: all who symbolize by imitation in this way belong to a group, linked by a kind of ritual: the tone of voice, the accent, the usual gestures, the turns of phrase, the most common concepts used by the professor—whose memory is at once consecrated and desecrated by imitation—all these components intervene in the celebration of the past; it is more a multiform caricature than a uniform photograph; it is the entire specter/spectrum *[spectre]* of memory that is reincarnated, from the best to the worse, the remembrance of good and bad grades, triumphs and humiliations; the professor brought back to life is both good and bad because he is impersonated. We might also notice how closely meanings are linked to concrete conditions of activity, how closely they adhere to symbols; a certain manner of using dialectical schemas may remain indissociable from the image of the professor who taught them, so much so that when we use these schemas we may have the impression not of thinking on our own but of speaking in the manner of that professor: the activity of expression, and verbal activity in particular lend their concrete substrate to these abstract aspects of an integral invocation through the body proper as the most available intermediary object.

Outside of the body proper, the most easily attainable intermediary objects are those that can be detached, manipulated, carried, or preserved, such as fragments of clothing or stone, a curl of hair, or some water from a river, like that Chateaubriand brought back from the Jordan River. Such symbolic objects are called "souvenirs *[souvenirs]*," and the belief in their operative force is so strong that they can produce powerful collective movements: when Lindbergh landed at Le Bourget airport after having crossed the Atlantic, the crowd ran to the hero to lift him triumphantly, but also to the Spirit of Saint-Louis to tear off pieces and keep them as souvenirs.[10] To pick up a symbol-memory *[souvenir-symbole]* is to retain something of the reality from which it is lifted, since this reality is deprived of one of its parts, small as it might be, and as a result, an absorption into the subject occurs through the intermediary of the bond of property; the souvenir is an *analogon* of the reality from which it was drawn, and it constitutes a mode of access to this reality through conscious knowledge but also through an operation of influence drawing its meaning from magical operations. According to the categories of the souvenir become symbol-image, the belongings of a person are to some extent in a symbolic relation with him. An ancient author mocks the admirer of a wise man who, after the latter's death, bought his clay lamp convinced that, studying under its light, he could imbue himself of the philosopher's knowledge; this is probably unusual with respect to philosophical thought since its disciples are generally less materially idolizing. Yet the quest for belonging is common in the form of a participation through object possession and in less purely reflective behaviors: some businesses in France today sell dresses or coats that belonged to actresses, even though our culture has a generally unfavorable opinion of the use of objects bought second hand; but the yearning to participate in the life of a famous and admired person through the use of a material *symbolon* is stronger than the reluctance to wear clothing that isn't new. For the same reason, houses where a celebrity has lived find more buyers and at a higher price. Each culture defines the class of objects allowing participation in the mode of a transfer of belongings; clothing and houses occupy a prominent place as intermediary objects probably because they are like envelopes of the body proper; next come usual objects such as pieces of furniture, then collectibles. In an adjacent category we find the objects directly produced by a person: handwritten letters, drawings, or craftwork.

Such objects are remarkable points—extreme terms of reality. They express the "hot spots" of situations and persons, through which they are articulated, in an effective and remarkable way, with the natural and social mode, according to a "savage" mode of perception and action; the idea that hair and fingernails retain vital force, even detached from the body, is roughly comparable to the belief that a noose used to hang someone carries good luck; hair and fingernails have the virtue of extremities: they express the insertion of the body in the outside world, materializing and expressing its limits, its active borders; anything that is mobile and visible is already virtually detachable from the individual in order to keep on expressing his force and possibilities of action; that which is sufficiently pliable and mobile in the body to serve expression, such as hair and the extremities of limbs, tends to be selected as an intermediary object preserving absolute properties; the

symbolic function is continuous with the skin appendages of various species, since these appendages manifest a relational category of the organism, existing for and towards the outside as organs of display [manifestation].
Hence there exists a category of intermediary reality between the organism
as a self-sufficient and necessary reality with basic organs, and the objects
of the external world subject to manipulation and organization and which
form into instruments or a territory: namely, the category of organs and
movements of display, which are linked to the outside and more laden with
expression than those organs necessary for life. It is precisely these organs
of display that are first recruited as symbols since they are detachable without endangering life, but also because their relative exteriority allows them
to be artificially overloaded with veneer, color, adornment, and jewels, and
to be considered as an intensification or a specialization of their perceptual
function (long fingernails, various hairdos); organs of display connect in a
continuous way to clothing and adornment (wigs); they thereby link back
to the world in a very different way than essential organs for functions such
as breathing and feeding; these are effectors that do not bear on objects and
do not operate on the world, but display and advertise a mode of being, a
state, or an attitude that are generally more durable than a simple action, and
often linked in a deep way to a function or a rank; to this same extent, the
mode of being of display organs may, among species whose appendages cannot be easily modified, call for an instrumental prosthetic complement that
affixes and stills, as a materialized (and thus detachable) symbol, the display
mediator; a scepter is a materialized figuration of the "hand of glory" with
its stretched index finger. The weapons of a warrior or the scepter of an
emperor are very directly symbolic appurtenances since they extend organs
of display in a prosthetic direction, and also because in the prosthetic relation, the suppression of the instrument-object robs the body of one of its
powers. Of course, according to a conceptual logic, even if the loss of a prosthetic object is akin to a mutilation for the one who knew how to use it,
it does not follow that its force or power could be transferred to any other
person taking hold of the object without prior learning; yet the implicit
logic of images enables precisely this belief in the transfer of power through
the prosthetic object, since the display of power transpires in attitudes and
appendages and not, strictly speaking, in motor organs as such; it is similarly

display that forms the trigger for the memory that restores the object and the situation; display, since it makes the displaying subject overflow towards the object, may be perceived as independent of that subject. This intermediary status between that of an organism and of an object from the milieu enables the formation of the symbol on the basis of the display perceived through the object. Display, indeed, is univocal only when it is directed and borne by an organism such as the scepter at arm's length; it becomes a tensed and metastable system when the same prosthetic object, detached from any organism, is both the object which, carried by the other, addresses the subject, and which the subject tasks with transmitting the power of his own organism to the world; the prosthetic object is then equally centripetal and centrifugal; the perceived scepter is pointed in a single direction; but the scepter becomes a symbol when it is all at once directed against the subject, and directed by the subject towards the world; both senses, both orientations cross each other and deploy between them the continuous spectrum of imaginary instances of experience, replacing the linear and discontinuous series of memory. The memory-image, originally strongly asymmetrical, thus progressively becomes symmetrical, because the bearer of the scepter vanishes while the subject takes hold of it; similarly, a symbolic weapon is all at once a threat against the subject and an object he can take hold of to threaten others. The symbol is an appurtenance that has simultaneously several owners and several orientations towards the object. By becoming symmetrical in this way the memory-image tends towards the status of an object, yet in a completely different way than objects from the milieu which are not made of the equilibrium between two opposite orientations provisionally neutralized. A symbol is but a pseudo-object loaded with all the potential energy of a metastable system, ready to spark a change of structure. We may take as another example that of the cross: it is a souvenir so long as it perpetuates the death of Christ; but it becomes a symbol within Christendom when it becomes also the sign of the *labarum* or that of the Crusaders, since its meaning is reversed according to the adage: *in hoc signo vinces* [You shall conquer for this sign]; this shift to the function of symbol is in fact the index of a change in the scope of Christianity in relation to temporal reality.

The evolution of the memory-image towards the state of symbol entails a certain process of abstraction, where "abstraction" means "an extraction from";

but it is an extraction of the elements of display [*manifestation*] from complete
situations: these extreme terms within situations, as key points conveying
forces, become concretized while the memory of the conveying organisms
and the particular circumstances recedes and fades away. The memory-image
becomes a symbol when the orientation or particular direction of the display loses its original univocity through the possible duality of orientations.
The memory of a weapon wielded by the subject, like that of a threatening
weapon wielded by others, only produces images. But these images form a
symbol when the weapon is understood as a threat to the subject, and, at the
same time, grasped as something to be wielded by the subject to threaten
others; these two directions of a weapon register the extreme terms of attack
and defense; the symbol-weapon is neither wielded by the subject nor against
him; it is the tension between these two images, like a weapon seen in profile
potentially harboring the gesture that will turn it against others or against
the subject; we may say in heraldic language that the symbol is always "passant" not "issuant," while the image is issuant and not passant. The formalization of a memory that produces a symbol is an operation transforming
the "issuant" objects located in relation to the subject and the situation into
"passant" objects waiting to be redirected in accordance with the project
from which they draw their orientation.[11]

In a concrete way, we could say that the mental world of symbols is that of
objects "seen in profile," while they are nonetheless key points within situations, objects, or organs of display [*manifestation*], loaded with meaning and
force; the relative detachment of these significant objects mobilizes them,
renders them available, makes them the toothing-stones of inventive imagination; symbols are "absolute objects," detached from the empirical situations of their emergence, yet having preserved their power, their capacity of
expression, their capacity to indicate potentials.

The subject for whom the majority of images are converted into symbols
partially loses his memories insofar as they are historical, dated, particular,
with oriented objects having a definite and univocal meaning with respect to
the subject himself; within the symbol, succession becomes simultaneity,
the individual acquires a universal scope, what belonged to others begins
to belong virtually to the subject, at the same time that he loses his own
appurtenances; symbols are not situated in relation to the ego, which means

they cannot adapt the subject, as acting organism, to his milieu or territory; they translate the force of things just as much the virtualities of action for the subject; they are powers without support, without subject, and without external milieu in which to be inserted. The world of symbols is a kind of pandemonium floating in between the situation of objects and that of subjects, interposed between the living and the milieu. In mental conditions, symbols may be taken for objective reality or they might inhabit the subject who feels possessed and loses his freedom and his power of initiating action; art practices a kind of exorcism which, rather than letting the universe of symbols float between the world of objects and the subject, stills it by representing it, ritualizing it, and inserting it within the objective world and social regularity; magic draws from the imaginary its means of evocation or influence in materializing symbols which it re-individualizes, christens with a proper name, or fashions after the semblance of a living being, to use it as a mode of access in the analogical operation of invocation or hexing. An effigy is an *analogon* of the person to be hexed, yet it is infused with the imaginary and constructed with the greatest possible number of symbol-objects borrowed from the actual individual. All such uses of the symbolic imaginary are naïve to some extent for they reprise a formalized content, that of the symbol, by trying to make it real again but without continuing the cycle of the image that was formalized into a symbol by losing its links as a dated and personal memory. But the cycle of the image cannot be reversed; a formalization has been completed, it is not from inside or without a constructive, productive, creative, or modifying operation on its structures that the insertion within the universe can be rediscovered; the symbol is a mixture of subject and object which has an instrumental value for invention; in magic, dream, or fantasy, it can only become degraded and yield the illusion of a false concreteness, an artificial world of appearances; the Platonic critique of the arts as generators of illusion applies essentially to arts seeking to rediscover an existence from symbols, inverting a becoming whose completion can only be found in invention—and in the recommencement of a new cycle of relations with reality—and not in an inversion of the cycle already accomplished. A memory in its most condensed form, that of the symbol, is but a moment in the becoming of the image, which has as much functional meaning with respect to the action to be undertaken after invention as with respect to the action already accomplished. Once an action is accomplished and an experience is had, by becoming formalized into a symbol, memory proposes instruments for a new action; the symbol absorbs the manifestation, but the manifestation does not deplete itself; it does not deplete itself in the imaginary either, since it is only a stage at the completion of which a new cycle of action becomes possible through the invented object.

It would certainly be interesting to study in themselves the direct uses of the imaginary as modes of expression, of communication, or of influence in the arts, in rhetoric and magic; however, since these are uses that interrupt the cycle of the image and prevent it from reaching its state of completion, the study of such modalities is of more interest for the history of groups and cultures than for the elucidation of the complete becoming of the image considered as a question of "general" psychology. But, it is worth noting that the cycle of the image is a genesis that is marked in each of its stages by a sedimentation, a reduction in the number of elements preserved and ultimately proposed as material for invention; not all motor tendencies receive a confirmation of a perceptual experience; only those that the imprinting of an intense situation stabilizes subsist, and, among memory-images thus gathered, only a few are formalized into symbols in order to organize the world of the imaginary serving as basis for invention. This is what explains the fact that the world of the imaginary appears richer than that of invention: images are more numerous than symbols when they are merely memory-images.

PART IV

Invention

To what situation does invention correspond? To a problem, which is to say, to an interruption due to an obstacle or a discontinuity acting as a barrier to an operative implementation [*accomplissement opératoire*] that is continuous in its project. What is problematic is a situation that dualizes an action, chops it up by separating it into segments, either for lack of a middle term or because the fulfillment of one part of the action destroys another equally necessary part; the two fundamental problematic modes are hiatus and incompatibility; both amount to an action's failure to adapt to itself intrinsically, across the various sequences and subsets it presupposes; solutions show up as restorations of continuity, enabling the progressiveness of operative modes along paths previously invisible within the structure of the given reality. Invention is the emergence of an extrinsic compatibility between the milieu and the organism and of an intrinsic compatibility between the subsets of the action. Detours, the fabrication of instruments, and the association of several operators all represent different means of re-establishing intrinsic and extrinsic compatibility. When a problem is resolved, the dimension of the final act of the result encompasses, in its dimensional characteristics, the operative regime that produced it; for instance, in a classical tale, a rolling boulder stuck in the middle of a narrow path cannot be moved by individual travelers trying to move it separately, since it is too heavy, though it is easily pushed aside by the travelers working together; here the problem cannot be solved as it is initially given, when the road is a place of passage where multiple individual itineraries do not compound *[couplage]*; rather the group of travelers exists virtually from the point of view of the result, since it is only at that moment that they can all resume their travel, even though they arrived at the obstacle at different times depending on their particular trip. The compounding of efforts, visible in the unity of the result, points back to the act of resolution and to invention; within the conditions of the problem, the lines of a possible solution already appear, albeit negatively; the accumulation of people stopped by the boulder, one after the other, progressively constitutes a simultaneity of expectations and needs, thus a tension towards the simultaneity of departures once the obstacle is removed; the virtual simultaneity of imagined departures points back to the simultaneity of efforts in which the solution lies. Anticipation and foresight are not enough since each traveller is perfectly capable of imagining how he would go on walking if the boulder were pushed aside; what is needed is that anticipation return to the present by altering the structure and conditions of the ongoing action; in this case, it is collective anticipation that alters each of the individual actions by constructing a system of synergy.

Hence there is a structuring return of the content of the anticipation onto the formula of the present action; it is a return of information, or rather a return of organization whose source is of the order of magnitude of the result—the regime of the operation thought of as carried out and complete. Invention sets up a certain kind of retroaction, a recurring input ("feedback") which goes from the regime of the completed result to the organization of the means and subsets within a mode of compatibility. In the example of the boulder, the organization of compatibility in the form of synergy amounts to setting the force of each traveler against a fraction of the boulder to be moved; since the boulder is not divisible this can take place only if the boulder is pushed at the same moment by all the travelers. The root of the solution is a communication between two orders of magnitude, that of the result (the road reopened to all) and that of the problem-event (a barrier across the path of each one), whose data are altered: within the new perspective of a collective (and no longer individual) result, the operation amounts to each traveler moving a fraction of the boulder; the collective result is still compatible with the individual result, the path being opened to each one when it is open to the group; similarly, the individual action of pushing is compatible with the sum of the actions of other individuals thanks to the additive simultaneity of parallel thrusts; it is this intrinsic compatibility that enables the extrinsic compatibility of the relation between a single person's force and the weight of a fraction of the boulder.

In such a case, invention is facilitated by the fact that the subjects are at the same time virtual operators; the interruption of the action caused by the problem-event prompts a shift to the order of magnitude of the result, which is that of compatibility; the different interruptions of the originally independent trips generates the collective of stopped travelers, thereby creating through a negative effect the field within which the compatible action can unfold; the association through a community of intentions within a homogeneous group is a particular case, since it requires neither instrumental mediation nor a division of labor. As soon as the problem can find a solution only in an order of magnitude very different than that of the individual and of the elementary gesture, because of size or complexity, it becomes necessary to resort to heterogeneous mediations, and the task of invention bearing on these mediations is considerable; but invention preserves its functional place as a transfer system between two different orders of magnitude; simple machines such as a lever or a capstan, even the inclined plane or the winch display in their structure the essential function of transfer such devices materialize. With a capstan or a hoist, a single operator, in each of his gestures, acts as if he were moving the fraction of the load that is compatible with his strength; yet he moves the entire, indivisible load, albeit only a small distance. Invention in such a case, while respecting the principle of conservation of work, consists in varying both factors, intensity of force and displacement, in order to adapt them to the capacities of the organism of the operator. The problem is solved when a communication is established between the action system of the subject who encounters the problem and the regime of reality of the result; the subject is part of the order of reality in which the problem is posed; he is not part of the order of imagined results;

invention is the discovery of mediation between two orders, a mediation thanks to which the action system of the subject may gain purchase on the production of the result through coordinated action.

For the problems related to moving loads (there is a problem when the action system and corporeal strength are not immediately efficacious), the most elementary inventions amount to using an adaptive mediator that links the regime of the result to the aptitudes of the operator; the human body, for instance, is ineffective for transporting a liquid; an intermediary solid is necessary, like a goatskin or a barrel that serves as an envelope with respect to the liquid, and as a maneuverable solid with respect to the human organism; the same goes for pulverized substances or small objects that must be placed in a bag or, better, a pouch with a strap appropriate for carrying on one's shoulder. When it is the volume of the load that causes a problem, the mediating object is a pole or a platter like those hunters use for large game. Finally, when the problem comes from the disproportion between the force of the operator and the mass of the load, the mediating object belongs to the general category of impedance adapters described in earlier examples. These various mediations have a common essence as adaptation systems; the molecules of a liquid or the particles of powder are of an order of magnitude that does not make them easily maneuverable by the human body without an intermediary object which gathers them by the billions; solid loads, though they cannot be divided, are manipulated with the aid of machines that bring about an adaptation of forces; in both cases the organism of the operator, in acting on the intermediary object, operates as though it dealt with a solid object of an order of magnitude that is homogeneous with it, and with physical-chemical characteristics compatible with the conservation of the organism (mid-range temperatures, non-sharp edges, non-toxic and non-corrosive composition, etc.). Intermediary objects are required to safeguard the body's integrity whenever the object is, in one of its characteristics, too heterogeneous with respect to the organism (extreme temperature, acidity, causticness, toxicity, etc.).

Through invention, the intrinsic compatibility of the organism extends to a situation, which initially, as a problem, does not admit such a compatibility; but there are different levels in the discovery of mediations that result in compatibility; if mediation consists merely in modifying or supplementing an operative mode, it is less complex than if it requires an intermediary object whose selection and use call for mediate operative modes; the detour through an instrument is not just an operative detour; it presupposes a cognitive detour—a subordination of the actonal chain[1] of selection or fabrication of the object to the pursuit of the end with a temporary substitution of the instrument-object for the end-object; an intermediary case between inventions of detour and instrumental mediations is the use of animals or more generally living beings as intermediary objects which one need not build, but only choose, capture, train, and develop: the large class of domestic animals and cultivated plants was likely among the first depositories of the inventive activity of the human species, at a time when instruments were still few and rudimentary. This category of modified living beings that preserve their spontaneity and capacity for self-reproduction is comparable to an intermediary object with multiple properties; training is the institution of a detour in behavior, in the animal, but the beneficiaries of this detour are humans.

The study of situations involving a detour has generally been conducted to measure the intelligence of various animal species; we should nonetheless note that the various experimental situations allow measurement only when basic conditions are similar; for a great many species, however, the pursuit of a goal in relation to which a detour behavior could occur cannot be dissociated from the preexisting organization of a territory; it is in accordance with the differentiated lines of this territory that a detour is possible, in the form of a change in itinerary, of relinquishing a main itinerary in favor of a less trammeled secondary itinerary that is not random and is already marked in the same way as the main itinerary. In other words, possible detours are part of the territory; they were predetermined at the moment it was surveyed, and they are the result of a learning experience, usually from early in life, in which the images directing action were formed. Outside of the territory, the detour behavior may not appear, since there is not a prior organization; the detour that is feasible without a prior organization of the territory is a detour at a short distance from the goal—the goal being perceptible but not directly attainable, which corresponds only to the terminal phase of a behavior. To this first reservation concerning the generality of the detour behavior as invention, a second can be added: the detour, for a given species, belongs to a definite behavior corresponding to a determined motivation, a certain level of vigilance, behaviors of predation or flight, etc. Sometimes the detour is spontaneous in a definite situation and is actually part of the action system of the animal, with imperceptible transitions from simple motor schemas (such as the twisted leap of the rabbit on the run) to more complex specific behaviors (the zigzagging flight of the hare) and to the "maneuvers" of females leading the predator away from their offspring (quail or seal); the detour emerges as a modality of flight or defense as much as an aspect of the pursuit of prey enabling the predator to get close without being seen or scented; in this case, the detour is not exactly a detour in relation to a goal but a specific mode of action; it is only in the final phase of the behavior that—close to shelter or nearing the prey—we can speak of a detour in the anthropomorphic sense of the term; what occurs then for the animal is the true substitution of a mode of action by another, for instance, the substitution of the final leap of the predator by extending the slow crawl of the approach. In a general manner, then, it is in terms of behavior flexibility that problems of detours corresponding to the majority of experimental situations are posed, rather than in terms of the invention of a new trajectory; to be able to detour, the animal must first reach the category of behavior within which the detour exists, despite types of stimulation apt to trigger, for instance, rectilinear leaping or flying, but not behaviors that include detour; it is this change of category or behavioral class that is not always possible or requires learning. Hence a detour made possible during exploration may not be available during flight because the behavioral class had changed. In such conditions, can the detour be considered as an invention within animal behavior?

Yes, but on condition of specifying that it is a detour implying a representation, an image, more than a direct perception; this type of detour implies the representation of effects that are distant from actions ("foresight") and the extended retention of a direction of activity, according to experiments by Hobhouse and Bierens de Haan; the perception of an end inhibits actions which deviate from that end. Lewin has indicated the difficulty young children have approaching a goal backward (for instance, trying to sit on a chair), even though backward walking belongs to defensive behavior in situations generating fear; conversely, backward walking is a spontaneous behavior among certain load-pulling species (ants and spider wasps). From this point of view, we should note that there are different species of detour depending on whether the path involves an alternating proximity or distance from the goal or displays instead progressive and continuous characteristics; in a case where a spiral chicken wire is spiraled around a goal, an animal will, if it is outside the wire, follow a continuous and progressive detour through the spiral, but if the animal is inside and the goal outside, the obstacle presents maxima and minima that are increasingly pronounced as the overall distance to the goal diminishes; a cat can solve the former but not the latter problem. W. and K. Mac Dougall attribute success in detour problems to an anticipatory intuition similar to the *Einsicht* [insight] noticed by Köhler in various types of tasks, particularly in labyrinth learning with visual cues; the presence of the *Einsicht* reveals itself through a sudden increase in success rates, thus a discontinuity in the error curve over time. Experiments with detours have been attempted on a large number of animal species; experiments with monkeys are now classic, as well as those with hens, which encounter much more difficulty than monkeys or dogs with a detour problem. Fischel presented tortoises with a detour problem by offering them a piece of worm behind a plexiglass partition; success comes all at once. A similar apparatus was used by Piéron with octopi, and by Bierens de Haan on the same animal. The latter let an octopus *see* a crab up close; a glass partition, invisible underwater, and running half way up the aquarium prevented the direct capture of the crab; when the stimulation was visual, what stops the octopus is the tactile and motor obstacle of the glass partition; even if, by chance, one of the octopus's tentacles brushed the crab, there was no integration of this tactile sensorial datum with the initial problem posed in terms of visual stimuli; the tactile datum is nonetheless an indication that might trigger the solution of the detour problem since the tentacle did effectuate a detour that enabled the capture of the crab. This observation is of great interest for the theoretical study of the detour as invention; it shows that the perceptual integration of data from several senses is an important adjunct in the discovery of solutions; the concrete mono-sensorial perceptions must be transcended by a centralized activity of synthesis in order for the intuition of the solution to appear; we recoup here, even within a perceptual situation, the *local activity* that serves as a receptive system for sensorial signals;

the cognitive context in which the detour situation may arise is more complex than the function of sense organs as receptors; when it can develop
as a mode of multisensorial compatibility, the image—an active system of
the reception of sensorial data—holds a reserve of solutions for concrete
invention, in the same way a roadmap is an always-ready reserve of itineraries. We now understand why the prior organization of a territory through
multiple and various explorations is one of the conditions for the resolution
of detour problems, for these provide the opportunity of developing images
that render data from the various senses compatible; the possible detours
preexist in the image, and the more precise the image is, the faster they are
discovered.

Moreover, the detour as a concrete invention finds a reciprocal form in
the shortcut, which emerges as an improvement of behavior, for example,
in the case of learning a labyrinth with several solutions, where it can also
occur as a sudden invention.

2. Instrumental Mediation

The recruitment of an object originally belonging to the external milieu
and used as instrument was long considered, especially by philosophers and
moralists, as a specific display of human intelligence, hence the label "*homo
faber*" chosen to designate our species. The Stoics often reprised the following theme: each animal species is endowed with specialized organs for defense,
attack, shelter construction, etc.; humans, by contrast, have neither organ-
tools (pincer or auger) nor innate operative knowledge to use them without
prior learning; they must fashion tools and learn to use them; but the equipment and innate knowledge of animals is limited, given once and for all as a
feature of the species, while human capacities are not limited; what at first
represents an infirmity, a lack of inbuilt equipment, also ensures an ultimate
superiority. Such ideas are found among Sophists and Lucretius along with
a more general idea of how progress is closely linked to inventive capacities
and their impact on society. It was then a conspicuous commonplace for
thought in antiquity, and it can even be found in mythology with Icarus and
Prometheus.

Yet the use of instruments does take place among animal species, under
conditions which, at times, point to a stereotyped activity generally found

among the various individuals of the species, and at other times are rarer and seem attributable instead to individual invention. In 1905, the Peckhams observed a wasp, *Ammophila urnaria*, tamping down the ground over its nest with a small rock held in its mandibles. Was this a case of individual invention? Minkiewicz, in 1933, observed solitary wasps in Poland performing the same operation with the scales of birch fruits, which implies a certain plasticity and adaptability to the parameters of the milieu in instrumental selection; in spite of this, Piéron considers that in such cases we cannot speak of invention—individual invention—but rather of an analogical conflation or instinctual extension; the maneuver is habitual to all members of the species, which owns the recipe. The tropical red ant living in mango-trees, *Oecophylla smaradgina*, brings several leaves together, with six or seven ants pulling them, then glues them edge to edge using a thread-secreting larva as shuttle. Ridley, Doflein, Bugnion, and Hingston have observed this construction of nests made of leaves in other ant species of the genus *Polyrhachis* or the *Camponotus senex*. There too, this behavior involving the use of a living being as tool or instrument is a species-wide recipe enabling a collective behavior with a division of labor (some workers keep the leaves in place edge-to-edge while others manipulate the larvae). We can thus speak of organization but not of individual invention, even if there is a use of instrumental mediation similar to that in human artisanal activity. Lansiaux and Roussy have noted the way some spiders use a small pebble as a web-tensing weight when a lower anchoring thread could not be attached for lack of available support point; this case is comparable to the various instrumental uses cited above, yet it arises in conditions in which the instrument replaces, as a fragment detached from other objects, an opportunity the situation could have offered on its own; the small pebble brought in corresponds to a reorganization of the milieu; this case establishes a continuity between simple organizations (tamping of soil or digging) and the use of an instrument detached from the milieu and re-attached to the organism as a prosthesis.

W. Köhler studied the use of instrumental mediations among monkeys in situations where, unable to reach a goal directly (for instance, a fruit suspended high above in the cage), these animals either used connected sticks, the end of one embedded in another, or a scaffolding of boxes or a ladder provided in their cage with other objects; the observed behavior implements a perceptual selection, with long objects (a plank or stick) recruited first as instruments. The construction of an instrument *per se* requires a higher capacity of integration and a prior experience of manipulation; only higher primates who spontaneously manipulate sticks placed at their disposal, before any finalized behavior, succeed later in embedding the segments of sticks to resolve the problem of the fruit suspended above the cage; we might say that in such a case it is the image of the embedding (as perceptual-motor reality) that is recruited at the moment of difficulty, and that the use of the instrument to be reconstructed is discovered through a mental image already constituted during open learning, comparable to an exploration for structuring the territory. We witness here the importance of the role played by the spontaneity of behaviors initially containing motor components ("need" for exploration, manipulation play) that serve as systems for the reception of perceptual data; it is through these motor components that an active mental image is constituted and can serve as solution for a problem. A mere perceptual investigation when the problem is presented does lead to selecting objects as mediators but without adequate discernment of their complex operative properties; hence, assembled boxes or a ladder given to monkeys are chosen for their perceptual qualities as scaffolding components, but without respect for the rules of equilibrium in their stacking or wedging against a wall (which would correspond to forcible embedding of the sticks); the monkey indifferently places a small box on a larger one then the reverse; it places the ladder vertically against the wall without slanting it; if the monkey reaches the goal in these conditions, it is by using these objects as momentary support to jump rather by climbing, which requires the mechanical conditions of stable equilibrium. Instrumental invention requires not only a perception, but also a complete mental image forged by the motor components involved in manipulation and exploration.

An adjacent problem to that of the instrument used to reach a goal is that of the instrument used to pull an object beyond direct reach, especially with the aid of a string or thread attached to that object, with or without obstacles (cage bars) that make the processing of relations more complex. Bierhens de Haan found goldfinches capable of resolving this problem on the first attempt, while others needed to learn the maneuver; Erhardt states that such traction actions are routinely used in the natural living conditions of several species of birds (tits and goldfinches), as well as the action of jamming a fruit into the hollows of bark to eat it (among nuthatches). Bullfinches proceed similarly to break open pinecone scales. Gulls and ravens break hard shells by dropping them from high above rocks.

In a certain sense there is a continuity between detour, instrument recruitment from the milieu, and indirect behaviors such as that of a bird lifting a hard shell in the air and letting it go so it will break on rocks; such indirect behaviors abound in the operative modes of various species; I have witnessed the European red ant make use of gravity to move loads: rather than carrying them one by one from a wooden plank five feet from the ground, the ant successively threw the loads (they were in fact ant corpses) then climbed down to the ground to complete transportation, after having unhooked a few dead ants stuck on wood fibers at the edge of the cut plank; however, the ant did not recuperate a number of corpses which, diverted by the wind, fell on a table rather than on the ground; this behavior is akin to that of the discovery of a shortcut, since the total length of travel and labor-time was reduced by a factor of fifteen compared to up-and-down round-trips. But is this an individual invention or a species-wide behavior? Certainly, it is a behavior finely adapted to the situation—effective, quick, and expedient—although it leads to a certain waste in the load; but I haven't been able to conduct sufficient observations to determine whether the use of free fall to lower loads is spread among ants; in all likelihood, this was a perfectly individual behavior and outside the anthill, which proves that behaviors we might call, with reference to human norms of task management, ingenious, are not merely collective among insects.

The most common argument against calling these accomplishments among animals 'inventions' maintains that such behaviors are widely found across the species; this is what Piéron calls a species-wide recipe; if the behavior is stereotyped it is indeed not an invention, yet the fact that a behavior is encountered often within a species does not prove that it does not result from a multitude of concurring and parallel inventions; the extreme complexity of the conditions of human action means that inventions are usually signaled by a dispersion of operative modes, while the use of a learned formula—a recipe—leads to uniformity; yet if we take into account the leaner framework and far more limited action systems of most animal species, the uniformity of operative modes does not prove the absence of an invention process, since the number of possibilities is limited. This is why it is reasonable to consider, as a criterion of inventive adaptation, a response, through organized and economical behavior, to random factors arising during the execution of a task, either using them if favorable, or neutralizing them if unfavorable; the problem of the capacity for invention among animals coincides here with their intelligence. Observations and experiments have been conducted, particularly by Fabre, on burying beetles trying to bury a mole tied by the experimenter to a stick that prevents it from being lowered: the beetles end up surfacing to assess the situation, discover the string, and cut it; Viaud comments on this experiment which he sees, contrary to Fabre, as a sign of intelligence in the beetles' reaction; Viaud adds observations he conducted in the Alsatian plain on burying beetles trying to bury a vole in ground crevices, exploring the shape of the crevice before orienting and slanting the flattened corpse of the vole so it better slides into the properly sized crevice.

In human life as in animal life, there is a constant necessity to confront the partial novelty of situations with an activity of organization of operative modes; the richer and more precise the mental image of the situation, the higher are the chances of discovering an adequate organization; the simplest invention is that which bears on operative modes because there is homogeneity among these modes, which involve motor schemas, and the representation of the problem; the discovery of practical solutions (of *praxis*) is very much analogous to the simplifications and structurations arising during learning; for a problem to be solved, it must first be posed in coherent, that is, homogeneous, terms, belonging to a single system, the same axiomatic; operative modes with their motor content constitute by themselves the most elementary axiomatic which has no need of being constructed, since it is given by the organism. But it is still necessary that all of the terms of the problem have been converted into operative terms, so that a distance between objects would be a path effectively taken, and a mass is something that has already been lifted with a given effort or has resisted efforts of moving it. This is why the condition for concrete inventions is prior exploration, manipulation, and organization of the territory in which the problem will arise and the instruments of a solution will be found; throughout this activity there are

translations into homogeneous operative terms of the dimensions and properties of things as though in an implicit algebra; the felt relations of objects
with capacities for action perform the most primitive formalizations.

3. The Properties Common to Detour and Instrumental Mediation

Both of these cases concern the selective recruitment of certain data from past
experience by the present representation of the concrete goal to be reached.
Invention, as an organization, is in this respect a detour through the past;
in past experience, in the course of explorations and manipulations, relations were established, sometimes fortuitously, between the organism and
the object constituting the goal; in a problematic situation, characterized
by discontinuity, the proximity of the goal and the intensity of the motivation create a strong slope, an important gradient field that interacts with
the whole population of images condensing past experience. This interaction between the field of finality (the gradient of the goal of the anticipated action) and the field of experience leads, paradoxically, to a simple
situation—but intense, because of the tension toward a goal that is near—
that of modulating a population of mental images bearing the results of explorations and manipulations that have required a very lengthy and complex
activity; an organization occurs because the simplest and smallest structure
(a goal to be reached in the present situation) governs a larger and more
complex set with a weaker gradient. This condition is formally the same as
that of an amplification through interaction between fields. If learning processes were as forcefully polarized as problematic situations, an organizing
invention would not be possible, because its condition, namely, the amplifying recruitment of images already previously constituted by the problem's
field of immediate finality, would lack its basic condition: a gain superior to
unity, thanks to a coupling as irreversible as that between the present and
the past; for amplification to exist, the images condensing past experience
must be as close as possible to a neutral state without being entirely neutral,
since then they would no longer offer any purchase on the field of modulation developed by the finalizing situation; we can understand then why
violently stimulating situations (intense emotions, excesses of reward or of
punishment) do not leave easily usable, mobile, and combinable images for
a later problematic situation, whereas disinterested learning, which is weakly

polarized, optimally prepares inventive organization; in order for invention
to have the best chance of arising, what is required is an alternation between
long durations in which activity is weakly motivated and weakly finalized
(free exploration and manipulation), and short durations with high goal gradients (problematic situations); we may call a *gain* the ratio of measures of
these durations entering into a relation of interaction and finding an equilibrium as fields of experience and of finality within the problematic situation.
It is then not solely the association of memories or the evocation of mental
images that enables an organizing invention; if a present image, developed
by the finalizing situation, triggers a single image from the past that carries
an experience—an image sufficiently polarized to balance and neutralize the
present image—the ratio is 1 / 1, which means there is no amplification; overly
accentuated images do not enable invention but only iteration and preservation; for images to be instruments of invention conforming to the finalized
situation where they organize themselves, they must be in a state close to
neutrality while remaining weakly charged; this state of weak polarization
corresponds to the end result of the process of saturation described above,
which occurs after the experience of the object; a strongly polarized image
of a scheme or project, of fear or desire, cannot be the material for a practical
invention bearing on reality, but only the content of phantasms; images that
express the desire to fly have hardly contributed to the invention of the air-
plane. The most modest of practical inventions is also the result of an act of
amplification which profits, in only a few instants, from a long and scarcely
finalized learning, producing mobile and detachable images following the
lines of force of field of finality.

B. Invention concerning Signs and Symbols

1. Objective Metrological Formalization: From Technics to Science

How did the shift occur, especially for humanity, from concrete situations
to a symbolic formulation that enables the solution not only of a countless
diversity of practical problems in each situation, but also of general and theoretical problems for which real difficulties figure as particular cases (as was
the case since antiquity for many problems of mechanics or hydrostatics)?

We can surmise that this shift from particular concrete cases to general and
theoretical cases is effectuated, on the basis of action, by the intermediary of

the partially theoretical and abstract formalization that the use of living auxiliaries in an action requires, auxiliaries whose actions one must organize in relation to a goal through commands and a univocal and coherent system of directing data toward the execution of a task. So long as each individual imagines, invents, and executes, practical thought can remain implicit, since it does not go beyond the operator who is the milieu of formalization and execution, of the project and its realization. The use of domestic animals to carry out a task already requires that the person who directs them has a more theoretical representation of the activity of operators, of the application of forces, of the resistance of masses, and of the direction of tools; but insofar as the driver stays by the side of the auxiliary animals, the effort of symbolization does not need to be developed into an independent system of signs. By contrast, when an individual calls upon others, servants or slaves, to execute a task, the transmission of commands cannot remain a step-by-step subjugation; in order to make the organized efforts of a team coherent, in order to synchronize activities and harmonize fragmentary executions, a communicable and thus expressible and formalizable conception of the project as a whole is necessary. Recourse to abstract representation begins with the use of domestic animals and becomes fully developed with slavery or forms of labor involving subordination and thus a formulation of the task in a univocal way through a system of commands. Architecture (in the sense of construction by a team with a leader), shipbuilding, or navigation are technics which have quickly developed the abstract positioning of problems; we sense their influence in the stereometry of the ancients, as well as in formulations that aim, in operative terms, to construct with a given component or to trace or further a line with specific properties; the form of the given command has remained in the style of geometry for centuries likely because it incorporated in its content a set of statements playing a role in the transmission of commands of rational execution. The ruler and compass are instruments of execution, even if, at a later stage of research, the geometer is for himself, as one person, the one giving the command and the one seeking to execute it with his own ruler and his own compass. Order and organization, commands given, and structures of execution happen to be formalizations of the task in accordance with the exigencies of information transmission of the one who knows and wants to the one who executes and obeys.

One particular aspect of the formalization of tasks towards the transmission of commands becomes visible with the emergence of complex automatic machines capable of receiving all of the commands before the start of the operation in the form of data and rules; it was then necessary to reinvent logically and in an explicit way the activities practiced by humans according to semi-implicit/semi-explicit rules; for instance, one of the first chess-playing machines obeyed all of the codified rules of the game of chess, but would place two or more pieces on top of each other on the same square: this rule, an implicit part of practical knowledge, had not been included in the given system as a command to the automatic player; only after succeeding in the complete transmission of the rules of the game of chess to an automatic machine was the system considered fully formulated. Recourse to an instrumental mediation in the form of another living being or a machine provokes, through the recruitment of supplementary effects that arise, a uniform and explicit translation of the terms of tasks and problems—which represents a reinvention of operative modes that renders them independent of the subject, and prepares the existence of an independent world of invented realities. Abstract formulations of geometrical problems in analysis became universalized at the time when the design of machines capable of tracing the set of all the curves was being sought.

A supplemental aspect of the necessity for formalizing operative modes, involving their explicit reinvention and preparing their objectification, is that of educating children or adults by means of clear expression rather than direct learning, practice and manipulation; the recipe must be converted into a logical modality expressible in numbers and figures. This difficulty is so great that it often leads to "theoretical," that is, simplified, formalizations, and to presentations that are merely pedagogical. However, the recognition of the logical value of inventions and of the possibility of clearly representing operative modes in a universal language coincides, in Western cultures, with the movement of progress during the enlightenment (see in particular the *Encyclopédie* of Diderot and d'Alembert as an example of explicit expression of the operative modes of professions). The quest for precise modes of expression integral to technics has led to the universalization of units of measure (for the sake of homogeneity and univocity) and of the internal system which connects them to each other (decimal metric system); metrology is still not a science in the sense of a universal symbolism of operations of conversion, but it prepares instruments for and opens a functional domain to it. Metrological universalization enables one to measure quantities and discover constancies through the conversion of one concrete form into another—a source of invention. The idea that nothing is lost and nothing created, whether in terms of matter or energy, translates, first, a metrological ideal extended to the whole universe. A large number of inventions figure as an organization of conditions of constancy, of conservation of energy or of matter in spite of changes from pluses to minuses or changes of physical state. Hence cable cars in which one end of a cable is attached to an ascending car and the other to a descending one implement an invention by the maintenance of a constant quantity of potential energy in the system for cars of equal loads; all the machine has to do is overcome frictions and ensure accelerations and decelerations at the start and destination, since they are not neutralized across cars. The more perfect the development of a symbolic measuring system is, the more compatibility can be carried out by linking perceptually heterogeneous realities together. Hence the cable car schema, in which compatibility is directly perceptible as ascending and descending motion, can give rise to that of the tramway or electric trains coupled through the same electrical circuit; the electrical dynamos of one of these vehicles functions as a receptor (thus as motor) while those of another functions as a generator (thus as brake), a reciprocity which produces the same conservation of mechanical energy, now through the conversion of electricity, as that of the cable cars, but here extending compatibility to synchronized acceleration and deceleration; a third threshold could be crossed through a second conversion, now into chemical energy in a battery, since the synchronization of the ascent of one vehicle with the descent of the other, or the slowing down of one with the acceleration of the other, would no longer be required. Metrological symbolism, in its extension, enables the comprehension and invention of ever-wider compatibilities; with cable cars, it is not only synchronization that is required, but also a parallelism and proximity of routes; with dynamos, synchronization is still required but not proximity; with buffer-batteries neither synchronization nor proximity are needed to preserve compatibility.

The cases of cable cars and the dynamos of tramways are merely pedagogical, that is, simplified, yet they nonetheless contain real invention schemas of the nineteenth century belonging to the framework of applications of the principle of the conservation of energy.

As for the conservation of masses—the condition of possibility of measures using the scale as an instrument (through the intermediary of weight) or, more directly, of elastic systems—it enabled the formalization of the basic metrology of chemistry in the era of Lavoisier, after having rationalized the technical study of combustion for lighting and of other oxidations (human respiration).

Hence the formalizations of operations—useful at the outset as means of communication to give commands or perform an educational training when the operator delegates the function of execution to a third party while retaining the management of the work—detach themselves progressively from this asymmetrical function of communication in order to become a universal and homogeneous symbolic system serving as a basis for abstract operations, and providing a higher level of extension, outside of homogeneous and concrete situations, to the activity on invention. Symbolic formalization, required to cross the distance and heterogeneity between conception and execution, weaves an abstract world, of representations of objects and formulas of relations, that forms the universal reserve of detours and mediations within the exercise of inventive activity.

This first level of formalization, continuous with operative processes of technics, prepares scientific invention and develops a representation of the world in which knowledge and power are convertible one into the other. We might say that this mode of formalization is objective, as independent as possible from references to a subject; it tends towards the execution of tasks by an impersonal, non-human, even non-living operator; it is a formalization for any operator whatsoever that provides a terrain for the development of scientific knowledge as a universal system of compatibilities.

2. Subjective Formalizations (Normative and Artistic)

But another mode of formalization is possible, separated from the first through a dichotomy that is necessary to preserve the homogeneity of operative modes; *everything that is not operative,* that is, everything in the relation with the world that is affective-emotional, may also be formalized and expressed according to subjective categories that authorize participation and action through the communication of a feeling or an emotion, or a definite mode of resonance *[retentissement]* or of motivation. In this sense, action, individual as well as collective, is distinct from an operation; it too has its modes of compatibility, which are norms and ritualizations, but not processes. The arts and religious modalities of collective life correspond to the formalization of action by opposition to operations, according to a dichotomy that is translated by the separation of leisure and work activity, even if celebrations punctuate the great phases in the patterns of work over the courses of the seasons. More specifically, it is artistic formalization that is apposite to the operative modes of work (the time of art is that of leisure), while religious formalization is the principle and guarantee of this dichotomy and of the alternating rhythm between leisure time and work time, highlighting transitions, changes of regimen, ritualizing the key moments of the beginning and end of labor and leisure, propitiating the start of work through the offer of first-fruits, thus facilitating the separation but also the compatibility of modes of work and leisure: the calendar is religious, with the complex structures of good omen and bad omen according to time and place, within an implicit logic of beginnings and endings, stoppages and resumptions.

The religious modality of formalization in our societies corresponds to the rhythm of holidays and commemorations, inauguration ceremonies, graduations, and rites of initiation or exclusion—everything that performs an action as an absolute origin or end of an existence; everything that institutes, voids, or converts in an essential way. At all such occasions, invention provides modes of expression and communication that are necessary for collective participation, and it operates a discovery of compatibility with the whole set of ideals of the group. A declaration of war or a treaty signature are actions existing as formalized and communicable performances tending towards a universal expression. Revolutions too, as well as a large part of political theory, unfold by inventing at each turn a new system of compatibility, creating norms and a new systematic framework for the relations among individuals and among groups; law, together with the legal universe as a whole, is a development that is contemporary with the formalization of action. Each new extension of the domain of human action is marked by an invention authorizing a systematic framework of compatibility embracing this domain (international law, then space law). In each era, normative inventions discover a compatibility for modes of existence that had neither meaning nor points of insertion in previous normative structures. Such inventions provide a symbolism of action by producing an expressible universe of norms while responding to problems; hence Christianity offered norms for relationships between those who had rights and those who didn't in ancient city-states; it provided a city of norms, resolving the problem of compatibility between empires, nations, and individuals, and overcoming, within the city, the limits of religious prohibitions (the Sabbath is made for Men, not Men for the Sabbath), and customary juridical obstacles (he who has not sinned, let him cast the first stone), or the norms of relations between rich and poor, nationals and foreigners. Axiological formalizations concern the key points and key moments of action, principally in the form of a system of axioms for decision-making that lead to a universal representation of the world and humanity, and which are expressed in a symbolism of action that can be taught and propagated. This symbolism sets up a system for the conversion of actions into one another, enabling them to be compared and relate to each other, even if they unfold in conditions that are heterogeneous and concretely dissimilar according to place, time, and the empirical surroundings of each subject. Invention in the normative domain also tends towards the universal.

As for artistic invention, to the extent that it performs a formalization of leisure, it also produces a complete and universalizable representation, participating in the specific logic of each genre and each form of art; successive inventions of symbolic forms recruit by enlarging the effects and modes of appearances of reality which initially were not recognized as citizens within the artistic domain; formalization proceeds in the direction of extension and the discovery of compatibility among originally heterogeneous data. If we consider only the still-recent instance of cinema, we can see that this art, initially considered as a formalization of the vision of motion, successively integrated sound, then color, by discovering the modes of compatibility of their simultaneous use; with every new incorporation, purists reacted, on behalf of the homogeneity of each art, by proclaiming the destruction of true cinema; but this art has developed; it is currently discovering the logic of its compatibility with the new world of broadcasting and production that is television, and with a technics authorizing this narrow compatibility: the recording of images on magnetic tape. The key to such successive extensions is the fact that a new element is not, subsequent to its incorporation, what it would have been in an isolated state, as a unique means of expression; hence sound was first speech in cinema, that is, a contribution of the actors' parts, and in this, of course, it doubled the image without mixing with it; a film became a tribune for speeches, tirades, or argumentation; then, with the broadening of the notion and technics of the sound track, sound integrated noises, and speaking came to the level of noises and sounds, becoming at times non-comprehensible or insignificant; in this new form, speech became compatible with the entire sonic content and with the image, whether it was emphasized or accessory; color too will be entirely compatible with the other compositional aspects when, within one work, and in alternation with these other aspects, it can be either conspicuous or barely perceptible, rather than being merely the opportunity to pick colorful subject matters.

What is truly the invention of an epoch, in the domain of artistic symbolism, is a mode of compatibility between previously isolated forms. In the seventeenth century it was architecture that played this role of permanent and universal panegyric of the arts because it placed the integration of sculpture, painting, fine woodwork, and the art of gardening and fountain craft, within organized synthetic wholes such as palaces or mansions. Renaissance Italy had paved the way in this area. Prior to the Renaissance, religious architecture had constituted the milieu and universal symbolic system integrating sculpture, painting, music, and singing. At the end of the eighteenth century and especially during the nineteenth century, it was literature that offered an open domain to particular modalities, attempting to make things visible and audible, absorbing with its specific means the plastic arts, painting, drawing (illustrations and engraving), making the book into the milieu of the compatibility of the arts, thanks to the development of the printed text. Cinema and then television took up the baton from the book and the newspaper as vehicle of the arts; it would be a mistake to treat them as separate arts comparable to music, sculpture, or theater; they form rather symbolic systems of compatibility resting on a technical invention in progress, as printing was at one time, annexing itself to large-run lithography and engraving; every step in technical inventions serving as platforms enables a broadening of the compatibility between particular arts, to the extent that cinema and television are like architecture in the seventeenth century or the book in the nineteenth century:

a house of arts, rather than an art seeking to stay within itself under the pressure of a professional group inhibiting the opening of a permanent invention.

Formalizations are always accompanied by domination; in the normative domain it was at times religious thought, at others political theory, and at yet others a legal research offering to "values" a compatible grouping by constructing a complete system in accordance with the dominant issue of the moment, which became like a vast house for all other problems; after the legal system of the French Revolution, a socioeconomic system followed which incorporated in turn all the other aspects of normativity by situating them with respect to its categories. This process is comparable to what we see at play in the arts where, in each era, there is a dominant art form functioning as a reference system for and containing the others. For this reason, the symbolic frameworks of action and of art are affected by historical relativity; their synthetic capability is that of an organizing dominance rather than an absolute universality; every system inserts itself in a chain of inventions.

3. Processes of Amplification in Formalization

The source of compatibility in inventions of formalization is also a process of amplification, of recruitment, through which a small and simple structure governs and modulates realities that are broader, more complex, and more powerful. In metrological formalization, compatibility is realized by the discovery—beyond complex realities such as volumes or densities— of a simple structure forming the basis of a system (fundamental units) and their mode of combination (for instance, the decimal system with its prefix "deca," "hecto," or "kilo"). The most complex relations between quantities to be measured find here a possibility of reduction and commutation; they become commensurable.

The same goes in the axiological domain; to invent a moral framework, for instance, means finding a system of fundamental units sufficiently simple and sufficiently close to the subject so that it can be anterior to any complex case submitted to a normative decision; the morals of each class or caste in ancient city-states had no common point and were not mutually compatible; the invention of a morality of compatibility, with Stoicism, consisted in setting up as a source of normativity a fundamental and primordial image simpler than that of any already codified activity and thus capable of modulating such activities: that of the role, of the persona, which may be equally that of the soldier or the emperor, and which possesses an intrinsic normativity as role-play (playing to the end, playing well). When the ancients discovered that slaves were humans rather than speaking goods or tools, they bestowed a normative structure on the master-slave relation by modulating it through the model of the simpler and more primordial relation of father to children (justice, protection, etc.): it is the smaller and simpler reality that serves as a paradigm for the broader reality and governs it. In Christian morality the rule of reciprocity (do unto others as you would have them do unto you) and, in a more concrete way, the model of fraternity as a basis for all human relations, give to a very simple and spare situation, less charged with social formalization than the relation of father to children, the power to model the infinite diversity of relations with others; fraternity is the standard situation, pure and simple, which is amplified in governing relations with others in accordance with the morality of charity. In this way a recently invented moral framework installs itself in the interval of indifference that remained below the threshold of previous morals, by means of a finer normativity; it does not contradict those morals but avoids having recourse to them, resolving the problem before the former normativity would come into play. Hence, in the episode of the adulterous woman about to be stoned, Christ makes the morality of charity bear on the interval of indifference separating the stoning in itself and the casting of the first stone; with the sentence, "he who is faultless, let him cast the first stone," he introduces an examination of one's own conscience that creates a situation of reciprocity between judging oneself and judging others; in order to throw a stone at the adulterous woman, one would have to throw it at oneself too; thus the first stone was never thrown because the new norm set itself below the law, in the interval between the judgment of oneself and the decision to act against others—between the inner self and the gesture. Kant proposes a still more universal normativity that no longer retains even the concrete being in all its affectivity, but only a good will and a respect for the reason in oneself as well as in others, which amounts to considering the human person as an end rather than a means. Increasingly simple structures, then, serve as the bases for normative formalizations, each representing another invention.

The various formalizations bring about compatibility in the form of an interaction between the various orders of magnitude of a staggered reality (family, city-state, inhabited lands); the invention of a new formalization amounts to discovering a smaller and simpler model closer to the subject and serving as paradigm for larger orders of magnitude; formalization thus gives an exemplary axiological value to an action ever more purely inchoate, which amounts to augmenting sensibility and, at the same time, the universality of the formalization, thanks to the inner structure of amplification.

In this form, invention, whether practical or symbolic (formalization), is the result of an interaction between a present field of finality and an accumulated field of experience. The act of invention is not essentially distinct from the organized modes of growth characterizing organisms: in the course of growth, a structure recruits and distributes resources provided by the milieu for an amplifying result; the weak and minimal endogenous reality governs and distributes exogenous reality. For the organizing interaction to be performed, organized materials must be homogeneous and sensitive to the fields distributing them by modulating their flux; and while the data of perception retain a relative heterogeneity and adhere to objects, images resulting from experience and expressing it are endowed with a relative homogeneity and fluidity making them mobile. All things being equal, the genesis of images, up to the oversaturated state which follows the encounter with the object, produces, for mental syntheses, an available content comparable to that which processes of integration provide the organism during growth; molecules in a metastable state, in their external relations, are almost neutral, rendering them easy to distribute with forces of a weak level; yet internally, they hold a high potential energy, which becomes available when they are distributed within the constituted organism; organization is possible because it is performed during the latency state of realities subject to organization. The genesis of images, the progressive saturation across phases, provides a reserve of contents in a state of latency, almost neutral externally, yet internally and intrinsically rich in possibilities of transformation. Such is the Imago with its polyvalent character: inside the complex Imago, the condensed experience constitutes a system of potentiality comparable to the large molecules of organic chemistry; the Imago that may be mobilized by a weak field brings with it a considerable reserve of accumulated experience; such too are the results of exploration and free manipulation, or "experiments just to see"; around each center provided by the perceptual and motor reference to the object, a polyvocal system of properties of things and the organism's modes of access is constructed that is externally closer to the neutral state than was the spontaneous motor initiative or the perceptual encounter. Organization occurs when simplicity rules a flux of complex realities, and this is possible because complex realities can provisionally be in a state of latency, enabling them to manifest as weakly polarized externally, and to free their content once they have been put into place.

C. Invention as the Production of a Created Object or of a Work

The process of invention may be formalized more comprehensively when it produces a detachable object, or a work independent from the subject, that is transmissible, that can be communalized, and that constitutes the basis of a relation of cumulative participation. Without wishing to negate the theoretical possibility or actual existence of cultures within certain animal species, we should note that the main limit of these cultures devolves from the paucity of means of successive transmission, the lack of an object that is constituted as detachable from the living beings that produced it, yet interpretable by other living beings that reuse it by taking the results of the terminal effort of their predecessors as a starting point. In other words, it is not so much the capacity of organizing spontaneity that animal societies lack but the power to create objects, if by creation we mean the constitution of a thing that can exist and have a meaning in a way that is independent from the living activity that made it. The creation of objects enables progress, which is a web of inventions one resting on another, with the latest subsuming the earliest. The organization of a nest or a territory vanishes with the couple or group that formed it; it is, at least, in the most elementary organic forms that the preservation of the object created or secreted by previous generations is the most effective as an organized support for later generations (coral, forest humus, etc.); these effects of cumulative causality resurface after that, in a clear and decisive way, only within the human species in the form of created objects having a meaning for a culture. There is no guaranteed progress so long as culture, on the one hand, and the production of objects, on the other, remain independent of each other; the created object is precisely an element of organized reality that is detachable because it was produced according to a code belonging to a culture enabling it to be used far from the time and place of its creation.

The character of universality and timelessness of the created object may disclose itself in various degrees, since cultures vary across societies; every object and every work have, in a given era, a limited horizon of diffusion; however, there exists in the created object a virtual universality and eternity corresponding to the inner feeling of the creating subject who thinks he is producing a *ktèma es aei*[2] in the terms of Thucydides, or declares like the Latin poet: *non omnis moriar,* "I will not entirely die." This virtuality consists in a permanent possibility of reincorporation in other works or in subsequent creations in the form of a schema or component, even if the individuality of the created object is not preserved across successive inventions.

The process of creation of objects emerges in various domains, yet it is particularly clear, at least in our societies, in the domain of technics and in that of the arts.

1. The Creation of Technical Objects

The continuity of what is created, with its double dimension of spatial universality and temporal eternity, emerges clearly only if we abstract from the destination of usefulness of technical objects; a definition by utility, through the category of needs, is inadequate and inessential since it draws attention to that through which such objects are prostheses of the human organism; yet it is precisely from this angle that universality and atemporality are the most directly impeded, for everything that adapts to the human being runs the risk of becoming a means of display [*manifestation*] and being recruited as supplemental appendage. A large number of technical objects are dressed up as objects of display, with local and fugitive meanings piling on them, overriding their technical content, dissimulating it, and at times imposing distortions on it. If we take the object of the so-called "touring" car (although this word means little in the context of most present uses), we find several layers ranging from the object of display (exterior) to the almost purely created technical object (in the scarcely visible or unknown parts for the majority of users: gears, transmission, or generator); the intermediary layer of reality, half-technics and half-language, is also that of the partially visible and describable organs, such as the engine which announces its cylinder capacity, its compression rate, the number of speeds, and the solutions used for accessory circuits (oil filter, etc.); there was the era of the long engine with a large number of cylinders in a line, then the V-engine and others in "flat-twin" designs, recently the slanted engine, not to mention the frequent incorporation in Italy of the cylinder volume in the denomination of the model or series.

Variations on the external layer are all at once infinite in number and rather limited; they are infinite because they are continuous, without the necessary gaps imposed by the state of things; all hues and all alterations of shape are possible, as in the domain of clothing; however, these alterations are limited by their compatibility with use, in the same way clothing is limited by the shape of the body, the necessity of allowing a relative freedom of movements and of preserving a minimal usefulness; if there is creation in the external layer of display, it is akin to the invention of a compatibility between the touring automobile and other technical products (for instance, the one-piece body for commercial vehicles and family station wagons) or between the car and other categories of objects according to a definite kind of lines and volumes, which is not without influence on clothing (sharp angles or rounded and loose shapes, trend towards large or small sizes); this aesthetics of created objects, giving them the semblance of a product of an era or civilization, is more a semantics than an aesthetics; it manifests itself simultaneously across a large number of categories of production and already lays deeper than simple external display; it registers and incorporates in objects a certain mode of communication between humans and things by exploring at each instant the most recent possibilities, as though humans must find in each object an opportunity of exploring the effect of the most recent discoveries, thereby participating to the extent they can in the whole field of contemporary activity, in accordance with a norm of presentness. Here we leave the layer of the external display of technical reality in order to shift to the intermediary layer of communication with the user, which is discontinuous, more reserved, and partially addressed to the connoisseur.

This semantics of presentness of what is created was translated, in the car of 1925, by the visible use of light alloys or aluminum whose functional meaning came from aeronautical construction at a time when canvas was

replaced by metallic surfaces; at the same time, we find light alloys in medi-
cal devices, in photographic enlargers, in a vast number of home appliances,
and even in furniture (doorknob and handles). The usefulness of the choice
of aluminum in small amounts, for example, on the dashboard of a car, is near
zero, since the total weight is only infinitesimally lightened; yet the inclusion
of this metal at the key point—the dashboard—enables the automobile to
speak, in its communication with the driver, the language of aviation; at that
time, because aviation itself was the "pilot," progressing in leaps and bounds,
aluminum was a more "technical" metal than others; in touring cars after
WWII, there was a proliferation of minor automatisms and controls used in
the navy and air force, where masses to be moved exceed human force, and
control panels are required. The use of a material displaying the present does
not only reflect, within a given technics, the prestige of a triumphant technics
in which the material has functional usefulness; this use also corresponds to
the transposition across many domains of a trend that arose in such a general
area that it inaugurates lasting training and radiates perceptual and operational norms; the house with large glass surfaces imposed its large, nearly flat
windows on the car, comparable to picture windows, and victorious over
the aerodynamics of shapes; like the cupboard integrated into stone walls,
the trunk of cars formerly brought from the outside onto the car body is now
part of the whole and is undergoing a sustained development. Each created
object thus takes part in a contemporary activity of creation according to
general modalities which unify solutions and align them with either a state-
of-the-art technics or with implementations whose constant use imposes
common norms on a whole population, for instance, in modern housing.
This communication among the middle layers of the created object causes
there to be, at each moment, not only parallel sets of created objects distributed across categories of use, but a world of created objects—a creation.

Nonetheless, in both the external and middle layers, we are dealing only
with an organization of extrinsic compatibility, comparable to the rules of
a language tending to become a *koinè*. Conversely, the organization of the
internal and properly technical layer makes the created object into a real
invention formalizing it concretely by giving it the features of an organism
through the search for conditions of intrinsic compatibility; we no longer
deal here with an act of display nor with a semantic relation to the universe

of technics and its progression, but with a direct and immediate adequation between the act of invention and the created object; the created object is in its very essence a reality instituted by the invention; this essence is primordial and may exist without display and without expression.

The display (external layer) and the expression (the middle layer) could not exist if they were not supported by the internal layer—the nexus of productive and resistant technicity upon which the external and middle layers develop like parasites, with an importance that varies in accordance with social and psychosocial circumstances. Situations of danger, of extreme difficulty, or war perform a purge of the inessential, letting the invented object emerge in its essential state; the primitive version of an invention is also "wilder" than its later version for mass distribution; the reaction of external layers back onto the invented object can, in certain cases, occasion a regression, as has happened recently in the domain of photography, where we see a generalized use of cameras whose optical attributes are very much below the actual possibilities of production, but which are endowed, as a counterpart, with a few rather limited automatisms that avoid gross errors in exposure time, and give access, without training, to the use of photography by a wider public knowing nothing of optics and photometry. By moving far afield of the place and time of the invention, the technical object may also undergo a split along the various layers, differently inflected according to use and social strata; thus photography first developed among knowledgeable amateurs and professionals who not only knew how to use a camera correctly, but also how to develop and print sensitive elements; a first split occurred when the vast majority of amateurs left it to artisans to develop and print their films; this is when the camera for the amateur became a camera with a roll of film easy to transport and ship, while the professional camera retained the sensitive plate on glass or plate film. The third dichotomy took place with the launching of industrial development and printing which no longer allowed the control or adaptation of each snapshot to variations of exposure time, especially for color pictures whose error tolerance is very small; it is to this industrialization that cameras with closed cartridges correspond, with very rudimentary optics and automatic settings of the diaphragm aperture, and no distance focus. The old amateur camera has not disappeared but has become specialized and perfected for photojournalism.

These two successive dichotomies produced a tripartite split at the end of which we find, first, at the purely technical layer, a camera chamber equipped with film plates, for scientific, geographical, and professional photography; the middle layer, corresponding to the predominance of expression, is concretized in photojournalist cameras with a wide set of optical and photometric settings; finally, the external layer of display is expressed in the wide dissemination of simplified but automated and closed cameras. We should note that this tripartite split corresponds to clearly separated functions in the uses of photography by various operators; a camera is in the hands of someone whose essential function, at the moment of operating, is to take a photograph; the photojournalist camera belongs to a journalist taking photographs for an investigation or during travel; the photograph has a professional value, but it is auxiliary; finally, the down-market cameras correspond to a leisure function of which they are a manifestation, and to which they are negatively adapted by virtue of their automatisms not having a sufficient extension to be applied to conditions outside of bright daylight and subjects located a few yards from the operator.

The technical object as a product of invention is characterized in an essential way by its organic character, which we might equally call a structural and functional self-correlation, as opposed to the divergence of adaptive evolution that specializes the product according to categories of users. In particular, in our chosen example, the foundation of photography as an invention should not be sought only in the camera, but in the compatibility of a photosensitive surface with the reduction of the camera obscura in a photographic camera; camera obscuras and photo-chemicals such as the bitumen of Judea were known before the invention of photography; the invention consisted in putting light to work, directly and automatically, on a photosensitive substance inside a small camera obscura forming an actual image of objects; the various successive improvements brought about more perfect conditions of compatibility between the photo-chemical phenomenon and the phenomenon of physical optics, especially through the discovery of a compound that retained its sensitivity for a long time after its fabrication, which also preserved, without alteration and until it was developed, the effect of light after exposure in the form of a latent image; the compatibility resides in the suspension of the chemical activity of the sensitive compound between fabrication and development, enabling the taking of the shot to be inserted within this temporal interval. To recall again the diverging specializations which follow the different layers, we can see that the use which gives priority to the most essential layer is also that which maintains the highest degree of compatibility between optical and chemical processes: with a professional camera using glass or film plates, and even with the most advanced photojournalistic cameras, each shot can be developed by itself. The Polaroid system, which features development and printing a few seconds or dozens of seconds after the snapshot, brings about a temporal and local compatibility between both processes whose interaction constitutes photography as an invention; moreover, this system implements a camera comparable to a professional photographic camera, at least with reference to the large format and the apparatus of the bellows; the Polaroid camera, rather than extending the divergent use which separates the display and expression aspects of the fundamental photographic apparatus, brings this diverging bundle together into a single unit, covering the whole spectrum of possible uses, from professional to leisure uses, including photojournalism and related applications, like the distribution of actors before a cinematographic take, through the retroaction of photographs on the actors poses. This new wave of invention in the domain of photography increases the compatibility between physical and chemical processes to such a point that it makes possible retroaction within the snapshot itself, a first photograph being used to improve framing, composition of subject-matter, and optical settings for the next photograph. Certainly, the invention of the Polaroid apparatus is the result of very advanced industrialization; yet, according to a common effect in technological matters, this true invention, bearing on the essential and constituting a major progress, restores some aspects of the activity of amateurs, in particular the extreme decentralization of the activity of operation, and a complete operative independence in relation to a centralized industrial universe. To the same extent, crossing the threshold of an essential improvement enables the re-convergence, as a base unit, of the various branches of an initially single technics, branches which minor advances in social and economic adaptation had superficially differentiated.

Other examples could be provided, if the question was to study the evolutionary facts of technical objects for themselves; but for the present study what is important is to note the fact that an invention or a major improvement upon an already-invented apparatus in order to perfect it is an act that institutes a compatibility between processes initially incompatible; for photography, it is the physical process of formation of a real image and the photo-chemical process that are made compatible through the phenomenon of the latent image; this compatibility belongs to the category of states of equilibrium, enabling the temporal succession of phases through the suspension of an activity. In other cases the compatibility is of a topological order; such is the invention of Marc Seguin, who created the tubular boiler for the production of thermal energy in mobile stations (locomotives, ships, and locomobiles). In a fixed station, in order to increase the yield of the furnace/boiler ratio, the heating surface was increased through the addition of exterior boilers to the main boiler's cylindrical body; this apparatus could very well have been generalized since we can easily imagine a proliferation of boilers around the boiler unit; but this apparatus cannot be applied, specifically, to a terrestrial vehicle, because of its great weight and size, its fragility, and the need for a heatproof lodging, channeling the flame around the boilers. Seguin made the simple cylinder boiler compatible with multiple accessory boilers by inverting the boiling schema and placing the other boilers *within* the main boiler, which not only increases the heating surface but diminishes the mass of water to be heated; the inversion of the accessory boiler schema means that water is no longer inside and hot gases outside, but that gases are in tubes parallel to the axis of the boiler with water around them. In this way the heatproof lodging is gotten rid of, the furnace directly sending the flame and hot gases in the tubes within the boiler; these tubes thus become multi-functional, since on the one hand they channel hot air, and on the other they serve as thermal exchangers; there is nothing else but these tubes between the furnace and the smoke-box located at both ends of the main boiler. In an almost paradoxical way, the outside envelope of the main boiler can become heatproof since all of the thermal exchange is condensed on the interior. The multifunctional character is completed by the fact that the reduced furnace produces only part of the combustion, which is extended inside the tubes throughout the boiler, when gas-rich coal is used; hence the invention contributes a wave of condensations and concretizations that simplify the object by charging every structure with a plurality of functions; not only are the former functions kept and optimized, but the concretion brings about novel properties, complementary functions that were not sought after, and which could be called "supernumerary functions," constituting the class of a veritable advent of possibilities coming to be added to the expected properties of the object. Through this amplifying aspect, invention is an opportunity for discovery in the area of technics, since the properties of the object exceed expectations; it would be partially wrong to say that the invention is *made in order to* reach a goal, to implement an effect entirely predictable in advance; an invention is occasioned by a problem that arises; but the effects of an invention go beyond the resolution of a problem thanks to the supernumerary aspects of the created object when it is really invented; these effects do not merely represent a conscious and limited organization of means towards a goal entirely known before implementation. In a true invention, there is a leap, an amplifying power, that goes beyond simple finality and the limited search for an adaptation. The supernumerary functions may sometimes be secondary and simply useful as additions; they can also become primordial so that the discovery takes over the initial intention; for an example of an only additive function, we may refer in the case above to the fact that the external wall of a tubular boiler may replace an outer frame because of its rigidity and perfectly rectilinear geometric shape, which the addition of extra boilers no longer overloads; this affordance has been used in locomotives, which brings gain of weight and space. By contrast, when Lee de Forest introduced a control grid between the cathode and anode in the original thermoelectric valve, he not only made possible the control of the electronic flux, providing a switch with an infinity of intermediary states between on and off: within a few years the vacuum triode became the central component of amplifiers for telephone electrical power, within the frequency band of musical sounds, then it displayed its remarkable properties for frequencies corresponding to Hertzian waves, not only in amplification and oscillation assemblies, but also in modulating and detecting functions. A new wave of properties of the electronic tube emerged with the introduction (for electrostatic insulation) of a grid-screen between the control grid and the anode; while carrying out its function of electrostatic screen, the grid-screen also produced an accelerating effect on the electron flux, increasing the inner resistance of the tube and making the flux nearly independent of the electrical potential of the anode; the introduction of a third grid very close to the anode, as suppressor of secondary emission, did not only fulfill this function of one-way barrier but also brought the possibility of modulation by electronic means; every invention, rather than being limited to solving a single problem, brings about a gain in supernumerary functions.[3]

In order to describe the main features of invention as formalization, however, it is not necessary to consider exclusively technical objects within the industrial sector; the industrial technical object belongs to the more general category of artificial objects that represent, in various domains, the achievement of a formalization leading to supernumerary functions. If we take, for instance, the arched vault as a process of construction, we can discern the multifunctional character of various components, acting on the one hand as relays in the transfer of compression forces, and on the other hand as part of the surface layer; each stone is in part roof, in part wall, and even the arch's keystone receives and transmits forces coming from other components; this communication of force affixes components one against the other through their sheer trapezoidal shape, requiring neither anchor nor cement; gravity, which creates the difficulty and poses a problem of equilibrium, is used as a means of cohesion in the final edifice. Gravity is integrated in the arch vault and works within the edifice; a segment of the arch vault would be, on its own, unbalanced; all the segments of the arch vault taken together produce a mutual equilibrium, so that not only is the whole balanced, without flat component susceptible to bending as beams do, but, moreover, the compensated disequilibria generate forces bringing the various parts of the building closer together, most notably upward: these supernumerary functions enable the arch vault to support another arch vault above itself, stacking several stories as in the bridge of the Gard River. The forces developed within the formalized whole that is the arch vault exceed its order of magnitude; the resolution of the problem through formalization creates an artificial object endowed with properties that exceed the problem. Genuine invention transcends its own end; the initial intention of solving a problem is only a trigger, a mobilization; progress is essential to inventions that constitute created objects because the object, endowed with new properties beyond those that solve the problem, transcends the conditions of the original position of the problem.

If invention were merely the organization of a given situation, without the creation of an object, this incorporation of supernumerary functions within the universe of producible things would not occur, since organization would be confined to the resolution of a problem; but as soon as a separate object arises, the constraints of that object entail a long detour, a larger unit of measure, that performs an incorporation of reality in the same way the evolution of life proceeds according to Lamarck: by incorporating within organisms properties that were left to the random effects of the milieu, properties which become, in more complex organisms, the source of regular functions.

This amplifying enjambment exceeding the conditions of the problem is necessitated, in the creation of objects by invention, by the obstacles which give rise to an organization limited to a strict and direct finality; thus, when stone construction was replaced with concrete, negative effects were encountered which prevented direct and non-amplifying replacement (possible cracks, uncontrolled dilation, or the poor resistance of concrete blocks to traction forces); concrete had to be reinforced with metal bars; these elastic components, working through traction, played their role best if they were constantly kept in traction, whence the technics of reinforced and pre-stressed concrete, which realized the amplifying enjambment characteristic of the invented object: pre-stressed concrete enables the construction not only of what was formerly possible with stone, but also beams and cantilevers that only wood or metal would have made possible, with the advantage [gain] of a homogeneous linkage to the whole of the construction, and with the added benefit of the identity of coefficients of expansion; the building made of pre-stressed concrete surpasses that which would have been possible with stone, wood, and iron. A secondary negative effect, then, which needs to be addressed in the search for compatibility required by the formalization of the created object (structural and functional self-correlation), is at first limited by mitigations, but subsequently becomes a positive part of the functioning of the whole. Hence in electronic tubes the secondary discharge of electrons by the anode was first a drawback, curtailed by the use of the third grid (suppressor) in the pentode structure; subsequently, this effect was favorably incorporated into the function of the whole in the photomultiplier cell, in which the secondary cascading discharge effect is systematically triggered from dynode to dynode to cause the amplification of an initially weak flux of photoelectrons. In order to be fully organized, the created object must be more complex and polyvalent than the strict project of problem resolution presupposed; it then displays new properties enabling it to solve, through an overabundance of being [*surabondance d'être*], other problems. It involuntarily incorporates other effects of the universe, since there does not usually exist a perfectly customized solution to a particular problem.

The incorporation—within a whole that is not only logically but actually and materially formalized, like an organism—of effects that were not sought by the finalized intention of problem resolution through organization, leads to a transcendence of the problem's conditions both potentially and in the universality of applications. This increase is comparable to a *functional surplus-value* caused by the work of natural realities incorporated in the created object so that it can be entirely compatible with itself; in this way, through the necessity of technical progress, the group of created objects incorporates more and more natural reality. A superficial non-dialectical view might lead one to believe that technics capitalizes an always greater sum of natural realities, impoverishing the universe of such realities; in fact, the group of created objects, incorporating ever more "wild" effects, becomes less and less arbitrary and less and less artificial in each of its elements; nature is re-created as necessitating formalization and concretization within the universe of technics. The more technics become objects, the more they tend to transfer nature into what is created; the progressive evolution of technics, thanks to the amplifying surplus-value of each invention that constitutes an object, transfers natural effects within the sphere of technics, resulting in the progressive naturalization of technics. The creative invention of objects is thus the last stage of a dialectical process transiting through perception; perception corresponds to the stage in which effect depends upon the milieu and is produced in the presence of the subject; through the surplus-value of invention, the effect enters into the system of the created object; invention takes nature into account as a necessary supplement to the simple practical and anthropocentric finality that only performed an organization by the most direct route; this supplement, required for the created object to become compatible with itself, performs an unexpected recruitment within the project of problem resolution, bringing about a solution broader than the problem. Progress, in the strong sense of the term, is the consequence of acts of invention; it goes beyond improvements targeted by the inventor and his intentions because, according to the expression of Teilhard de Chardin, "the rooms are greater than the house" that was planned to be built. Invention completes perception, not only because it makes real in an object what perception apprehends, but also because it adds effects to the initial conditions rather than selecting them for information capture as does perception in selecting among possibilities offered by the situation. For this reason, inventions that create objects, thanks to the recruitment of effects, convey to scientific discovery data that perceptual observation cannot extract from reality.

Moreover, this amplification effect through the recruitment of natural effects within technical invention has practical and social consequences that parallel its theoretical consequences. The mechanism of economic surplus-value that Marx describes in *Capital* expresses, in the sphere of human work, one of the consequences of the implementation of technical inventions that enabled the industrial revolution; this means that the labor of worker operators was incorporated in the schema of inventions and was recruited as a natural effect; but the amplification effect is not restricted to the domain of operator labor, it is merely visible in a privileged way in this domain—a particular case greatly concerning human societies. Nor is amplifying dialectical evolution only human, social, and political; it characterizes the entire domain of objects created by invention, not only in their relation with human society, but also in their relation with nature; through the intermediary of created objects, the relationship of humans to nature is subjected to an amplifying dialectical evolution whose active grounding lies in invention, effectively expressing the cycle of the image, by the expansion of the terminal phase of creative invention outside of the individual.

A complete study of the applications of this conception of the technical object created by invention exceeds the scope of this study of "general" psychology, for not only the consequences but also the conditions of the genesis of an invention imply collective contents and historical aspects, together with the specific way in which knowledge and power are transmitted in the form of constituted objects or of production processes, and with the exigencies of the conditions of reception, which are not just economical but cultural (see *On The Mode of Existence of Technical Objects*). Leroi-Gourhan has studied phenomena of diffusion, transmission, and transposition of technics within the framework of ethnology, with complex phenomena such as those occurring when a population is presented with objects displaying a more advanced development than its own (metal tools imported into a stone-tool culture) in *L'Homme et la matière* [*Man and Matter*] and *Milieux et techniques* [*Milieus and Technics*]. From this point of view, our societies have posed the problem of the relation of recurrent information between the producer and the consumer—who is in truth an operator-user and not a consumer when it comes to technical objects; a complete market study in this area should include the study of an invention's distribution channels, since a technical object carries, in itself, both implicit and explicit information about its conditions of use and the choice of models; conversely, the finalization of the features of a model by a manufacturer is a study not only of intrinsic but also of extrinsic compatibility since it entails the adaptation of the object to a system of virtual uses that do not at all correspond to a univocal concept; accordingly, in the rural French milieu of small farms mixing polyculture farming and livestock, efficient production using agricultural machinery has long confronted a lack of adaptation of machines to the actual functions of labor; these machines, particularly tractors, were conceived in relation to an ideal use in flat areas with monoculture farming in large contiguous fields, since such regions had been the first to cross the economical threshold of industrial machinery; the tractor was reinvented after 1950 in France for regions of polyculture farming on small or midsize farms, and it was quickly adopted, showing that, for the most part, it was not a matter of prejudice to be overcome or economic conditions yet to be obtained; in its new form, the tractor is no longer just agricultural (made to pull a plow) but becomes, all at once, a stationary generator of motive power, a road-ready vehicle with tires and higher speed, and a universal support for tools directly fed with the mechanical power from the engine, creating a close compatibility between the towing effect and the power source effect: the invention of an intrinsic mode of compatibility between these two effects made the extrinsic compatibility possible by adapting the multifunctional tractor to a continuous spectrum of uses, from either traction or engine power, to both simultaneously. A similar study could be conducted on the automobile market in France; the failure of some models (the Renault Frégate) is not caused by technical deficiencies, but by a deficiency of knowing with respect to its necessary extrinsic compatibility, in particular its dual purposes (transporting people and things); the success of the 4L model conversely corresponds to a good study of the plurality of needs. More generally, the perfecting of a technical object in the direction of concretization and the enhancement of its level of internal compatibility produces an external adaptability that is termed "versatile" in the U.S. and may be compared to flexibility in the sense of the word in psychology. The multifunctionality of uses corresponds to one of the essential functions of invention as a creator of compatibility; the fact that an invention is a creator of objects plays an essential role here since an object can be a real synthesis while the concepts of use and finality, univocal and limited, remain abstract; they enable the organization of the production of a thing towards a pre-established end, but not the creation of an object as a materialization of an image, as a continuous spectrum linking extreme terms like the tractor and the engine or the car meant to transport people and the car meant to transport merchandise. The object can totalize and condense information gatherings that express needs, desires, and expectations; the recurrent circulation of information between production and virtual use makes the image and the created object communicate directly, enabling a compatibilizing invention, while a conceptual definition according to finality deploys only a single-function abstraction, eschewing invention. For the same reason, a purely economic study of the genesis and use of technical objects is insufficient since it does not account for their mode of existence, which is a result of an invention condensing, in one object, a sheaf of information contained in the reality of an image that has reached the end of its becoming.

All of technics cannot, of course, be reduced to the production of objects; numerous technics amounted and still amount to discovering processes, that is, organizing efficient action according to the postulate of praxeology; however, it is when technics encounters the object and shapes it that it constitutes itself as a specific and independent reality able to surpass temporal and cultural barriers. Out of the vast Roman empire, which was a masterpiece of organization across multiple domains, what has reached us in an active way is what was created as an object: aqueducts, roads, bridges, and houses. If all roads lead to Rome, it is because the Romans of antiquity have invented the construction of roads as stable objects, concretizing the technics of communication, fast travel, commerce, and transportation, while formalizing the entire reach of the image of power whose seat was Rome but which drew its sustenance from the provinces through the continuous circulation of things and human beings. This network of objects has survived the empire because it transcended, through invention, the particular finality of each of its actions, and incorporated a nature *[une nature]*.

2. Other Categories of Created Objects, in Particular, the Aesthetic Object

The existence of several layers around an object responding to mental images is not the exclusive characteristic of the technical object; it is also found in the domain of the sacred, linked to the profane by different zones that mediate and protect it, but also hide to some extent what is essentially sacred— what constitutes the source and resistant nexus of sacredness (see the study on *Technicité et sacralité [Technicity and Sacredness]*, part of a course of social psychology delivered at the Faculté des Lettres of Lyon and published in the *Bulletin de l'ecole pratique de psychologie de l'université de Lyon*).[4] It is likely that the sacred object cannot be multiplied like the invented technical object; yet sacredness is propagated to some extent through contact and intention, or through the fragmentation of a unique primitive object; finally, the ritualization of sacrifice constitutes a spatial and temporal reticulation that universalizes sacredness and creates an interaction between nature and the sacred that is formally comparable to that which characterizes the development of technical objects. Perhaps even the dialectical process described above may also occur through the dissemination of the sacred through paths analogous to those of technicity. This would allow us to posit that, in part, sacredness corresponds to a creative activity concretizing the genesis of images with an incorporation of effects contained neither in the finalizing intention nor in the project of ritualizing, and with a similar opacity of univocity with respect to conceptual analysis.

The category of aesthetic objects lends itself more easily to observation, or perhaps even analysis, in our societies; the mode of existence of these objects reveals a plurality of more or less deep layers, that is, more or less proximal to the result of invention, with mode, of a superficial type, and styles, which imply a dissemination across a group of amateurs who are partially initiated and sometimes capable of reproducing, imitating, and organizing a limited world according to the norms drawn from the created object, such as the way furniture is arranged to showcase artworks, constituting their milieu.

However, the topological analogies between the various layers of objects do not constitute the essential part of the effects of the invention activity as the endpoint [*terme*] of the genesis of images; the essential part of invention resides in the effect of amplification by the recruitment of initially unexpected realities and the integration of these realities, with new powers surpassing the origin, into a formalized system; the development of this formalization, which is a consequence of the cumulative character of inventions, entails the incorporation of realities that were at first non-human into a world that has meaning for humans. Indeed, this is also what occurs in the evolution of the different arts, to the extent that they produce works independent of their creators and broader than the conditions of their invention. A work is less broad than the conditions of its invention when it is directed by a predetermined and predetermining finality, which gives itself the possibility of choosing an object to alter by detaching it from the conditions of its natural existence. Hence, selecting a landscape, a house, or trees in order to paint them, based on the already picturesque character of these objects, is to extract through selection an already-constituted aspect, remaining at a superficial layer of reality, altered according to the time and place. Such activity, rather than amplifying, captures and reduces; it exhausts its subject the way one exhausts a source of natural energy, since it takes from the world homogeneous realities; the obsolescence of such forms of art is comparable to that of technical objects in which the superficial layer predominates, making them accessories of a defined attitude; the decorative object and the hit song belong to this superficial category; for a current example, we may take that of opticalized objects unconnected to meaning, use, or nature, from clothing to jewelry and automobiles to furniture; what these cases lack, with respect to invention, is the discovery of compatibility; the opticalized motif is produced separately and is imposed in a violent way onto forms whose genesis did not anticipate such an encounter; there is now opticalized commercial adhesive tape that can be taped on any object in whatever manner. Art operates here through the addition of a pre-established, superficial film on things whose essential character is not modified; it is not creative because it is not demiurgic, it is only a masking and additive form of art without an activity of incorporation. Of course, optical motifs may have a meaning and be integrated when they underscore the remarkable points of an object such as a rocket, a target, a test pattern, a buoy, or a milepost; but in such cases these motifs are precisely those of a shape, size, and color adapted to the object and its situation.

Such superficial use is not recent: in other periods, there were profusions of ribbons or flowers on clothing, furniture, etc.

The middle layer in the production of created aesthetic objects is that in which activity is neither a random coating nor an amplifying invention but an elaboration that stays in place, as it were, without an increase or decrease of limits, without gain or loss, remaining within a closed and chosen universe of connoisseurs who form a coterie. A way of acting and a set of processes are preserved and transmitted through time with neither learning nor forgetting; this modality represents, as in the case of technical objects, the attitude and tendency of those who, without being creators, make use of the arts as accessories to their main activity, as a hobby practiced with taste and distinction, but in a relatively marginal way with respect to a central activity, such as the way a journalist uses photography; a journalist's requirement for a photograph is that it be technically skillful and a satisfactory accessory to his investigation or discovery, which is that of a reality essentially expressed in the written text. Similarly, a dedicated amateur expects an art object to be satisfying and skillful within a marginal and limited universe that produces its own norms; for this reason the amateur tends to be conservative, that is, inclined to appreciate techniques that are relatively old; today in France, according to M. Ignace Meyerson, a widespread cultivated public appreciates Impressionist paintings.

According to this schema of dialectical reversal, the activity of creators in the arts should be archaizing, or at least it could appear as primitive. And this is true. The music of Xenakis (for instance, "Terretektohr" presented in April 1966 by the ORTF) is disconcerting to professional musicians; a violinist from the orchestra showed, with perceptible sadness, the objects given to him as instruments: a whistle, another gourd-shaped object, the kind of things usually reserved for the drummer of the ensemble; the violinist resigned himself to using these objects "with the imposed rhythm"

but could not accept calling it "music." Yet, despite the nobility of this attitude of refusal within elevated norms, Xenakis's piece is nonetheless a work
that integrates very primitive sounds and noises produced by easy-to-build
instruments which have existed for thousands of years; we might say they
are raw sounds just as much as they are musical sounds; this work integrates
the effects of a "wild' sonic matter and incorporates it into such a complete
formalization that it determines, during the performance, displacements of
the localizable source of sound across the performers as if they were part
of the aesthetic perception. In the domain of architecture, we have referred
to the power of discovery of Le Corbusier's thought, and the simultaneously
futuristic and raw character of his use of materials, whether rough or industrial, without dissimulation: what comes out of industrial work is, like concrete, raw in a certain way; the marks of constructive human activity, such as
the traces left by wooden molds, may be retained for the final perceptual
mode of the building; the final work integrates the phases of its fabrication
in perceptual modalities, which thus remain perpetually present in the constituted work, as though it were in the very process of being made. Aesthetic
amplification recruits present effects, such as the imprint of wood boards in
the concrete that fills the voids, making them into a compatible system for
the whole duration of the work. The work provides a futural dimension to
the ephemeral gesture; it temporally universalizes it; it also bestows a dimension of spatial universality to a local reality by inserting it into a whole in
which it plays a full and prominent role as the single representative of its
species in this place; smooth pebbles from the closest river were incorporated into the façade of the Arbresle Convent, giving the building the power
to display native reality in its perceptible materiality; this materiality formalized by invention, the only one in the world of its kind within the relation
of compatibility it maintains with the universe of other artworks, confers a
spatial universality to what constitutes it, as if it were meant to manifest the
local character of things insofar as they are the unique particular aspect of a
multiform universe, like a word or expression within a language that can be
indefinitely enriched; the archaism of raw reality and the local character of
the perceptual display of matter: these are the sources of the effects that art
in the strong sense—as inventor of created objects—recruits and displays
by dilating them towards the time to come and the universality of a space.

Any inventor in the realm of art is futuristic to some extent, which means he exceeds the *hic et nunc* of needs and ends by enlisting within the created object sources of those effects that live and multiply in the work; the creator is sensitive to the virtual—to what calls forth, from the depths of time and with a humility situated in a distinct place, the course of the future and the amplitude of the world as a place of manifestation; the creator saves the phenomena because he is sensitive to what, in each phenomenon, calls for amplifying manifestation, the sign of an enjambment pointing towards the future. He is the person in whom the genesis of images reveals the desire of beings to exist;—to exist, or rather to exist a second time by being born again in a meaningful universe in which each local reality communicates with the universal and where, rather than being buried in the past, each instant remains the origin of an echo that multiplies and becomes more nuanced as it diversifies.

There is a logical relation between the three types of formalization of an object, so that the same object can, over time or by migrating from one culture to another, change category (sacredness, technicity, art). Contemporary cargo airplanes are revered by the indigenous people of Port Moresby ("cargo cult") who built landing strips and a perfunctory control tower in their villages to invite the planes to land; such a category shift is possible because they attribute the creation of the planes to their ancestors and consider whites as mere thieves and the current holders, but not the true builders, of the planes. The passage from technicity to the sacred without any modification of the object is made possible by pushing the origin of the object into the past, not a historical past but the absolute past of original, ancestral, and mythical sources. The category of the sacred is that of the absolute and original past, that is, implying and bearing the present existence of the individual and collective subject; the paternal abode or the domain of ancestors, as an object constructed and organized by primordial beings with respect to our existence, is clothed with sacredness. Conversely, the aesthetic object is entirely coherent with respect to itself only within a perspective whose vanishing point lies in an indeterminate future; the sacred eludes any causality that is historically assignable by going towards the indefiniteness of the past, in the same manner that the true aesthetic essence eludes any assignable finality by going towards the indefiniteness of the future; the sacred is beyond causality and the aesthetic is beyond the functional; however, within the technical object that is of the present, the close interaction of the causal and the functional produces the greatest possible proximity between the created object and natural reality, both of which diverge within the sacred and aesthetic categories.

Technical invention is perfected by the inner resonance of the produced object, that is to say, by the situation in which each subset modulates all the others; a "naïve" invention orders its different subsets according to a finality and in a unidirectional manner, in order to reach a result—the various subsets thus act as recruited and situated accessories; finality thereby remains provisionally superior to the relays of causality that are subjected to it; but perfecting consists in elevating the level of intrinsic compatibility by tightening the linkage between subsets, which amounts to bestowing on each of them a power to modulate the structure of the others, as in an organism, according to a process of individuation.

It would be possible to study the conditions that facilitate invention among individuals and groups; a rather large number of technics for facilitating invention (or for increasing the level of creativity) have been presented, for instance, Osborn's "brainstorming." Such technics are often stated in the form of negative rules: the rejection of prejudice, customs, hierarchic relations, of systematic and critical attitudes (the "think up or shut up" of Osborn); positive rules are fuzzier (try inverting solutions that already exist, attempt to suppress one element, etc.); in truth, the spirit of these methods, beyond their general aspect of opening a field of research, tends to eliminate the modes of mental activity producing strictly univocal representations, such as systematic deduction, to make room for the genesis (in the form of images) of complex and non-univocal representations, through transposition, inversion, or change of scale. Technical invention can therefore serve as a paradigm for processes of creation that take place in other domains: more generally, problem resolution in groups is fostered by everything that increases the polyvocality of representations and the plurality of attitudes in each member of the group; role change is one of the means for progressively substituting a structure of hierarchizing finality with a state of inner resonance in the group; the group becomes an organism to the extent that each member modulates the others; it is then that a group becomes capable of creation, rather than remaining a hierarchized system of execution.

There is a possible linkage between creativity within the group and the inventive attitude in the individual: the Socratic dialectic is one of the most illustrious examples of it.

The group discovers meanings and succeeds in solving a problem by inventing itself as an organism. The concrete distribution of doctrines, of attitudes, and of specialties across members of the group gives, in a way, living substrates to representations: each state of the relations between members materializes an attempt to combine principles. A group organizes itself to the extent that, through its exchanges, each of the members "modulates" all the others.

Conclusion

Recapitulation

The first three parts of this course studied the genesis of the image across the stages of a direct cycle of growth, development, and saturation of a sub-individual component of the mental activity under consideration, more or less like an organism or an organ within a larger organism. The last part sought to show how, when the saturation point of that component is reached (a saturation point that depends on the capacities of each living being to organize information), there is, in the course of a critical process globally designated as invention when its results are positive, a change of structure which is also a change in the order of magnitude, through the implementation of a reciprocity between the sub-individual elements (images in a state of symbol) and the directing lines of a super-set which, during the three preceding stages, did not exist in a state of actuality, but only in the form of constraints, limits, or sources of information that are outside the living being. This means that invention, induced by a need for internal compatibility, occurs through and is expressed in the position of an organized system that includes the living being through which it emerges as a subset.

Formally comparable to a change of milieu (the wish to find a new milieu is in fact one substitute for failed invention), invention is distinguished from the images preceding it by the fact that it performs a change in the order of magnitude; it does not stay within the living being as a component of its mental equipment but steps over the spatio-temporal limits of the living to connect with the milieu which it organizes. The tendency to transcend the individual subject which is actualized through invention is, in fact, contained virtually in the three previous stages of the image cycle; the amplifying projection of the motor tendency, prior to the experience of the object, is an implicit hypothesis of deployment within the world; the perceptual classes, serving as a subjective system for the reception of incident information, posits a universal application; finally, the symbolic bond of memory-images, while it expresses the attachment of the subject to the situations that constituted its history in a centripetal direction, it also and above all prepares for the use of reversibility, which converts this bond into a pathway towards things. In none of the three stages of its genesis is the mental image limited by the individual subject who carries it.

It is this relative exteriority that is realized in invention by the position of created objects serving as organizers of the milieu. A created object is not a materialized image, nor is it placed arbitrarily in the world like an object among other objects in order to overload nature with an artificial supplement; it is (through its origin) and remains (through its function) a linkage system between the living and its milieu, a double point in which the subjective world and the objective world communicate. Among social species, this point is triple since it becomes a pathway of relations between individuals, organizing their reciprocal functions. In this case, the triple point is also a social organizer.

For all these reasons, the system of created objects—within the double perspective of the relation with nature, which tends, through the working of this system, to become the organized super-set of compatible territories, and of the relation with the social as a super-set of functions that may be organized as synergy—constitutes the envelope of the individual.

Implications of the Present Proposal

It is worth specifying, first, the relative character of the created object; the created object is in fact a point of the milieu reorganized by the orientated activity of an organism. We can oppose neither human constructive operations to those practiced by animals, nor the fabrication of instruments smaller than the organism and borne by it to the setting up of roads, paths, storerooms, or limits in a territory serving as milieu to the organism, and thus larger than it. The tool and the instrument, just as much as paths and protections, are part of the envelope of the individual and mediate its relation to the milieu. We must characterize this mediation *topologically*. Whether instrument, tool, or specific structure of a territory, the object bearing the results of an activity of invention has received a supplement of coherence, of continuity, of intrinsic compatibility but also of compatibility with the non-elaborated remainder of the milieu and with the organism. These two external compatibilities, with the "wild" milieu and the living individual, are the result of the intrinsic compatibility that enables a single object to perform a simultaneous plurality of functions. A pathway, in order to exist according to internal compatibility, must be endowed with coherence and stability as a physical object (impermeability, the equal distribution of loads on the ground, etc.), and the search for this internal compatibility is what appears foremost to be the goal of conscious and willful invention: there may be several formulas of compatibility according to the materials used; the Roman road is founded on a system of rigid sublayers; it is founded like a building; today's roads are relatively elastic constructs but they must be extremely waterproof and have optimal drainage; their formula is the flexible continuity of their surface, much more so than the hardiness of each supporting block. When it ages, the Roman road is eroded one flagstone at a time, while the contemporary road loses its equilibrium across long undulations or buckles. External compatibility with respect to the subject may be summarized in terms of a viability for a definite mode of circulation and performance (horse-drawn conveyances prohibiting sharp rises but allowing for sharp curves, loaded mules, fast engine-powered vehicles, etc.): it is the characteristic of adaptation to a living being, whether direct or through a new and smaller mediation (vehicle). External compatibility with respect to the general milieu is generated by the layout of the road, according to the relief and composition of the terrain, including risks of avalanche, of mudslide, and so on; the road, as a resurfacing, develops supplementary mediations that connect it to the wild milieu around it: bridges, viaducts, tunnels, tree hedges, anti-avalanche reinforcement, preventative planting, sometimes at great distances, like outposts. Internal compatibility, then, which makes the road into a consistent construction, appears as a two-way transfer system between the living being and the milieu; when this compatibility is established, it enables the individual to move through the milieu in a continuous manner; but conversely, it also enables the preservation and reinforcement of engineering structures, of safety, and of protection. This self-constituting character of the created object is so strong that invention is, generally, a manner of treating a problem as solved in a non-tautological way; if one road is already built, it will be less difficult to build another a few feet away, thanks to the ease in transporting machines, workers, and materials; the solution consists in making this "solved problem" equivalent to a gradation of operations mutually enabling each other until completion: leveling, laying a gravel base, etc., until the last surfacing layer, whose finishing work requires an already perfectly leveled roadway. The created object is cumulatively organized by operations linked in a coherent manner, bringing the order of magnitude of the "wild" milieu closer to that of the individual operator. The category of the "created" is thus broader than that of invention, for it comes into being as soon as there is a cumulative and coherent effect of organization between the individual and the milieu, bringing an intermediary mode of mediation into existence; but it can also integrate inventions because of the created object's character of internal coherence and multiple compatibility, which develops optimally when the "solved problem" method can be used. The progress of the created object consists in a development of the intrinsic compatibility of the object, which extends the reach of the coupling between the milieu and the living being: all created objects that are means of communication of a human origin, for instance, follow this development, derived from formerly used natural pathways, but increasingly tending towards internal modes of compatibility that enable a more extended and more universal penetration of the natural milieu. It is not each created object, apart from the other, that we should consider, but the universe of mediation they form and in which each partially serves as a means to the others.

If we consider the created object as a mediator of the relation between living beings and the milieu, it is less arduous to find the link between inventions among animal species and humanity; the use of instruments is indeed rather rare among animals, yet nothing forces us to consider the building and fabrication of instruments as the preeminent instance of invention; instruments and tools are but a relay in the creation of objects, one more mediation between the created object and the living being creating it. Since a large number of animals are endowed either with specialized organs or with specialized operative modes connected to these organs, instrumental mediation is not necessary, given this preadaptation. There is a direct relation of operative modes and organs to the activities that create objects, such as the building of a nest, the digging of a lair, and more generally the construction of a territory. The created object exists as soon as a defined activity overdetermines the natural world, imparting to it a topology that expresses the presence of living beings according to a selective mode of behaviors. Simple visual or olfactory marking already represents a coherent demarcation, itself related to locations functionally connected to other activities (rest, food gathering, shelter, etc.). By the same token, marking acquires a meaning for intra- and interspecies social relations. The most concrete and complete created objects such as nests and lairs are also nexuses in intra- and interspecies social relations, as well as mediators of the relation between living beings and the milieu. In some cases, the created object is highly multifunctional, such as the termite-hill which, in addition to having to a high degree all of the usual functions of the nest (thermoregulation), is also a pathway to the objects on which termites work. The created object is, first of all, the world as a reality organized into a territory; it is also the envelope of concrete individual existences in such a tight way that for some species the created object is almost fused with the organism, as in corals. Is the coenenchyme a created object or an organism? We understand with such cases the continuity between functions of growth and the activity of creation—a genus of which invention is a species; growth and invention converge in the production of the network of created objects.

We cannot deny, however, that there is a difference, at least of degree, between the current capacities for the production of created objects by humans and by the animals most gifted in this respect. One of the main reasons for this difference lies in the multiplication of mediations, among humans, between the created object and nature, on the one hand, and the created object and the operator, on the other hand; the network of two-way pathways from nature to humans and humans to nature displays an indefinite anastomosis and a multitude of relays; hence the orders of magnitude made to communicate and interact in this way are much larger than in the animal realm, even in the best cases (social termites) in which the operator's activity cannot avail itself of a complex chain of mediations. The only angle through which an equivalence to the plurality of human mediations can be seen among animal species is that of the anatomic-physiological specialization of individuals working cooperatively or in the serialization of successive specializations of individuals across their life course (bees): in such instances we encounter a plurality of developmental phases and the character of an organized cycle that we witness in the becoming of the mental image tending towards invention.

Within this perspective provided by the analysis of the created object, the study of the mental image could become a particular case of the study of a larger set of phenomena; it is through the final phase of invention that the cycle of the mental image might reveal that it belongs to the general category of self-organizing processes of activity, one of whose major aspects in human societies is the organization of work. We could then understand how, guided originally by the vector of motor tendencies projecting encounters with objects, the mental image is charged with exteroceptive information before being formalized into symbols of reality in order to serve as the basis of an organizing invention. To this end, besides exceptional cases where a spectacular and large-scale reorganization propagates through a society and becomes a new landmark, there is a continuous web of implicit reorganizations, interwoven in work, but which are neither generalized nor propagated outside of the field of application for which they were meant; and yet, such minor reorganizations are also inventions, and the force of distributed inventions within a task, each too minimal to propagate outside of the situation, may be as important as a massive act of invention that organizes a situation in one blow, together with all analogous situations. This is especially the case in the animal activity of object creation, which minutely adjusts tasks to themselves and to the milieu during their performance; this is also the case of artisanal production. Each task comprises a certain number of organizing actions, and if the scope of each of these actions is inferior to the dimension of the task, the created object remains essentially dependent on the particular conditions of its insertion within the milieu, on its end, and on the particular means of its realization; these inventions do not emerge outside of the operator who may reproduce them in the course of analogous tasks but not formalize them as an absolute; this is the case with animal or artisanal activity in which invention is distributed throughout its execution. Conversely, if the act of invention is concentrated over several tasks, it is formalized into an invention detachable from its conditions of performance, as in industrial work. Finally, a remarkable particular case is that of the dimensional adequation between an artwork and an organizing invention: the created object is entirely organized in a single act, without residue or fuzzy areas, but this action does not exceed the limits of the created object, which thus remains particular and unique: the art object, a stable intermediary between artisanal fabrication and industrial operation, is a completely organized object, and, in this respect, absolute, albeit singular. Within the artisanal object, invention remains within the limits of the performance of tasks, bringing about partial organizational linkages; within the industrial object, invention exceeds the performance of tasks; within the artwork, invention and the performance of tasks occur at the same time and have the same dimension.

The study of the mental image and of invention thus leads us to praxeology, "the science of the most universal forms and the most elevated principles of action within all living beings," according to the 1880 definition by Alfred Espinas in the article titled "Les Origines de la technologie" [The Origins of Technology], published in *La revue philosophique de la France et de l'étranger.* Praxeology, together with the research of Slutsky, then Bogdanov (*Tectologie,* Moscow, 1922), has developed in the direction of the economy and the organization of human activity. Hostelet has also confirmed this trend towards the study of human activity, as well as Thadée Pszczolowski (*Les principes de l'action efficace [Principles of Effective Action],* Warsaw, 1960] cited by Kotarbinski in *Les origines de la praxéologie [The Origins of Praxeology].*[1] But it is reasonable to think that, after having separated humans from animals, and utilitarian action from action in general, praxeology could become a general praxeology, integrating the study of the most elementary forms of activity, which would in fact fit rather well with other investigations by Espinas. At this juncture, the cycle of the mental image progressing towards invention may well appear to be an advanced level of the activity of living beings considered, even in its most primitive forms, as autokinetic systems interacting with a milieu. The autokinetic aspect that manifests itself through the motor initiatives in less advanced life forms is translated—within life forms endowed with complex nervous systems—by a spontaneity of functions which triggers, before the encounter with the object, the cycle of the image, and which is concluded by invention.

Notes

Preface

1. The course on *Imagination and Invention* was first published as copies distributed to students, then in the *Bulletin de Psychologie* between November 1965 and May 1966. I published some passages from this course—those concerning invention in the domain of technics—in Gilbert Simondon, *L'invention dans les techniques: Cours et conférences*, ed. Jean-Yves Chateau (Paris: Le Seuil, 2005). For an introduction to the elements of Simondon's thought, see my *Vocabulaire de Simondon* (Paris: Ellipses, 2006).

2. This course, which was distributed to the students and then published in the *Bulletin de Psychologie* (from January to May 1965) was published in 2006 by Éditions de la transparence, with a preface by Renaud Barbaras, under the title *Cours sur la perception (1964–1965)*. It was reissued by PUF in 2013.

3. Gilbert Simondon, *On the Mode of Existence of Technical Objects*, trans. Cécile Malaspina and John Rogove (Minneapolis: Univocal, 2017), 43.

4. Simondon, *L'invention dans les techniques: Cours et conférences*, 84. The quotation is from the second course, *L'invention et le développement des techniques*. It is a brief justification for the inclusion of considerations on technology in a course on psychology which might at first appear surprising. For a more general account of the relations between psychology and technology, see the preface to *L'Invention dans les techniques*.

5. In an earlier version of the manuscript, Simondon had considered using "Mental Images and Invention" as the title (or subtitle) of his course.

6. See below, Conclusion, Recapitulation.

7. Taine studied the imagination of artists in *On Intelligence*, book 2; Ribot studied that of inventors in the domain of technics and the sciences in his *Essai sur l'imagination*

créatrice (Alcan, 1900); Bergson refers to Ribot's work in his article "Intellectual Effort," in the course of an analysis of the relation of the dynamic schema to the image in the effort of invention, where he takes the example of the construction of a machine. "Intellectual Effort," first published in 1902, collected in *Mind-Energy,* trans. H. Wildon Carr (Westport, Conn.: Greenwood Press, 1975), 186. Sartre says, cavalierly and perhaps without having really tried to understand Bergson, that Bergson did not clearly say what a dynamic schema is nor how it functions. *The Imaginary: A Phenomenological Psychology of the Imagination,* trans. J. Webber (London: Routledge, 2004), 62, cf. 60–62; see also *The Imagination,* trans. K. Williford and D. Rudrauf (London: Routledge, 2012), 57–60. Now, it is notable that Sartre constructs a theory of the imagination without really taking artistic creation into account, other than in its results (from the point of view of its reception), and still less did he consider technical invention. Perhaps this is one of the conditions of his misapprehension, indeed his injustice with respect to Bergson. It could be said that Bergson did not develop the analysis of technical invention in a way that would be sufficiently detailed and precise to be justified, explanatory, and convincing, but it is not without interest even if it is lightly sketched. Simondon will, in a certain sense, take it up and develop it, bring precision, and, in so doing, bring a justification which was not, until then, as apparent or effective. One could of course consider that Simondon, as he often does, profoundly rectified Bergson's theses in bringing so much precision, a view which is certainly plausible; but one might also consider that, by means of that precision, the interest and the depth were finally able to appear, and, in any case, it brought the capacity to find support in a learned and inventive science and to resist quick critiques. Such is still the ambiguity that follows a provision of precision in philosophy; but, when critique takes this form, it becomes an eminently Bergsonian way of critiquing and philosophizing (see the first page of *The Creative Mind*: "What philosophy has lacked most of all is precision.").

8. As we will see, it is not possible to merely claim that what interested Simondon above all was the technological question of invention, and that his philosophical considerations of the image were therefore only a psychological pretext required to address it: the first three substantial parts of his course deal with the image and, we will emphasize this point once again, the image is studied in such a way that it provides a genetic and transductive foundation for the comprehension of invention.

9. See below, Preamble.

10. See below, Introduction, A. 1.

11. Gilbert Simondon, *Cours sur la perception,* op. cit. In the following year, 1966–1967, Simondon gave a course on *La sensibilité* and on *Sensibilité et perception,* in the context of the course *Initiation à la psychologie moderne* (see the *Bulletin de Psychologie,* December 1966 to May 1967). Simondon's interest in the problems of perception, so

prominent in these courses at the Sorbonne (and there are still others), already appeared in his principal thesis on *Individuation* the third part of which ("Psychic Individuation") begins with a chapter on the individuation of perceptual unities and their segregation. See *Individuation in Light of Notions of Form and Information,* trans. T. Adkins (Minneapolis: University of Minnesota Press, 2020).

12. Sartre, *The Imaginary,* 120.

13. Sartre, *The Imagination,* 4 (translation modified).

14. Sartre, *The Imaginary,* 120.

15. Sartre, *The Imaginary,* 3.

16. Simondon, *Cours sur la perception,* 229.

17. Sartre, *The Imaginary,* 5.

18. Sartre, *The Imaginary,* 7.

19. Sartre, *The Imaginary,* 8.

20. Sartre, *The Imaginary,* 10.

21. Sartre, *The Imaginary,* 11.

22. Sartre, *The Imaginary,* 12.

23. Sartre, *The Imaginary,* 14.

24. See *The Imagination,* 41–70.

25. See below, Preamble.

26. See *The Imaginary,* 97.

27. See below, Part IV, C. 1.

28. See below, Introduction, A. 1.

29. See below, Introduction, A. 1.

30. This was not Bergson's central project in *Matter and Memory.* For Bergson it was first of all a question of characterizing not the general nature of the image (as a material reality), but material reality as in image such that we can perceive it (whether it be present or not). "Matter, in our view, is an aggregate of 'images.' And by 'image' we mean a certain existence which is more than that which the idealist calls a *representation,* but less than that which the realist calls a *thing*—an existence placed halfway between the 'thing' and the 'representation.'" Bergson, *Matter and Memory,* trans. N. M. Paul and W. S. Palmer (Cambridge, Mass.: MIT Press, 1990), 9. Simondon does not really take up Bergson's thesis, to the extent that he does not take up Bergson's problem, but he will show that that the Bergsonian formula which makes the image an intermediary is absolutely justifiable if one aims to characterize its nature: an "intermediary reality between subject and object, concrete and abstract, past and future" (the title of the first section of the Introduction below).

31. See below, Introduction, A. 1.

32. See below, Introduction, A. 1.

33. See below, Introduction, A. 1.

34. See below, Introduction, A. 1.

35. This is probably because Favez-Boutonier's course on the imagination had presented Bachelard's conception at great length.

36. Bachelard, *Air and Dreams: An Essay on the Imagination of Movement,* trans. E. R. Farrell and C. F. Farrell (Dallas: Dallas Institute Publications, 1988), 3.

37. Bachelard, *Air and Dreams,* 12: "How many times, at the edge of a well, with its old stone covered with wild sorrel and fern, have I murmured the names of distant waters, the name of a world buried in water"

38. Bachelard, *Air and Dreams,* 5.

39. Bachelard, *Air and Dreams,* 5.

40. Bachelard, *Air and Dreams,* 7.

41. Bachelard, *The Psychoanalysis of Fire,* trans. C. M. Ross (Boston: Beacon Press, 1964), 20.

42. Bachelard, *La terre et les rêveries de la volonté: Essai sur l'imagination des forces* (Paris: Corti, 1947), 3.

43. Bachelard, *La terre,* 4.

44. Bachelard, *La terre,* 5.

45. When he thematizes the relation to the work of art as such (at the very end of *The Imaginary,* in the second part of the conclusion: "It seems that it is time to draw some conclusions" (188). Sartre organizes his remarks as a polemic against the idea that the work could be considered as a *realization*: "It is then thought that there was a passage from the imaginary to the real. But this is in no way true." "We must not tire of affirming," he says, that "what is real" is only "the results of the brush strokes, the impasting of the canvas, its grains, the varnish spread over the colours," but the work of art as such, that which is "'beautiful,' on the contrary, is a being that cannot be given to perception and that, in its very nature, is isolated from the universe" (189). If one wishes to define the "existential type of the work of art," of the "art object" (a problematic that is indeed consonant with that of the "mode of existence" of technical object in Simondon, and of the images whose cycle leads there), one must say that the "work of art is an irreality" (188). Is it not this conception of the image and of imagination, constructed in the form of a conceptual opposition that is exclusive, resounding, metaphysical, and, in any case, essential with respect to perception, that prohibits the thought of a "realizing" imagination, even in the artistic domain (and what if it were in the domain of technical objectivity!)? Or indeed, is it rather the absence of a consideration of the possibility of an inventive imagination in the technical domain (where it is not only material objectivation, but effective functioning that is required), which renders possible this conception that opposes, absolutely, the perceived and the imagined,

the real and the image (contra Bergson who, in return, analyzed the technical invention of a machine, even if less clearly and precisely than Sartre would have liked (see "Intellectual Effort" in *Mind-Energy*, 186).

46. See below, Introduction, A. 1.

47. See below, Preamble.

48. See below, Preamble

49. See below, Introduction, A. 1.

50. See below, Introduction, B.

51. See below, Preamble.

52. See below, Preamble.

53. Sartre had perceived the "relation of existence and of action between the object and the subject, one woven in images and symbols," as well as the importance of action, of movement, of affectivity, and of knowing (*savoir*) in the image; but the condition for movement, action, or activity to be sources of images and *analogon* for them is that they be, first of all, objects of consciousness, of experience, lived experience, of perception, through which a body of knowledge is formed. Making the image a consciousness and considering it as incompatible with perception, refusing any possibility of an unconscious, ignoring the problem of the realization of a work starting in imagination, Sartre did not conceive that the movement might be the first origin of images, the first images, by itself.

54. See below Part I, A. 1. Cf. G. Simondon, *Cours sur la perception*, 100.

55. See below, Part I, A. 2.

56. See below, Part III, A. 1.

57. See below, Part I, A. 2.

58. See below, Part I, A. 1.

59. See below, Part I, A. 1.

60. See below, Part I, A. 6.

61. See below, Part I, A. 6.

62. See below, Part II, A. 2.

63. See below, Part II, B. 1.

64. See below, Part II, B. 2.

65. See below, Part II, C. 1.

66. See below, Preamble.

67. See below, Conclusion, Recapitulation.

68. See below, Conclusion, Recapitulation.

69. See below, Part IV, C. 1. My presentation here is principally focused on the problems of the relationship between imagination and invention. For an account of the relations specific to invention, particularly in the domain of technics, see my introduction to the courses and lectures collected in *L'invention dans les techniques*, op. cit.

Preamble

1. [Throughout *Imagination and Invention,* Simondon writes very long sentences articulated by semicolons—a pattern that's already visible in *On the Mode of Existence of Technical Objects* and *Individuation.* Rather than breaking them up into smaller sentences, we have reproduced his semicolons throughout. They represent an ideal of the unity of thought manifested through syntax at the level of the sentence rather than the paragraph—Trans.].

2. [All ellipses are Simondon's.—Trans.]

Introduction

1. [Throughout this paragraph, Simondon is closely summarizing book 2 of Taine's *On Intelligence,* "Of Images." We have followed T. D. Hayes's 1871 translations of the technical terms.—Trans.]

2. [See Fontaine's fable "The Milkmaid and the Milk Jug" in which Perrette, carrying her milk to market and dreaming of what she will buy after she sells it, drops the milk jar.—Trans.]

3. [English in original throughout the book. In *Individuation,* he attributes the concept to Arnold Gesell, a founding figure of American developmental psychology (207); Gilbert Simondon will develop the concept in relation to Gesell in Part 1 A. 4, below.—Trans.]

Part I

1. [The French *conduite* has been rendered throughout by "behavior": the English "conduct" tends to have a normative connotation which it does not have for Simondon.—Trans.]

2. [English in the original; Simondon had also mentioned this text in *Individuation* and gave it the same title there (cf. p. 545). We have been unable to find an article with this exact title; however, it may be a reference to an article by Arnold Gesell and Louise Ames, which outlines the four cycles Simondon sketches in *Individuation.* See Arnold Gesell and Louise Ames, "The Ontogenetic Organization of Prone Behavior in Human Infancy," *The Pedagogical Seminary and Journal of Genetic Psychology* 56 (1940): 247–63.—Trans.]

3. [Donald Landes notes, in his translator's introduction to the *Phenomenology of Perception,* that the concept of a body schema *[Körperschema]* in early twentieth-century German neurology was translated into French and English as a "body *image*"—an interpretation Merleau-Ponty implicitly rejected in retranslating it as *le schéma corporel;* he explicitly rejected it in chapter 3 of part 1 of the *Phenomenology of Perception,*

"The Spatiality of One's Own Body and Motricity," many of the concepts and arguments of which are at play in part 1 of *Imagination and Invention.*—Trans.]

4. [This expression, *le corps propre,* is also a technical term in Merleau-Ponty, traditionally translated into English as "the lived body" or "one's own body." We use all three expressions in the text.—Trans.]

5. [English in the original.—Trans.]

6. [*Neighbours* (dir. Norman McLaren, Canada, 1952).—Trans.]

7. [Edgar Morin, *L'Esprit du temps,* Paris: Grasset, 1962.—Trans.]

8. [*Violon d'Ingres* (dir. Jacques Brunius, France, 1939).—Trans.]

9. [Georges Friedman, *The Anatomy of Work: Labor, Leisure, and the Implications of Automation,* trans. Wyatt Watson (Glencoe, Ill: Free Press, 1961).—Trans.]

Part II

1. [In English. Simondon seems to use *déclencheur, amorce,* and "releaser" interchangeably in the next two sections.—Trans.]

2. [The course on instinct is published in Simondon, *Communication et Information* (Paris: PUF, 2015).—Trans.]

3. [Simondon is referring here to Benjamin Mendelsohn's inter- and postwar writings about victimology. Mendelsohn was widely recognized as the "father of victimology" for his work, but his typologies of victimhood were widely and vigorously criticized for their tendency to place blame on the victim. See, for instance, Mendelsohn, "Une nouvelle branche de la science bio-psycho-sociale: Victimologie," *Revue Internationale de Criminologie et de Police Technique* 10, no. 2 (1956): 95–109.—Trans.]

4. [English translation forthcoming, University of Minnesota Press.—Trans.]

Part III

1. ["Imprinting" in the section title above is English in the original.—Trans.]

2. [This passage also comes from "On Images," in book 2 of *On Intelligence.* See p. 38.—Trans.]

3. It is necessary to have heard the *Miserere* oneself to appreciate the magnitude and precision of such memory for music. [This note, in fact, appears to be Taine's. See *On Intelligence,* book 2, p. 41.—Trans.]

4. [From here onward Simondon uses the word *empreinte* for imprinting. *Prégnation* is not used again.—Trans.]

5. [Literally "Fight between a Bay Horse and a Bay-Brown Horse in a Stable," commonly referred to in English as "Arab Horses Fighting in a Stable."—Trans.]

6. [From Corneille's *Le Cid,* Act I, scene VI:

Don Diego: Rodrigo, hast thou courage?

Don Rodrigo: Any other than my father would have found that out instantly!—Trans.]

7. [Emphasis added by Simondon. See Berkeley, *Principles of Human Knowledge and Three Dialogues* (Oxford: Oxford University Press, 1999), 12.—Trans.]

8. For a study of the various categories of the imaginary and a discussion of terminology, see Mrs. Favez-Boutonier's seminar on *L'imagination*, pp. 92ff., particularly the commentary on the thesis of M. Ortigues in *Discours et symbole*.

9. [The English translation of *The Formation of the Symbol* took its title from Piaget's subtitle. See Jean Piaget, *Play, Dreams and Imitation in Childhood*, trans. C. Gattegno and F. M. Hodgson (London: Routledge, 2002). For the passage Simondon quotes below, see p. 280.—Trans.]

10. [Over the next few paragraphs, Simondon uses the word *souvenir* in two senses. One means, as it does in English, a material token of a past experience; the other refers to a discrete memory.—Trans.]

11. [An "issuant" is a heraldic figure half covered by a vertical or horizontal field while "passant" means it is shown in full and walking.—Trans.]

Part IV

1. [The concept of the actone is from Henry A. Murray, *Explorations in Personality* (Oxford: Oxford University Press, 1938). See p. 41, n. 8, for a definition.—Trans.]

2. A thing for the ages.

3. A more recent example is the Guimbal turbine integrated with the alternator within the pressure conduit.

4. [The course was published as *Psychosociologie de la technicité* in the bulletin pratique de psychologie et de pédagogie, Lyon, in three issues: November–December 1960 (*Aspects psycho-sociaux de la genèse de l'objet d'usage*); January–February 1961 (*Historicité de l'objet technique*); March–June 1961 (*Technicité et sacralité*). See *Sur la technique* (Paris: PUF, 2014).—Eds.]

Conclusion

1. Tadeusz Kotarbinski, *Les origines de la praxéologie* (Paris: Académie Polonaise des Sciences, Centre Scientifique de Paris, 1965).

Bibliography

1. This bibliography appeared at the beginning of the manuscript and was presented as "suggested reading."—Ed.

Bibliography[1]

Articles in the *Vocabulaire de la Philosophie* by André Lalande, 5th ed. (Paris: Presses Universitaires de France, 1947) and the *Vocabulaire de la Psychologie* by Henri Piéron, 2nd ed. (Paris: Presses Universitaires de France, 1957).

Bachelard, Gaston. *Air and Dreams: An Essay on the Imagination of Movement.* Trans. Edith R. Farrell and C. Frederick Farrell. Dallas: Dallas Institute Publications, 1988.

Bachelard, Gaston. *Earth and Reveries of Repos: An Essay on Images of Interiority.* Dallas: Dallas Institute Publications, 2011.

Bachelard, Gaston. *Earth and Reveries of Will: An Essay on the Imagination of Matter.* Trans. Kenneth Haltman. Dallas: Dallas Institute Publications, 2002.

Bachelard, Gaston. *The Flame of a Candle.* Trans. Joni Caldwell. Dallas: Dallas Institute Publications, 1988.

Bachelard, Gaston. *The New Scientific Spirit.* Trans. Arthur Goldhammer. Boston: Beacon Press, 1984.

Bachelard, Gaston. *The Poetics of Reverie.* Trans. Daniel Russell. Boston: Beacon Press, 1971.

Bachelard, Gaston. *The Poetics of Space.* Trans. Maria Joas. Boston: Beacon Press, 1969.

See especially, Bachelard, Gaston. *The Psychoanalysis of Fire.* Trans. C. M. Ross. Boston: Beacon Press, 1964.

Bachelard, Gaston. *Water and Dreams: An Essay on the Imagination of Matter.* Trans. Edith R. Farrell and C. Frederick Farrell. Dallas: Dallas Institute Publications, 1983.

Bergson, Henri. *Creative Evolution.* Trans. Arthur Mitchell. Mineola, N.Y.: Dover Publications, 1998.

Bergson, Henri. *Mind-Energy: Lectures and Essays.* Trans. H. Wildon Carr. Westport, Conn.: Greenwood Press, 1975. An article on intellectual effort, first published in 1902. Collected works in Henri Bergson. *Oeuvres.* Paris: Presses universitaires de France, 1959.

Bergson, Henri. *Time and Free Will: An Essay on the Immediate Data of Consciousness.* Trans. F. L. Pogson. Mineola, N.Y.: Dover Publications, 2001.

Boirel, René. *Théorie générale de l'invention.* Paris: Presses Universitaires de France, 1961.

Delacroix, Henri. *Les grandes formes de la vie mentale.* Paris: Alcan, 1934.

Delacroix, Henri. Article on "Invention" in Dumas's *Nouveau traité de psychologie.* Vol. 4. Paris: Alcan, 1930, 447.

Descartes, René. *The Passions of the Soul.* In *The Philosophical Writings of Descartes.* Vol. 1. Trans. John Cottingham, Robert Stoothoff, and Duguald Murdoch. Cambridge: Cambridge University Press, 1985.

Diel, Paul. *Symbolism in Greek Mythology: Human Desire and Its Transformations.* Trans. Vincent Stuart, Micheline Stuart, and Rebecca Folkman. Boulder, Colo.: Shambhala, 1980.

Dufrenne, Mikel. *Le poétique.* Paris: Presses Universitaires de France, 1963.

Durand, Gilbert. *The Anthropological Structures of the Imaginary.* Brisbane: Boombana Publications, 1999.

Eliade, Mircea. *The Forge and the Crucible: The Origins and Structure of Alchemy.* Trans. Stephen Corrin. Chicago: University of Chicago Press, 1978.

Eliade, Mircea. *Images and Symbols: Studies in Religious Symbolism.* Trans. Philip Mairet. New York: Sheed and Ward, 1969.

Favez-Boutonier, Juliette. *La volonté.* Paris: Presses Universitaires de France, 1945.

Favez-Boutonier, Juliette. *L'imagination.* Paris: Centre de Documentation Universitaire, 1963.

Freud, Sigmund. *Five Lectures on Psycho-Analysis, Leonardo and Other Works.* Ed. James Strachey. Standard Edition, vol. 11. London: Hogarth, 1957.

Freud, Sigmund. *The Interpretation of Dreams.* Ed. James Strachey. Standard Edition, vols. 4 and 5. London: Hogarth, 1953.

Freud, Sigmund. *Introductory Lectures on Psycho-Analysis.* Ed. James Strachey. Standard Edition, vols. 15 and 16. London: Hogarth, 1963.

Gurney, Edmund, Frederic W. H. Myers, and Frank Podmore. *Phantasms of the Living.* London: Rooms of the Society for Psychical Research, 1886.

Hermetic Treasure: The Book of Images without Words (Mutus Liber) *and the Symbolic Treatise on the Philosopher's Stone.* Ed. Emmanuel Henri Lalande (Marc Haven). Utrecht: Inner Garden Press, 2015.

Husserl, Edmund. *Ideas Pertaining to a Pure Phenomenology and to a Phenomenological Philosophy—First Book: General Introduction to a Pure Phenomenology.* Trans. F. Kersten. The Hague: Nijhoff, 1982

Janet, Pierre. *L'automatisme psychologique: Essai de psychologie expérimentale sur les formes inférieures de l'activité humaine.* Paris: Alcan, 1899.

Jensen, Adolf. *Myth and Cult among Primitive Peoples.* Trans. Marianna Tax Choldin and Wolfgang Weissleder. Chicago: University of Chicago Press, 1963.

Jung, Carl Gustave. *Symbols of Transformation: An Analysis of the Prelude to a Case of Schizophrenia.* Princeton: Princeton University Press, 1976.

Jung, Carl Gustave, and Charles Kerényi. *Essays on a Science of Mythology: The Myth of the Divine Child and the Mysteries of Eleusis.* Translated by R. F. C. Hull. Princeton: Princeton University Press, 1969.

La Boétie, Etienne de. *Discourse on Voluntary Servitude.* Trans. James B. Atkinson and David Sices. Indianapolis: Hackett Publishing Company, 2012.

Lacan, Jacques. "Les Complexes familiaux dans la formation de l'individu: Essai d'analyse d'une fonction en psychologie." In *Autres écrits,* ed. Jacques-Alain Miller. Paris: Éditions du Seuil, 2001.

Lacroze, René. *La fonction de l'imagination.* Paris: Boivin & Cie, 1938.

Lagache, Daniel. "Fantaisie, Réalité, Vérité." Communication faite au congrès de Stockholm sur le Fantasme. *Revue Française de Psychanalyse* vol. 28, no. 4 (1964).

Lagache, Daniel. *La jalousie amoureuse: Psychologie descriptive et psychoanalyse.* 2 vols. Paris: Presses Universitaires de France, 1947.

Levi-Strauss. *The Savage Mind.* Chicago: University of Chicago Press, 1966.

Lévy-Bruhl, Lucien. *Primitive Mentality.* Trans. Lilian A. Clare. New York: The Macmillan Company, 1923.

Lucretius. *On the Nature of Things.* Trans. Martin Ferguson Smith. Indianapolis: Hackett, 1969. Book 4.

Malebranche, Nicolas. *The Search after Truth.* Trans and ed. Thomas Lennon and Paul Olscamp. Cambridge: Cambridge University Press, 1997. Book 2, parts 1 and 2.

Meyerson, I. "Les images." In *Nouveau traité de psychologie.* Ed. Georges Dumas. Paris: 1932. Vol. 2, pp. 541–602.

Moles, Abraham. *La création scientifique.* Geneva: Kister, 1957.

Montaigne, Michel de. *The Complete Essays.* Trans. M.A. Screech. New York: Penguin, 1993. "Apology for Raymond de Sebonde."

Morelle, Paul. *Histoire de la sorcellerie.* Paris: Richard-Masse, 1946.

Osborne, Alex F. *Applied Imagination: Principles and Procedures of Creative Problem Solving.* New York: Scribner, 1953.

Pascal, Blaise. *Pensées and Other Writings*. Trans. H. Levi. Oxford: Oxford University Press, 1995. Section 2 of Brunschvicg's edition, p. 82.

Payne, Phoebe Daphne, and L. J. Bendit. *The Psychic Sense*. London: Faber, 1943.

Piaget, J. *Play, Dreams and Imitation in Childhood*. Trans. C. Gattegno and F. M. Hodgson. London: Routledge, 2002.

Plato. *The Symposium*. In *Complete Works*. Indianapolis: Hackett, 1997.

Revault d'Allonnes, G. "La Schématisation." In *Nouveau traité de psychologie*. Ed. Georges Dumas. Paris: 1932. Vol .4.

Ribot, Théodule. *Essai sur l'imagination créatrice*. Paris: Alcan, 1900.

Ribot, Théodule. *La psychologie des sentiments*. Paris: Alcan, 1896.

Sartre, Jean-Paul. *The Imaginary: A Phenomenological Psychology of the Imagination*. Trans. J. Webber. London: Routledge, 2004.

Sartre, Jean-Paul. *The Imagination*. Trans. K. Williford and D. Rudrauf. London: Routledge, 2012.

Schuhl, Pierre-Maxime. *Imaginer et réaliser*. Paris: PUF, 1963.

Schuhl, Pierre-Maxime. *Machinisme et philosophie*. Paris: Alcan, 1938.

Spinoza, Benedict de. *Ethics*. Trans. E. Curley. New York: Penguin, 1996.

Stendhal. *Love*. New York: Penguin, 1975.

Taine, Hippolyte. *On Intelligence*. 2 Vols. Trans. T. D. Hayes. New York: Henry Holt, 1875.

Taton, Réné. *Causalité et accidents de la découverte scientifique*. Paris: Masson, 1955.

Van Lier, Henri. *Le nouvel âge*. Paris: Casterman, 1962.

Voutsinas, Dimitri. "Hypnose, suggestion, hystérie." *Bulletin de Psychologie* 14 (Nov. 5, 1960): 161–89.